THE SCOTS ABOLITIONISTS
1833–1861

THE SCOTS
ABOLITIONISTS
1833–1861

C. DUNCAN RICE

Louisiana State University Press
Baton Rouge and London

Copyright © 1981 by Louisiana State University
   Press
All rights reserved
Manufactured in the United States of America

Designer: Joanna Hill
Typeface: Linotype Caledonia
Typesetter: Service Typesetters
Printer and binder: Thomson-Shore, Inc.

LIBRARY OF CONGRESS CATALOGING IN
   PUBLICATION DATA

Rice, C. Duncan (Charles Duncan), 1942–
   The Scots Abolitionists, 1833–1861.

   1. Abolitionists—Scotland.   I. Title.
HT1164.S35R53   326'.09411   81–3789
ISBN 0–8071–0861–8   AACR2
ISBN 0–8071–0898–7 (pbk.)

In memory of
Dr. James Inglis Rice, M.B.E., M.B., CH.B.

Contents

Preface and Acknowledgments

I have consciously aimed this study at Americanists and historians of English reform, as well as specialists in Scottish history. The way in which Scottish abolitionists used the slavery issue as a vehicle for other concerns raises the question of whether American abolitionists whose behavior we have explained in other ways may not sometimes have been doing the same. Again, the Scottish antislavery movement shows how much Victorian reform loyalties were molded by the tension between province and metropolis, and how often events in America became a metaphor for arguing out domestic concerns.

However, I have not written a blow-by-blow comparison between the response to slavery in Scotland and in other societies. The book concentrates on the Scottish movement against slavery. In general, I have left specialists in other areas to decide for themselves whether my conclusions have any bearing on their work. I have mentioned the activities of English and American reformers only when they had an important bearing on what was happening in Scotland. Howard Temperley has already studied the conservative English abolitionists, and Douglas Riach the radical Irish ones. Douglas Stange's work on the important West Country group is not yet available. For comparison and background, I have therefore had to discuss them at rather greater length than I would have wished. But my narrative only covers the antislavery connection between Scotland and America, within a fairly narrow time period. I have not fully examined the Scottish response to slavery before 1833, since I am now working on another book on that subject. I have not gone beyond 1861, where the Scottish-American connection has been exhaustively covered by Helen Finnie.

The biases the book reveals are three. Unlike many friends and colleagues, I do not believe that the promotion of social change is necessarily an unqualified good. It follows that I have not applauded one abolitionist rather than another because he or she was more "radical" or "uncompromising." Second, I believe that even in the 1980s history remains part of our written culture. I have therefore tried hard, some will say too hard, to make my work readable. Third, I am convinced that history as a discipline will die in the perilously near future if our profession does not occasionally break away from some of its own scholarly conventions. Respect for evidence need not carry with it a contempt for the word *perhaps*. Our subject will gain validity, and our investigations ultimately be speeded, if we sometimes overcome our timidity about leaving the shelter of our own footnotes. I am not ashamed that there are many places in this book where I have set out brazen hypotheses which are not documented to normal professional standards.

A great number of friends have helped me in preparing this manuscript. George Shepperson has greatly influenced my views of the way in which Scots used American phenomena for their own purposes. I have been helped on purely Scottish problems by Donald Withrington and Nicholas Phillipson, and on the nature of the American reform impulse by David Davis. My views on reform have also been greatly influenced by Bill Breitenbach, who intends to become the Perry Miller of his generation. If he makes everyone think as hard as he has made me, he will. His exhaustive criticism of the manuscript, together with that of Jane Pease, Howard Temperley, and Nicholas Phillipson, forced me to make extensive changes. I was also helped greatly by the advice of Roger Anstey, Elisha Atkins, Michael Bernstein, Ruth Claus, Seymour Drescher, Bill McFeely, Iaian MacIvor, Edmund Morgan, Bill Pease, Lewis Perry, Douglas Riach, Stanley Engerman, and Douglas Stange, all of whom also read the whole thing. This would have been a much worse book without all the help I have received, but I cannot pretend it is anyone's fault but my own that it is not better than it is.

Finally, it is hard to imagine having worked on the book, or indeed anything else, without the support of my wife.

Abbreviations Used in the Notes

AHR	*American Historical Review*
AQ	*American Quarterly*
ASP	Anti-Slavery Papers, Rhodes House, Oxford. Accession numbers are given only for the correspondence in Bodleian Brit. Emp. Ms. S 18
ASR	*British and Foreign Anti-Slavery Reporter*
AUL	Aberdeen University Library
BCMB	Minute Book of the Bristol and Clifton Ladies' Anti-Slavery Society, Dr. Williams' Library, London
BCR	*Special Report of the Bristol and Clifton Ladies' Anti-Slavery Society; During Eighteen Months, from January, 1851, to June, 1852; with a Statement of the Reasons for its Separation from the British and Foreign Anti-Slavery Society* (London, 1852)
BM	British Museum
BPL-C	Child Papers, Boston Public Library
BPL-E	Estlin Papers, Boston Public Library
BPL-G	Garrison Papers, both incoming and outgoing, Boston Public Library
BPL-M	May Papers, Boston Public Library
BPL-P	Phelps Papers, Boston Public Library
BPL-W	Weston Papers, Boston Public Library
CUL	Cornell University Library
EP	Estlin Papers, Dr. Williams' Library
EUL	Edinburgh University Library
GESMB	Glasgow Emancipation Society Minute Books, 4 vols., Smeal Donation, Mitchell Library, Glasgow
GESR	Annual Reports of the Glasgow Emancipation Society
GUL	Glasgow University Library

JAH	*Journal of American History*
JNH	*Journal of Negro History*
JSH	*Journal of Southern History*
LC	Library of Congress
MVHR	*Mississippi Valley Historical Review*
NEQ	*New England Quarterly*
NYPL	New York Public Library
NYHS	New-York Historical Society
SNL	Scottish National Library
SHR	*Scottish Historical Review*
WLG	W. P. Garrison, *et al., William Lloyd Garrison, 1805–1879. The Story of His Life Told by His Children* (4 vols.; Boston, 1885–1894)
WMQ	*William and Mary Quarterly*

THE SCOTS ABOLITIONISTS
1833–1861

CHAPTER I   The Scottish Background
and the Atlantic Context

Even modern Scots are sometimes unsure how far they are Scottish and how far British. This uncertainty was more pressing for
the abolitionists who are the subject of this book. Their country
was in the process of emerging from its "last purely Scotch age."
Their parents' generation had grown up when "almost the whole
official state, as settled at the Union, survived. . . . All our nobility
had not then fled. A few had sense not to feel disgraced by being
happy at home." Even after the flight of the aristocracy, the Scots
abolitionists and the middle class from which they sprang remained recognizably Scottish in language, education, and religion.
They viewed the increasing interference of the London government in their affairs with mixed satisfaction.[1] At the same time,
they shared many of the goals and assumptions of other British
subjects. In important respects, too, they were citizens of an
English-speaking Atlantic community, and their reform activities
have real similarities to those of their American counterparts. The
Scottish antislavery movement after 1833 had much about it that
was distinctive. Yet it was always part of a larger whole. Its idio-
syncracies, which are the subject of this book, stand out in relief
only against the background it shared with the wider movement
in England and the United States.

No aspect of the nineteenth-century antislavery movement is more
important than its internationalism, and none is more crucial to an
understanding of the Scots abolitionists. Certainly there is a real

1. H. Cockburn, *Life of Lord Jeffrey* (2 vols.; Philadelphia, 1852), I, 125, 126;
H. Hanham, "Mid-Century Scottish Nationalism," in R. Robson (ed.), *Ideas and
Institutions of Victorian Britain* (London, 1968).

sense in which the British and American abolitionists were romantic nationalists. But even if their shared anxieties over slavery had not drawn them together, they lived in a time of internationalism as well as nationalism. Even in the mind of Giuseppe Mazzini, an insistence on the role of nationalism as history's motive force was paralleled by a deep belief in the brotherhood of liberal men and women throughout the world. "We believe," he wrote, "in the *unity* of the human race, and in the moral *equality* of all the children of God."[2] These decades show a conscious radical cosmopolitanism, a reluctance to allow the new nations to maintain the barriers among men raised by the selfish dynastic power lusts of the past.

In Britain and America too, internationalism tinged benevolent activity at all levels. It is at its most obvious in the peace movement, and in the campaign for an ocean penny post. It is also closely linked to the free-trade views shared by most of the reform community, and it is of great importance in the Atlantic antislavery movement. William Lloyd Garrison's masthead for the *Liberator*—"My country is the world, my countrymen all mankind"—was a watchword for abolitionists whose other views were quite at odds with his. The romantic enthusiasm that both British and American leaders shared with continental Europeans of the same generation brought them to a cosmopolitan enthusiasm as deep as their local ones. "Moral force," wrote one of them, "cannot be bounded by geographical lines, rivers or oceans." In the same way, George Thompson, the most influential of the Scottish leaders, could defend himself from the charge of meddling in American affairs by announcing that "as a citizen of the world he claimed brotherhood with all mankind." "True charity," remarked one West Country abolitionist, "begins at home. But it is a very false charity that stops there."[3] He was preaching on the text from 1 Corinthians 12:13—"For by the spirit are we all baptized into one body, whether we be Jews or Gentiles, and have all been made to drink of one spirit."

2. G. Mazzini, "To the Italians," *La Roma del Popolo*, I, rpr. in *Essays* (London, 1894).
3. E. Wright to B. Green, March 17, 1835, in Elizur Wright Papers, LC; *Liberator*, October 11, 1834; S. A. Steinthal, *American Slavery: A Sermon, Preached at Christ Church Chapel, Bridgewater* (Bridgewater, 1853), 17.

The international ethic in itself might just as easily have inspired British concern over slavery in Cuba, Brazil, or for that matter Islam, as in the United States. However, the history and form of the Atlantic community made the system in America a more convenient and indeed a more pressing first objective. British evangelicals were haunted by their own personal accountability for the sins of Americans, not only because they were fellow Protestants and, in a sense, fellow countrymen, but also because American society had first been molded by British government and British law. None of them ever put it better than Captain Charles Stuart, the eccentric Scot who converted Theodore Weld to abolition.

> The United States of America are our sister land. Like us, they boast of freedom—like us, they are pouring the Bible and light all over the world—and like us, they disgrace their professions and tarnish their fair name, by keeping slaves. Freemen, like us; and, like us, slave masters.
>
> They lay this sin to our charge, and unquestionably the guilt of its origin is ours. They are our progeny—they were long the subject of our laws. We tempted them, and they consented. The guilt of the consent and the continuance is theirs; but, as the crime of the temptation was ours, we owe them, on this head, all the amends which holy love can make.

Where abolitionists were not sensitive to this strain of British guilt, American proslavery writers were quick to point it out.[4]

It was logical that Britons determined on world emancipation should begin with America. By the 1830s they lived in a genuine Atlantic community, which shared a consensus of ethical concerns and which was specially suited to benevolent cooperation. The antislavery movement was only one of the good causes that drew strength from the close institutional, cultural, and religious ties between the two countries. In the early nineteenth century these ties were strengthened by a dramatic improvement in sea communications, whereby the crossing eventually came to take much less time than covering the same distance by land. It is not often realized that this acceleration came before the introduction of

4. C. Stuart to editor of London *Patriot*, January 11, 1833, rpr. in *Liberator*, April 12, 1834; *Liberator*, February 2, 1835, March 3, 1835, May 30, 1835.

steam passenger ships. By 1830 the six or eight weeks of the eighteenth century had been clipped to between twenty and thirty days, as a result of dramatic improvements in hull design and rigging plan. Even more important, the Atlantic traveler could now take advantage of increasingly regular and frequent packet services rather than wait in port for the uncertain departure of a particular vessel. The first steam packets, in the fifties, improved reliability slightly but not much: the North Atlantic was not noted for light airs. A transatlantic voyage had become a much less daunting prospect than in the eighteenth century, years before anyone seriously thought of regular steam services. By the time of West India emancipation, indeed, the crossing was probably less alarming than the journey from Edinburgh to London had been fifty years before, when passengers still made their wills before setting out. Doubtless the increased convenience of travel did much to encourage the stream of philanthropists and churchmen who crossed the Atlantic in both directions during this period. Most prominent American reformers visited Britain at one time or another before the Civil War, among them Elihu Burritt, Garrison himself, Henry C. Wright, and Harriet Beecher Stowe. These pilgrims would all have agreed with Wendell Phillips when he wrote that the sympathy they inspired was "the sheet anchor of our cause."[5]

British travelers going in the opposite direction were not always as conscientious as might have been wished in passing on that sympathy, though opposition to slavery was very much part of assumed liberal orthodoxy at home. However, few failed to denounce the South roundly upon their return. Apart from men like George Thompson, Charles Stuart, and Joseph Sturge, who went to America with the specific intention of investigating and attacking

5. F. Thistlethwaite, *America and the Atlantic Community: Anglo-American Aspects, 1790–1850* (New York, 1963); H. I. Chapelle, *The Search for Speed Under Sail, 1700–1855* (New York, 1957), 255–97; R. Carwardine, *Transatlantic Revivalism: Popular Evangelicalism in Britain and America, 1790–1865* (Westport, Conn., 1978); G. C. Taylor, "Some American Reformers and Their Influence on Reform Movements in Great Britain, from 1830 to 1860" (Ph.D. dissertation, University of Edinburgh, 1960); B. Quarles, *Black Abolitionists* (New York, 1969), 116–42; J. H. Pease and W. H. Pease, *They Who Would Be Free: Blacks' Search for Freedom, 1830–1861* (New York, 1974), 48–67; W. Phillips to G. Thompson, July, 1839, in BPL-G.

the system, many visitors published accounts of the atrocities they had seen, or more often heard about, in America. Among the most important were Edward S. Abdy, who went to the United States to examine its prisons for a British government commission; George Combe, the Edinburgh phrenologist; and Charles Dickens.[6] There were also many more obscure visitors, like the Reverend George Lewis of the Free Church of Scotland, who was surprised to find that black people did not smell after all—"their presence is just as sweet as their masters' "—and who rather pathetically shared his picnic oranges with the slaves of his fellow travelers. Most of those who wrote about their journeys placed slavery's atrocities squarely before the public, specially stressing its sexual malpractices. "There is no subject," noted Governor James H. Hammond of South Carolina, ". . . on which in especial learned old maids like Miss Martineau linger with such an insatiable relish."[7]

These individual contacts were paralleled by institutional ones, which the abolitionists were also able to turn to good use. An obvious area of effort was in the reform societies themselves. The societies in the two countries, devoted to foreign and domestic missions, temperance, pacifism, and other good causes, tirelessly exchanged publications and personnel. Delegates or lecturers in one cause or another went back and forth across the Atlantic, especially at the time of the May anniversaries, when Americans habitually appeared at London meetings and Britons at New York ones. Abolitionists were often able to get useful publicity from the affairs of other movements, as Frederick Douglass did at the World's Temperance Convention of 1846 by denouncing delegates who lacked antislavery credentials or were on record as excusing slaveholders.[8] On a less sensational plane, every personal contact between reformers, and every exchange of publications, increased British knowledge of the world of American benevolence, and

6. M. Berger, "American Slavery As Seen by British Visitors, 1836–1860," *JNH*, XXX (1945), 181–202.

7. G. Lewis, *Impressions of America and the American Churches* (Edinburgh, 1845), 147; J. H. Hammond, *Two Letters on Slavery in the United States, Addressed to Thomas Clarkson, Esq.* (Columbia, S.C., 1845), 15.

8. F. Douglass, *My Bondage and My Freedom* (New York, 1855), 86–89; *Correspondence Between the Rev. Samuel H. Cox, D.D., of Brooklyn, L.I., and Frederick Douglass* (New York, 1846).

British understanding of the position of abolitionist colleagues across the Atlantic.

This kind of activity, however, counted for less in the Atlantic community than the ties between branches of the different denominations. Such ties were nowhere more important than in Scotland, but they had a significance for Christians in all parts of Britain. Like the great reform societies, each denomination would invite foreign delegates to its general assembly or other annual meeting. American leaders therefore appeared regularly at the Yearly Meeting of the Friends, the Annual Conference of the Wesleyans, the Yearly Synod of the Unitarians, and so on. All of them exchanged epistles and advice with corresponding bodies overseas, and these could be used as vehicles for persuasion on the slavery issue. Again, denominational periodicals, which were read in both countries, brought British opinions on slavery to the evangelical public in America and vice versa.

Such contact provided British abolitionists with an area in which they could feel they were doing something direct for the cause. Whatever the oblique relevance of working against the slave trade, for free production in India, or for opening Africa, it was only as church propagandists that they could do the same work as their colleagues in America, and do it as well or better. In spite of the expansion of cheap publications in the first half of the century, the pulpit remained a centrally important organ of middle-class propaganda. For a minister to be won over to the point where he would expound abolitionist views to his congregation was a great triumph, and the official conversion of a complete denomination a glittering one indeed. The British worked hard through church channels towards these ends, and at first they found the American clergy most receptive to their influence. England was the country of John Wesley, Scotland that of John Knox, and the views of their modern Christian public were listened to with appropriate respect. British church leaders, indeed, had great stature in America in their own right.[9] It was crucially important to American abolitionists that they and their churches should take an acceptable position on slavery. Otherwise their implicit approval, even if it was only the approval of silence, could be used by the proslavery hosts

9. For example, see *Liberator*, April 10, 1840.

in the United States to convince doubters that their peculiar institution was acceptable after all. "My work is to make slavery disreputable," wrote Frederick Douglass, "and I cannot do this while Christian churches in this country [Britain] are extending the hand of Christian fellowship to the slaveholders and endorsing their character as slaveholders."[10]

The Atlantic community of churches gave British abolitionists real scope to work among their own countrymen. They constantly pleaded that they should use their influence to the utmost to bring pressure on denominational brethren in America. First they suggested personal persuasion, by individuals or through the churches themselves. Thereafter they argued for ostracizing Americans who visited Britain for church purposes or for special occasions like the Great Exhibition. Unless they could plead a demonstrable antislavery commitment, they should not only be shunned socially, but also banned from normal religious privileges.[11] There were clear tactical problems in bringing up so explosive a subject, since the friction it risked might often impair cooperation in other areas of humane concern. Nevertheless, the British denominations, and even individual congregations, poured resolutions and remonstrances across the Atlantic from the thirties onwards.[12] In retrospect, it may be doubted whether such initiatives had much effect beyond irritating proslavery men and encouraging abolitionists in their already firm conviction of their own rectitude. In Britain, however, each remonstrance attracted attention when it was issued, and then did further service by being printed in the papers or being made up into a pamphlet or broadsheet for more permanent circulation. This and other forms of contact through the church connection were more important than any other form of

10. F. Douglass to J. Scoble, May 9, 1846, C16/75, in ASP.
11. S. A. Steinthal, *American Slavery: A Sermon*, 20–23; Jane Wigham to M. W. Chapman, August 18, 1847, in BPL-W; *Slave*, April, 1851; *Anti-Slavery Advocate*, March, 1854; *BCR*, 16–19; *Proceedings of the General Anti-Slavery Convention, Called by the Committee of the British and Foreign Anti-Slavery Society, and Held in London, from Friday, June 12th, to Tuesday, June 23rd*, (London, 1840), 121, 126–28, 133; P. Pillsbury to E. Baines, July 5, 1854, in Leeds *Mercury*, July 8, 1854; *ASR*, September 1, 1860.
12. For example, see *An Expostulation with Those Christians and Christian Churches in the United States of America, That Are Implicated in the Sin of American Slaveholding*, by a Committee of the Reformed Presbyterian Church in Scotland (Glasgow, 1848).

activity in maintaining British interest in American slavery.

There was less future in secular efforts against slavery on the other side of the Atlantic. But the British abolitionists also tried hard to keep their country's fashionable periodicals at an acceptable standard of antislavery commitment. From organs like the *Westminster* and the *Edinburgh*, through *Blackwood's*, down to more obscure sheets like the *Eclectic* and *Fraser's*, they all were circulated and read avidly in the United States. The *Edinburgh*, in fact, had a higher American sale than the *North American Review*. It was still acceptable to ape British attitudes in the world of letters, and these journals were genuine culture carriers, with a disproportionate role in forming American opinion. Abolitionists were well aware that these lordly periodicals would be well received even in households where their own literature was anathema. As Phillips put it, "The prejudice which treads underfoot the 'vulgar' abolitionist—dares not proscribe the literature of the world." During his 1846 visit to Britain, Garrison actually spent most of his time trying to make contacts among those influential in editorial circles. His British colleagues continually tried to influence the press. With some magazines, notably Thomas Carlyle's vehicle *Fraser's*, they failed dismally.[13] With others they were moderately successful. Many of the major British reviews published antislavery short stories and articles which, though received well in the abolitionist press, were no doubt read in American circles closed to literature from more radical sources.[14] This was another part of the web of the Atlantic community where British abolitionists, Scottish ones among them, could usefully weave.

Another part of the common experience shared by the Scots was the Emancipation Act of 1833. It was a watershed for all British abolitionists. Apart from its emotional and institutional legacy, it

13. A. Hook, *Scotland and America: A Study of Cultural Relations* (Glasgow, 1975), 94; W. Phillips to G. Thompson, July, 1839, in BPL-G. See also [?] to G. Smith, May 15, 1839, in Gerrit Smith Papers, NYPL; Phillips to O. Johnson, June, 1840, in *Liberator*, July 24, 1840; W. M. Merrill, *Against Wind and Tide: A Biography of William Lloyd Garrison* (Cambridge, Mass., 1963), 193–94; ASR, January 1, 1950, February 1, 1850, March 1, 1850, April 1, 1853, March 1, 1854; *Anti-Slavery Advocate*, November, 1852.

14. For example, see *Eclectic Review*, April, 1841; *Blackwood's*, January 1853; *Westminster*, April, 1853. See also ASR, February 2, 1853.

freed them, within their context of transatlantic cooperation, to take their place in an international coalition of reformers. Their commitment had now become intense enough to drive them into the attack on slavery in countries whose affairs were, strictly speaking, none of their business. The anxieties which had first stirred their interest in slavery were complex, but that interest, once raised, was maintained by a steady widening of their sense of moral responsibility. To that extent their agitation belied the all-too-common view that all idealisms except those of the present are a cover for bad motives. On the other hand, they were never blind to the advantage of using slavery and antislavery as issues to attack enemies of long standing. Scots abolitionists, for instance, found it hard to resist pillorying rivals who failed to take a correct tactical position in a campaign that was unanimously approved. Yet they were moral men and women who had become convinced that slavery was an evil, and who were determined to do what they could to overthrow it throughout the world.

In America, the Emancipation Act, which was the first major national manumission, had an electrifying effect. William Lloyd Garrison himself, who visited Britain to watch the legislation go through, was actually most displeased with its terms. In his view, it was "a complete triumph of colonial chicanery over the philanthropy of the British people . . . not an example for us to imitate, but a precedent for us to shun." But its compromise clauses on apprenticeship and compensation did not make its impression on the American mind any less deep. Its significance was especially great for free northern black communities, who held celebratory August 1 meetings until the Civil War. As late as 1914, Marcus Garvey thought it worth arranging for his Universal Negro Improvement Association to be launched on August 1. Evidence from the British liberation was widely circulated in America, in the hope of presenting the West Indies as a working showcase for successful emancipation.[15] The most perceptive American leaders

15. *Liberator*, December 10, 1833, July 24, 1840, April 13, 1841; W. L. Garrison to S. J. May, December 4, 1834, in BPL-G; E. D. Cronon, *Black Moses* (Madison, Wis., 1955), 16; J. M. McPherson, *The Struggle for Equality: Abolitionists and the Negro in Civil War and Reconstruction* (Princeton, N.J., 1966), 155n, 185n; J. A. Thome and J. H. Kimball, *Emancipation in the West Indies: A Six Months' Tour in Antigua, Barbados, and Jamaica* (New York, 1838).

were aware that emancipation had involved a compromise unacceptable in many committed antislavery circles. It had also been gained by methods inappropriate to a country where there was no central Parliament upon which pressure could be brought from without. What they understressed, if indeed they recognized them, were the difficulties the West Indies encountered in using free labor after 1833 and 1838. This meant that the British success gave all the more encouragement to the cause in the United States. It galvanized American feeling against slavery in much the same way as Lincoln's Emancipation Proclamation, thirty years later, quickened antislavery sentiment in Brazil and Cuba.[16]

In Britain, the West Indian campaign had built up a momentum that could readily be turned into the wider campaign for universal emancipation. By 1833, the British public had absorbed a mass of propaganda on the cruelty of black slavery. The repugnance the abolitionists had created did not have to distinguish between the system in colonial and foreign parts of the English-speaking world. In the twentieth century, it is difficult to comprehend the impression the antislavery fight had made on the evangelical middle-class mind. Few modern readers of *John Halifax, Gentleman* will notice the significance of the hero's death after thirty-three years of marriage. Among her Victorian public, Mrs. Craik could assume that few would fail to pick up a number that was metaphorically symbolic of liberation from earthly bondage, as well as being Christ's age when he died.[17] In a few years the shortcomings of the apprenticeship system that had succeeded West India slavery again turned British philanthropic attention to the affairs of the Empire. In August, 1833, the movement was ready for further action. It was easy for leaders like Garrison, or his friend George Thompson, to point to new horizons in the United States.

At a purely institutional level, too, 1833 had left an important legacy. The techniques of agitation used prior to 1807 and 1833 were copied by other British reform campaigns, most notably by the Anti-Corn Law League. Equally important, the great victory left each British city with a miniature antislavery movement of its

16. Pease and Pease, *They Who Would Be Free*, 51–53; O. Johnson, *William Lloyd Garrison and His Times* (Boston, 1880), 97.
17. D. M. Muloch [Mrs. Craik], *John Halifax, Gentleman* (1856; rpr. London, 1974), 461–62.

own, which lacked immediate objectives. They had stocks of pamphlets, papers, tracts, and even some funds ready for use. They also had manpower and womanpower, eager for employment most conveniently to be found in continuing and expanding the antislavery agitation. For most committee members, even for some rank-and-file supporters, an end to the movement would have meant that an agreeable and socially acceptable way of passing the time had gone. In an age without electronic media, the movement was a form of entertainment for two generations, especially for dissenters, among whom the reading of novels and other light literature was not permissible. Even in rural Cranford, which had none of the loneliness and tension of the great northern cities that the novelist Mrs. Gaskell herself knew, the ladies occasionally met one another at antislavery and other reform lectures.[18] There was also a small minority to whom the end of the agitation was even more threatening. For those who had been salaried or part-salaried lecturers or officials in the campaign, antislavery was a livelihood for which they had developed special knowledge and special skills. For both groups, it was attractive to maintain the old activities. Their motives were too simple to be committed in writing, perhaps too far blurred by the overwhelming conditioning in good works to be admitted even in private. Nevertheless, the British antislavery impulse broadened after West India emancipation in part because abolitionists were reluctant to let a cause that had become a part of their lives wither away from the stark fact of success.

In either case, the whole idea of antislavery had now taken on connotations which made that success, splendid though it was, seem a limited one. To say that the British movement was a spontaneous moral revulsion against social injustice raises more questions that it answers. By the end of the eighteenth century, however, the concept of slavery had acquired a series of nuances that made it acutely distasteful to committed Christians. This was not just a matter of semantics, and it did not just mean that concern for the helpless slave became a convenient token by which the devout could self-righteously identify themselves to each other and to outsiders. The abolitionists shared the urge of most Protestant reformers to attack the transgressions of others, both to

18. E. Gaskell, *Cranford* (London, 1853).

demonstrate their own purity and to transfer some of their own sense of sinfulness, but the attack on slavery had peculiarly soothing moral connotations. Enslavement to Satan had so long been a metaphor for sinfulness that it was easy to make slavery itself the symbol of sin. The slave's loss of physical free will could easily be conflated with the Christian's concern over moral free agency. The role of the liberator became an echo of Christ's mission as man's redeemer. The slave himself, suffering in innocence, provided a ready symbol of Christ's own atonement for human sin. By the same token, his plight was uniquely interesting to believers who conceived themselves both literally and metaphorically as bondsmen of the Savior. Slavery's symbolic values tied in closely to those very religious anxieties that afflicted evangelical Christians who had passed through the psychological turmoil of a conversion experience.[19] The motives behind the evangelical assault on slavery went far beyond crude economic concerns, and they were bewilderingly complex.

More to the point of 1833, the imperative that sprang from this matrix of spiritual concern was not blunted by local success. Though the evangelical assumed the totality of his personal sinfulness, he acted out his humility and gratitude for personal redemption through accepting the obligation of universal love. His urge towards benevolence therefore went beyond concern for abuses for which he was individually or even nationally responsible. In limitless gratitude, he was as much bound to follow the Savior's injunction in one part of the world as another. At the same time, the theological and intellectual resonances of slavery made it equally symbolic of his own state of sinfulness, wherever the sword of benevolence was to be carried against it. All was God's kingdom. Though it was clearly good tactics to begin with the enemy within the gates, few evangelicals felt that this would commute their obligation for future foreign service. Wherever it

19. C. D. Rice, "Controversies over Slavery in Eighteenth- and Nineteenth-Century Scotland," in L. Perry and M. Fellman (eds.), *Antislavery Reconsidered: New Perspectives on the Abolitionists* (Baton Rouge, 1979), 24–48; D. B. Davis, *The Problem of Slavery in Western Culture* (Ithaca, N.Y., 1967), esp. 219–390; idem, *The Problem of Slavery in the Age of Revolution, 1770–1823* (Ithaca, N.Y., 1975); R. T. Anstey, *The Atlantic Slave Trade and British Abolition, 1760–1810* (London, 1975), 126–41, 157–235.

survived, slavery was the prime symbol of the personal sinfulness with which they had struggled and were still struggling. The years before 1833 had only been a first round. Twenty-five years later, the old Roxburghshire revivalist James Douglas of Cavers could still point to Satan's reign in the American South. Slavery was "Mammon and Moloch combined, that horrid being besmeared with blood, still standing erect, joined with blood and cemented by gore."[20] British abolitionists, and the Scots foremost among them, were internationalists by religious conviction, and they were drawn to America by the nature of the Atlantic community in which they lived. Having driven Mammon and Moloch from the British Caribbean, they regrouped quickly to attack them in the new theatre of the model republic.

In organizational terms, indeed, 1833 was as important for William Lloyd Garrison's visit as for the emancipation itself. He was already thinking in terms of an Atlantic alliance of abolitionists. He was quick to inform *Liberator* readers of his achievements, under six headings:

> 1st. Awakening a general interest among the friends of emancipation in this country, and securing their cooperation with us, in the abolition of slavery in the United States. 2d. Dispelling the mists with which the agent of the American Colonization Society has blinded the eyes of benevolent men, in relation to the design and tendency of that Society. 3d. Enlisting able and eloquent advocates to plead our cause. 4th. Inducing editors of periodicals and able writers to give us the weight of their influence. 5th. Exciting a spirit of emulation in the redemption of our slave population, among the numerous female anti-slavery societies. 6th. Procuring a large collection of anti-slavery documents, tracts, and volumes, which will furnish us with an inexhaustible supply of ammunition.[21]

Activities of these sorts went on continuously until after the Civil War. Garrison's visit was the first real attempt to organize British sympathizers in explicit support of the American campaign. His drawing the old Agency Committee lecturer George Thomp-

---

20. J. Douglas, *The American Revival* (Edinburgh, 1858), 2. The image drawn here is that of Moloch the child slayer, as in *Paradise Lost*, I, 392–93.
21. *Liberator*, September 7, 1833.

son into the attack on slavery throughout the world marks the launching of a genuine British movement against slavery in the United States. After Garrison's departure, Thompson set about forming a chain of universal abolition societies throughout the country. Foremost among them were the emancipation societies of Glasgow and Edinburgh, which dominated activities in Scotland up to the Civil War. The mutual interest in slavery upon which Garrison capitalized was only one aspect of the middle-class Atlantic community, and Britons and Americans had anxiously been exchanging epistles on the subject since the Seven Years' War.[22] But the early organization of British support would have been very different without the work of Garrison and Thompson.

Even after 1833, neither British nor Scottish reformers became so absorbed in the American problem that they ignored developments in the Empire. The abolitionists destroyed the apprenticeship system in 1838 and, as far as they knew, did the same for East India slavery through the impressive but inoperative Act of 1843. They remained concerned over the West African slave trade and paid considerable attention to Thomas Fowell Buxton's African Civilization Society and the Niger Expedition of 1841. Throughout the forties, they squabbled unhappily over the problem of whether free trade in sugar would ruin the West Indies and worsen slave conditions in Cuba and Brazil.[23] With the exception of a small group in Glasgow, they also lobbied against the plans of the pseudoabolitionist McGregor Laird for a "toll-free bridge" to carry labor from West Africa to the West Indies. Indeed they opposed all schemes for meeting Caribbean labor problems by importing Indian coolies or Sierra Leonean recaptives. All such proposals, they suspected, were sinister planter ramps to resurrect the slave trade.[24] In the forties and fifties they also continued their debate over the West Africa squadron, its morality, and its efficiency. As late as the eighties, in fact, they were still

22. B. Fladeland, *Men and Brothers: Anglo-American Antislavery Cooperation* (Urbana, Ill., 1972), 3–194.
23. H. R. Temperley, *British Anti-Slavery, 1833–1870* (London, 1972), 18–67, 93–110; C. D. Rice, " 'Humanity Sold for Sugar!' The British Abolitionist Response to Free Trade in Slave Grown Sugar," *Historical Journal*, XIII (1970), 402–18.
24. *Cf. British Friend*, May 31, 1843, February 29, 1844, April 30, 1844; GESR, 1843, 69ff.

prepared to campaign vigorously against the East African traffic.[25] But the dominant antislavery theme of these years was a North American one. The concern of British abolitionists over imperial problems never drew them away from their duties as citizens of an Atlantic community.

There was still a network of antislavery societies throughout Britain after 1833, and its principal interest was in the South. In 1839, an attempt was made to unify these efforts through the foundation of the British and Foreign Anti-Slavery Society. At anniversaries, or at meetings to discuss major events or hear star speakers, it could raise audiences of up to six thousand.[26] Its followers split up violently in 1841, in a direct reflection of the schisms in the American movement. Yet they continued their work for the rest of the decade. In the fifties they were given a new stimulus by the romantic British passion for Harriet Beecher Stowe and *Uncle Tom's Cabin*. This fashionable enthusiasm could not disguise the extent to which the traditional sources of antislavery support were beginning to weaken. The old societies were only revived by the imminence of the Civil War and the attraction of a new field of benevolence among ex-slaves. During and after the conflict, they were strong enough to make a substantial contribution to the Freedman's Aid Movement.[27] At various points between 1833 and 1861, British abolitionism was strong enough to support four separate periodicals.[28] Only the Scottish support for the American movement is described in this book. At many times the Scots, like the Irish abolitionists, were a law unto themselves. Nevertheless, they always worked against the backdrop of a wider national movement of considerable strength, in which they were only a small group of actors, albeit a distinctive one.

25. C. Lloyd, *The Navy and the Slave Trade* (London, 1949), 104–14, 187–274; W. E. F. Ward, *The Royal Navy and the Slavers* (London, 1969), 193–200.

26. *ASR*, May 18, 1842, June 28, 1843, June 1, 1853.

27. C. Bolt, *The Anti-Slavery Movement and Reconstruction: A Study in Anglo-American Cooperation, 1833–1877* (Oxford, 1969), 54–140; H. M. Finnie, "Scottish Attitudes Towards American Reconstruction, 1865–1877," (Ph.D. dissertation, University of Edinburgh, 1975), III, 3–418.

28. *Anti-Slavery Reporter*, published in London from 1839 to the present; *Slave*, in Newcastle from 1853 to 1856; *Anti-Slavery Advocate*, a Dublin, Manchester, and Bristol cooperative, from 1852 to 1861; and *Anti-Slavery Watchman* in Manchester, 1852.

The men and women who are the subject of this book lived in a society still fascinatingly different from that of England. This does not mean that their generation had any of the glamour of the eighteenth century. Part of the distinctiveness they shared with all modern Scots was a growing sense of belonging to a nation that had slipped from the standards set up by its own past. By 1830 the age of Brougham had succeeded the age of Hume. Indeed Scottish culture was beginning its descent into a lesser era of diffidence and whimsy, its culture one part kailyard and one part capitalist ethic. Scotland's imperial contributions were still great ones; her infantry regiments were still unmatched; her evangelical commitment put her in the vanguard of Protestant religion; her university system was among the most vital in the world; and she was still producing some of the finest scientists, doctors, and engineers of the time. Yet the glamour of the golden age had gone. No one could now realistically remark, as Thomas Jefferson had done in the year of the French Revolution, that in moral and physical science, "no place in the World can pretend to a competition with Edinburgh."[29] As he looked back to the days of his boyhood, even Henry Cockburn, Whig and modernist though he was, could not shake off a nostalgia for the men he had not been able to appreciate when he had had the chance.[30]

The second Scottish renaissance, like the first, was brought to a standstill by the death of its leaders. Four centuries had not made William Dunbar's lament any less true:

> Art-magicians and astrologgis,
> Rhetoris, logiciannis, and theologgis,
> Them helpis no conclusionis slee:—
> *Timor mortis conturbat me.*

> I see that makaris amang the lave
> Playis here their padyanis, syne gois to grave;
> Sparit is nocht their facultie:—
> *Timor mortis conturbat me.*[31]

29. Quoted in Hon. Lord Cameron *et al.*, *Edinburgh in the Age of Reason: A Commemoration* (Edinburgh, 1967), 10.

30. H. Cockburn, *Memorials of His Time* (Edinburgh, 1856), 47.

31. "Lament for the Makaris. 'Quhen he was Sek,'" in *The Poems of William Dunbar*, ed. W. Mackay Mackenzie (London, 1932), 20–23.

Henry Mackenzie, the Man of Feeling, and his friend the author of *Waverley*, both died in the year of the First Reform Act. They were the last major survivors. If Victorian Scotland was one of the world's cultural leaders, it was largely by association with its own past. This did not prevent its citizens from drawing a certain self-confidence from the knowledge that they lived in a country that only a few years before had been the most glittering province of the European Enlightenment.

Their antislavery past, on the other hand, was less creditable. Eighteenth-century Scotland is an extraordinary case of a small society that developed a heavy economic commitment to slavery at the very time when its intelligentsia were vehemently criticizing it. Both commitment and critique are richly documented. The paradox is that they seem to have been quite without effect on one another until Waterloo, if not later. Throughout the Enlightenment the Scots moralists and essayists wrote, spoke, and debated on slavery at great length. Their consensus that forced labor was both immoral and socially undesirable was complete, and their writings made a real contribution to Atlantic antislavery ideology. They seldom seem to have considered whether their views affected the youths who read their treatises and sat under them in the lecture hall, although one of them, James Beattie of Marischal College, once wrote cheerfully that "for upwards of twenty-five years . . . [I] have laboured in pleading the cause of the poor Africans. This, at least, I can say with truth, that many of my pupils have gone to the West Indies, and I trust have carried their principles with them, and exemplified those principles in their conduct to their unfortunate brethren."[32]

Beattie was whistling in the dark. Only five West Indian Scots allowed their moral scruples to mold their response to slavery. It is true that four of them became abolitionists of major national importance. One of them, Zachary Macaulay, had in his youth become dissipated along with Glasgow students who were then listening to the lectures of Adam Smith and John Millar. Another, James Stephen the elder, had sat under Beattie and his group at Marischal College. A third, James Ramsey, had also been taught

32. Fragment, n.d., in M. Forbes, *Beattie and His Friends* (London, 1904), 236n.

by Beattie's master Thomas Reid and been one of Beattie's friends in their student days. A fourth, William Dickson, the Thomas Clarkson of Scotland, was an enthusiast both for Beattie and his writings. The fifth, Hercules Ross of Rossie, was a not very intelligent M.P. in the Dundas interest and appears to have had few intellectual contacts.[33] These five men notwithstanding, the whole surviving body of correspondence sent home from the colonies by young Scots of respectable family and sound education, contains only one expression of moral doubt over slavery. This was written by a South Carolina loyalist who lamented that his fortune was to be lost although he had had to overcome his scruples over slavery to earn it.[34] The most prestigious literati of the home country conspicuously failed to make it seem either immoral or abnormal to maintain the individual or national commitment to slavery. Since the literati were an elite closely allied to the aristocracy of wealth and birth—and since many of the emigrants were themselves the younger sons of that aristocracy—the gulf between critique and commitment is a major historical puzzle.

Prior to 1833, Scotland contributed more to the theory than to the practice of the antislavery movement. The secular enlightened attack on slavery owed as much to the Scots literati as to any group of scholars.[35] Disapproval of slavery seems to have been universal among Scots intellectuals extraordinarily early—by the mid-fifties if not before. By 1771, William Smellie's first edition of *Encyclopaedia Brittanica* was able to announce that the slave trade was "scarce defensible on the foot either of religion or humanity," without attracting any special attention. Slavery was denounced in the great works of moral philosophy, criticized in the college lecture rooms, and debated repeatedly in the convivial and literary

33. H. Ross to C. Haliburton, July 29, 1791, to R. Cooper, July 25, 1791 (copy), to W. Wilberforce, September 8, 1791 (copy), Ms. Gen 533/35, 36, 37, in GUL.
34. G. Ogilvie to A. Ogilvie, April 25, 1778, in Box 9, Ogilvie-Forbes of Boyndlie Ms., uncataloged, AUL.
35. The most important direct contributions were A. Smith, *An Inquiry into the Nature and Causes of the Wealth of Nations* (2 vols.; London, 1933), I, 344–46; J. Millar, *Observations Concerning the Distinction of Ranks in Society* (2nd ed.; London, 1773), 251–312; G. Wallace, *A System of the Principles of the Law of Scotland* (Edinburgh, 1760), I, 87–96; J. Beattie, *Elements of Moral Science* (2 vols.; Edinburgh, 1790–93), II, 150–223; D. Hume, "Of the Populousness of Antient Nations," in *Political Discourses* (2nd ed.; Edinburgh, 1752), 155–262; C. D. Rice, *Rise and Fall of Black Slavery* (London, 1975), 163–77.

clubs that were the most vital center of the Scottish Enlightenment. There was no serious published attempt to present a theoretical defense of slavery. On the other hand, it does not seem to have occurred to anyone that the new moral sensibility carried with it a duty to remonstrate with those friends, relatives, and countrymen who were then heavily involved in the West Indies. In the last third of the century, it must have been impossible for any literate Scot to avoid exposure to antislavery ideas. Even a professor whose brother was a pillar of the Guineamen's lobby could use his lectures on Greek culture as a peg on which to hang an antislavery homily.[36]

Most genteel eighteenth-century Scots appear to have shrugged off any responsibility to put theory into practice. Clearly the four emigrant Scots—Ramsay, Macaulay, Stephen, and Dickson—made important practical contributions to the national campaign against the slave trade. But the Scottish cities appear to have had much less grassroots enthusiasm for abolition than the English ones. As for the intellectuals, apart from the common sense group, among whom James Beattie and his friend Sir William Forbes the banker must be included, the only major scholar who gave the London committee any help was John Millar of Glasgow. The sole member of the intellectual elite of the bench whose name they could use was Francis Garden, Lord Gardenstone, a notorious eccentric and suspected Jacobin. Whatever enlightened views were expressed in the salons of Edinburgh and Glasgow, most normal Scots probably shared James Boswell's response to the evangelical campaign:

> Go, W——, with *narrow* scull,
> Go home, and preach away at Hull,
> No longer to the Senate cackle,
> In strains which suit the Tabernacle.

A Scottish abolition committee did at least set a precedent for future organization, and published one pamphlet.[37] On the whole,

36. Entry under "Negroes," in W. Smellie (ed.), *Encyclopaedia Brittanica* (1st ed.; 3 vols.; Edinburgh, 1771); A. Dalzel, *Substance of Lectures on the Ancient Greeks, and on the Revival of Greek Learning in Europe* (2 vols.; Edinburgh, 1821), II, 246–48, 251, 267–69.

37. [J. Boswell], *No Abolition of Slavery, or, the Universal Empire of Love: A Poem* (London, 1791), 8; *A Short Address to the People of Scotland on the Subject of the Slave Trade, with a Summary View of the Evidence Delivered Before*

however, the modest Scots contribution to the campaign for slave-trade abolition was out of all proportion to the intellectual concern the problem had attracted during the Enlightenment.

This gap may be explained very simply. First, Scots who had been most exposed to the secular enlightened critique of slavery were not yet the ones influenced by the evangelical imperatives of the sort that had driven the Clapham sect into action and that later came to have a similar effect in Scotland. Second, the success of the treason trials of 1793 in blunting the national appetite for radical activity inevitably had an effect on agitation against slavery and the slave trade. The minister of Jedburgh, for instance, did everything in his power to check "the diffusive contamination of anarchical principles" during the years of the French Revolution. But he still came under considerable suspicion as a Jacobin, because he organized a petition against the slave trade in the Synod of Merse and Teviotdale and because he published one of his own abolitionist sermons. He took the hint, and after 1792 he gave no more public support to a cause his heritors thought so dangerous.[38] In the new century, however, there was considerable shaking among the dry bones, because of increased evangelical anxiety over the symbolic and theological connotations of slavery, and because of the waning of the memory of Bloody Braxfield's judicial persecution of Scottish radicals. Perhaps, too, the abolition of the slave trade was a distinct enough writing on the wall to slow the movement of able Scots to the West Indies.

Yet it was not until 1814 that a first meeting against slavery was held in Edinburgh. Lord Cockburn noted that it was the first Scottish gathering held for any reform purpose since the treason trials. An Edinburgh Abolition Society was formed in 1823, and there were soon comparable bodies in Glasgow and Aberdeen.[39] Glas-

---

a *Committee of the House of Commons* (Edinburgh, 1792). The Minute Books of the London Abolition Committee, Add. Mss. 21254–21256, in BM, though they cover the period from 1787–1811, contain only scattered references to cooperation from Scotland.

38. T. Somerville, *My Own Life and Times* (Edinburgh, 1861), 263–66.

39. Cockburn, *Memorials of His Time*, 282. Minutes for July 22, 1823, December 8, 1824, in Minute Books of the Committee on Slavery, I, in ASP; *First Annual Report of the Edinburgh Society for Promoting the Mitigation and Gradual Abolition of Slavery* (Edinburgh, 1824); *Second Annual Report ... Abolition of Slavery* (Edinburgh, 1825); C. D. Rice, "Abolitionists and Abolitionism in Aberdeen: A Test Case for the Nineteenth Century Anti-Slavery Movement," *Northern Scotland*, I (1972), 65–87.

gow alone was eventually able to find 38,000 signatures for one of its petitions against slavery. Though the west was a stronghold of religious radicalism, this was not bad for a community that was built on Virginia tobacco and West Indian sugar, a decent equivalent of the 41,000 gathered at the same time in Manchester, and well ahead of the 17,000 from Edinburgh. A major Scots contribution to the West India fight was the 1830 pamphlet of the Reverend Andrew Thomson, which probably did more to push the British movement into its immediatist phase than any other publication. However, the country's involvement was not yet in any sense greater than that of other parts of Britain, perhaps simply because, as one abolitionist put it, "the West India party is no where stronger" than in Glasgow.[40] Still, the campaign did create a local tradition of commitment, which left its own legacy and could later be referred to piously by those who turned to help the movement in America.

At the same time, Scottish society as a whole gradually changed its attitude to slavery and its connection with the slave colonies. By 1830, disapproval of slavery could be assumed in all respectable and literate Scots homes. In a sense this disapproval became theoretical again in the thirties. Whereas the earlier critique had not shaken commitment to slavery, West India emancipation removed the commitment itself. The Scottish textile industry relied upon southern slave cotton right up to the Civil War, and indeed Clydeside shipbuilders were eventually able to sell a number of vessels to the Confederacy. But the national involvement was entirely different from what it had been in the eighteenth century, when there must have been few articulate Scots families without a relative working as a manager or bookkeeper or in some other post in one of the slave islands. The new opponents of slavery looked outward to an empire that was no longer based on plantation slavery. Scotland was still producing a surplus of educated young men, but very few now went to the Caribbean. Instead they sought their fortunes in England, as some had always done, or in

40. *Anti-Slavery Monthly Reporter*, July 31, 1826, cited in Fladeland, *Men and Brothers*, 177; A. Thomson, *Substance of the Speech Delivered at the Edinburgh Society for the Abolition of Slavery, on October 19, 1830* (Edinburgh, 1830); D. B. Davis, "The Emergence of Immediatism in British and American Anti-Slavery Thought," *MVHR*, XLIX (1962), 231; J. Cunninghame to T. Chalmers, 1817, Ms. 4.6.8, in Chalmers Papers, New College, Edinburgh.

Canada, the Middle East, or the Antipodes. The web of Scottish connections in the South had been cut apart by the American Revolution, when the overwhelming majority of Scots became loyalists and were pillaged for their pains. As for the West Indies, there is no economic reason to believe that young Scots of parts would have stopped going there of their own accord, or suddenly concluded that the system had become economically unviable.[41] Perhaps they too began to absorb new moral perceptions from evangelical Christianity. In any case the expansiveness of West Indian and Guianan agriculture was checked by the Abolition Act of 1807.

By the end of the Napoleonic Wars young Scotsmen were seeking different career paths. Partly because of a shift in the opportunities available to them, the way was opened for the antislavery critique to be applied universally. After 1833, it widened into a denunciation of those nations that still tolerated slavery. America, inevitably, was the country where the work was to be begun. In a sense the new commitment was molded just as much by the prior success in overthrowing imperial slavery as it was by economic change or even self-fueled moral change. In the light of this logic, it is no paradox that Scottish enthusiasm for antislavery seems to be higher after 1833, when the country had got rid of its own West Indian entanglement, than before. This is not an imputation of hypocrisy. It was simply easier for Scots to indulge their doubts over slavery when countrymen who had previously been up to their ears in the institution had been forcibly pulled out of it. Scots could only afford the luxury of unanimity over slavery because, willy-nilly, their own commitment to plantation agriculture had been broken.

Even so, there would have been little Scottish concern about the sins of the South if Scots had not developed deep evangelical concerns over slavery that were quite foreign to those of the secular Enlightenment. To some extent new moral imperatives sprang from the revivals of the Haldane brothers at the turn of the century. These have some similarities to the Second Great Awakening in America, and they added greatly to the strength of the indepen-

41. I. C. G. Graham, *Colonists from Scotland: Emigration to North America, 1707–1783* (Ithaca, N.Y., 1956), 150–83; S. Drescher, *Econocide: British Slavery in the Era of Abolition* (Pittsburgh, 1977).

dent or Congregationalist churches, and thereafter to the Baptist ones. By the end of the century, too, the established Church of Scotland, like English episcopacy, had produced a strong body of highly educated evangelicals. This was quite different from the situation in the days of the old highfliers or orthodox Presbyterians, when enthusiastic religion had been the antithesis of intellectual respectability. The new evangelicals were often learned, often even fashionable, and they followed their own group of philosophers, the common sense school founded by Thomas Reid and later led by Dugald Stewart. By an extraordinary religious alchemy, these years saw the whole weight of the Scottish intellectual elite shift from the moderate party of the Old Kirk to the evangelical one. In the eighteenth century a sophisticated evangelical like Sir Harry Moncrieff had stood alone among the highfliers, an anomalous prince on an obscurantist dunghill. In the nineteenth century, the days when the moderates, tinged with skepticism and deism, could attract brilliant dilettanti like Jupiter Carlyle of Inveresk had faded into the past.[42] In short, this was a change from a situation wherein high learning and vital religion were antithetical, to one wherein they were compatible if not inseparable. This revolution in religious history has never been explained or even documented, though it clearly had some connection with a change in the psychological matrix of conversion experiences.

In either case, the result was that the enlightened critique of slavery came to be absorbed by men of acute religious sensibility. Their awareness of its symbolic values would impel them to translate theoretical disapproval into action. The new views were much more explosive than the old, and they were all but universal. By 1818, for instance, Sir Walter Scott could assume the readers of *The Heart of Midlothian* would pick up the metaphorical point that Jeanie Deans's nephew died in slavery in the colonies soon after she had tried to liberate him from his own and his father's bondage to sinfulness.[43] In the early nineteenth century, both

42. On the world of the moderates, see A. Carlyle, *Autobiography* (Edinburgh, 1860); H. G. Graham, *Scottish Men of Letters in the Eighteenth Century* (London, 1901); J. Ramsay of Ochtertyre, *Scotland and Scotsmen in the Eighteenth Century* (2 vols.; Edinburgh, 1888).
43. W. Scott, *Heart of Midlothian* (1818; rpr. London, 1957), 459.

among evangelicals in the Church of Scotland and in the voluntary or dissenting denominations, there were new groups of men who had absorbed not only the enlightened distrust of slavery, but also the deep religious commitment that would impel them to translate that distrust into action. This combination drove them first to help overthrow West Indian slavery and thereafter to work in support of the American movement.

During the first third of the century, Scottish evangelicals, many of them leaders in their denominations, frequently and explicitly linked their opposition to slavery to their own deeper religious anxieties. As early as 1796, Dr. William Innes, a Haldane convert who later became a pillar of the Baptist connection, pointed to slavery as a symbol of total societal bondage to sin. Dr. Thomas Chalmers, the Free Church leader, saw slavery as an obstacle to the redemption by example that was the main mechanism of evangelism. Dr. Andrew Thomson, his friend among the evangelicals of the Old Kirk, moved to an immediatist view on slavery because of his position on personal accountability. James Douglas of Cavers, the most influential lay Congregationalist of his time, was haunted by slavery because it was the symbolic opposite of free agency under God. Dr. Ralph Wardlaw of Glasgow, another independent leader, saw the overthrow of slavery as an act of atonement for national sins, as well as a first victory in the wider battle against enslavement to sin. The eschatological importance of emancipation was that of an act of redemption—redemption of the abolitionists as well as redemption of the slaves.[44]

Doubtless, Scottish evangelicals, like English and American ones, also found slavery alarming in purely secular terms. It represented an extreme form of the reduction of labor to a commodity, of a process upon which an industrializing society depended, though in a less flagrant way than the world of the plantations. Though the middle class would ultimately gain from the new relationships, they

44. W. Innes, *Important and Interesting Observations on the Abolition of the Slave Trade* (Edinburgh, 1796), 5, 8, 15, 21; T. Chalmers, *A Few Thoughts on the Abolition of Colonial Slavery* (Glasgow, 1826); Thomson, *Substance of the Speech Delivered at the Edinburgh Society*; J. Douglas, *Slavery, Sabbath Observance, and Church Reform* (Edinburgh, 1833), 3–4; R. Wardlaw, *The Jubilee: A Sermon Preached in West George Street Chapel, Glasgow on . . . the Memorable Day of Negro Emancipation in the West Indies* (Glasgow, 1834), 16, 17–18, 34; Rice, "Controversies over Slavery," 24–48.

did not adapt without strain to the removal of paternalistic restraints on the operation of the labor market. Abolitionism may
have given them an ideal release for their inchoate distrust of the
disturbingly harsh society in which they lived and from which
they profited.[45] What this kind of concern cannot explain, however,
is the quality of urgency in their commitment to antislavery, both
before and after 1833. Their distrust of slavery took on the attributes of a moral imperative simply because slavery's range of religious meanings could bring out practically every anxiety to which
the evangelical mind was a prey.

The point about such concerns is that they were just as effective
a fuel for antislavery activity after West India emancipation as
before. The problems that slavery symbolized—accountability,
atonement, redemption, and free agency—were not national but
cosmic ones, and they lost none of their force because freedom
had come to the British Caribbean. In the particular case of Scotland, the universal abolition movement they produced was all the
stronger because there was no longer an incentive to be discreet
about an institution in which so many countrymen had previously
been involved. The close Scottish-American connection made it
logical to begin with the United States.

It was probably because of this shift to a foreign country that
the contributions of Scottish abolitionists after 1833 were for the
first time greater in proportion than those of the country at large.
Whatever its force for the abolitionists, antislavery had now ceased
to be a pressing domestic issue. The Scots it concerned were no
longer in their usual position of competing on unequal terms with
national leaders who had more political power than they. In the
West India events, abolitionists had only played a provincial supporting role. It was doubtless pleasant, in the campaign for world
abolition, to find themselves in a position where *no one* had any
political mechanism for influencing the American situation. It was
also specially easy for Scottish evangelicals to channel their ener-

45. This hypothesis owes something to four very different books: K. Polyani, *The
Great Transformation* (London, 1944); H. Perkins, *The Origins of Modern English
Society, 1780–1880* (Toronto, 1969); F. Weinstein and G. M. Platt, *The Wish To
Be Free: Society, Psyche, and Value Change* (Berkeley, 1969); Davis, *Problem of
Slavery in the Age of Revolution,* 453–68.

gies into a foreign benevolent campaign: the affairs of Washington were no more remote to them, in some important ways, than
those of Westminster. In one sense, indeed, they were less remote, for they were at least assured with some frequency that
their contribution to the American cause was an important and
special one. "I hardly think you in England," wrote Wendell Phillips, "are aware of the extent to which the names of our English
colaborers are household words among us."[46] The fact that on this
occasion he really meant Scotland and Scottish, or at worst Britain
and British, was a slight insult to bear in exchange for such flattery.

A striking characteristic of the Scottish movement was its almost
total lack of concern over antislavery unity. There is a splendid
Scots toast that Americans, for some reason, always find appealing:

"Here's tae us!"

"Wha's like us?"

"Dam' few, an' they're a' deid!"

This kind of cheerful arrogance may be a partial explanation of
the independence of Scottish abolitionist behavior after 1833. But
it was also linked with the form of the Scottish antislavery tradition, the nature of the country's connection with America, and
the peculiarly satisfying uses to which the issue could be put in
expressing specifically Scottish antagonisms, both at home and
abroad. The Scots may have used benevolent and church activity
as a sort of supplement to a political life they apparently found
inadequate. In either case, their antislavery disagreements reached
an extraordinary level of vehemence. They were able to use these
disagreements as a means of gaining capital in feuds that had absolutely no reference to what was happening to black people in
America or anywhere else.

That phenomenon is the concern of this book. The use of the
slave as a pawn in white squabbles was nothing new, and it was
certainly not confined to Scotland. Even in Jane Austen's *Emma*,
he was brought up as a means of drawing attention to the "gov-
erness trade." British Tories habitually used his presence in the
land of the free as evidence of the bankruptcy of democracy.

46. H. Hanham, "Mid-Century Scottish Nationalism," 151, 153, 156, 164–66; D.
Daiches, *The Paradox of Scottish Culture: The Eighteenth-Century Experience*
(London, 1964); Phillips to J. Murray, Jr., May 29, 1849, Ms. 2086 f.206, in
Watson Autographs, SNL.

Working people, too, could trot him out as proof of middle-class hypocrisy. The Scots were as agile at this kind òf game as anyone else. Indeed they introduced a new refinement of their own, for they used not only the slave, but also disagreements over the best means of helping him, as a way of projecting their own likes and dislikes, foreign and domestic. It was only in Ireland that discussion of slavery was put to equally elaborate uses.[47]

This book, however, is concerned only with the Scottish response to slavery and antislavery. The strength of the country's antislavery movement after 1833 is not at issue, but the story of its disunity is a fascinating one. After 1841, when news of the disagreements among the American abolitionists reached Britain, the Scots gleefully plunged into this new conflict. As the movement became increasingly fragmented, they were able to turn its controversies to good use in several directions—to express their distrust of centralization in the metropolis, to assist them in their endless church vendettas, and to help fuel their distrust of those richer or poorer than themselves. This does not mean that the evangelical anxieties which had first drawn them to the cause were any less real, or that the pity they expressed for the slave was any less genuine. But it was an added bonus that in helping liberate the American slave, Scotland could once again use "events in the New World to bring into focus its own situation in the Old."[48]

It was not an accident that it was over slavery that the abolitionists did this most often. Slavery impinged on almost all the most important aspects of the Protestant middle-class consciousness. The intensity of Scottish concerns over it is also fine evidence of the reality of a middle-class Atlantic community in the middle third of the century. For a few years, indeed, that concern was so deep that even the Scots were able to work for American emancipation without major disagreements. This brief honeymoon is the subject of the next two chapters.

47. J. Austen, *Emma* (1816; rpr. London, 1964), 238; N. W. Senior, *American Slavery: A Reprint of an Article on "Uncle Tom's Cabin"* . . . *and of Mr. Sumner's Speech, with a Notice of the Events Which Followed That Speech* (London, 1856), 38–39; D. Riach, "Ireland and the Campaign Against American Slavery, 1830–1860" (Ph.D. dissertation, University of Edinburgh, 1975).
48. G. A. Shepperson, "Writings in Scottish-American History: A Brief Survey," *WMQ*, Third Series, XI (1954), 173.

CHAPTER 2

The Scottish Societies
Formation and Composition

The background and benevolent interests of Scottish antislavery leaders after 1833 are of considerable interest. It must be said at the outset, however, that these men and women would have been appalled by the suggestion that their commitment to help the slave was a distinct part of their Christian life, or even that their religious and quasi-religious concerns were in any way separate from their secular ones. Abolitionism was one of a series of interdependent benevolences, and only one. Slavery did have special connotations, but abolitionism and other good causes complemented one another. They would ultimately stand or fall together, for they were all aimed at the identical problem of removing the barriers to salvation presented by the infinite forms of sin. Antislavery only acquired its special place because slavery created more religious anxiety than did any other aspect of the cosmic tension between good and evil. Even the most ill-educated Christians had long been accustomed to think of man's struggle with sin as a fight against "enslavement to his passions."[1] At home and abroad, social maladjustments of all sorts could be translated into these terms.

In Scotland as in England and America, there were also secular reasons for the intensity of concern over slavery. Because it was the *reductio ad absurdum* of the categorization of labor as commodity, slavery was the most alarming of all social abuses, the horrifying extreme of the distinctiveness between employer and employed. It cannot have been easy to adjust to the changing

1. Elizabeth Mure, "Some Remarks on the Change of Manners in My Own Time," *Selections from the Family Papers Preserved at Caldwell* (3 vols.; Glasgow, 1854), I, 270. I am indebted here to D. B. Davis, *The Problem of Slavery in Western Culture* (Ithaca, N.Y., 1966).

relationships of an industrializing society, and it was accordingly comforting to attack their caricature across the Atlantic. This was true, perhaps particularly true, of the members of the urban middle class who were financially successful. Outwardly they had adapted readily to the nineteenth century, but by the same token they were probably the first to feel physically and psychologically threatened by their increasing distance from the faceless labor force upon which their position depended. It is not in the slightest bit odd that so many Scots abolitionists were prosperous, any more than it is strange that almost all of them were heavily involved in other good causes, both at home and abroad. Nor is there a paradox in saying that in Scotland as in other countries, the urgency of the attack on slavery was quickened rather than the opposite by worsening domestic problems. Abolitionism was in part fueled by local anxieties. It gathered strength when the consistent threats to religion and to stable society at home became more apparent than in the relatively innocent days of the eighteenth century.

The most alarming of all nineteenth-century Scotland's domestic ills was the problem of the unchurched poor. They were at the same time a serious threat to organized religion and an alarming hint that the organic bonds of traditional society were slackening. In Glasgow in particular, the threat was compounded by its connection with Catholic immigration. In the previous century, remarked one Victorian historian, the city had been "totally destitute of these hordes of Milesian helots." In 1792 there had just been enough of them to fit up the Mitchell Street tennis court as a temporary "mass-house." Five years later they opened a little chapel in the Gallowgate, in 1815 an ostentatious Gothic church in Clyde Street. Four years later there were 8,245 of them. By 1851 massive immigration had brought the total up to a terrifying 90,000. Even at the 1841 census, before the Famine, an incredible 5 percent of the total Scottish population was Irish-born. This was distributed fairly widely, in small towns and even in rural areas.[2]

The "Patlanders" were only an especially distasteful aspect of

2. J. Strang, *Glasgow and Its Clubs; or Glimpses of the Manners, Characters, and Oddities of the City, During the Past and Present Century* (London, 1856), 116–18; J. Handley, *The Irish in Scotland, 1798–1845* (2nd ed.; Cork, 1945), 89–90.

a wider problem. Evangelical Christians were perhaps less realistic than their ancestors in their hopes for a godly society that would promote universal salvation. Throughout Scotland, they spent the whole period in a state of acute anxiety about the numbers of the irreligious poor in general. This was not necessarily because there were more of the poor or because they were poorer, although, relatively speaking, they may have been. What mattered was that they tended to be forced increasingly into discrete communities of their own. This made them more visible, more distinct, and therefore more threatening in every possible sense.

Even Edinburgh, though it remained a professional and bureaucratic capital instead of an industrial one, was much affected. The city had come very far from the days when a lord of session and a laborer might live on different floors of the same tenement, and the principal of the university could joke with the water cadies at the Tron. The rich and fashionable who had been able to resist the pull of London had moved to the gorgeous terraces and squares of the first and second New Town. Even the more modest middle class would soon begin to move into new areas away from the old center. The lands and closes of the Old Town, where all the intellectuals of the golden age had once lived, had become a scandalous and terrifying slum. In a smaller town like Aberdeen, where the spectre of the unchurched poor walked less obviously, it was still the main anxiety of the churches.[3]

Indeed this concern was reflected in every Scottish city—in Dundee, Paisley, and Kircaldy, and in old market towns like Dunfermline, Dumfries, Ayr, and Kilmarnock, where the textile industry had gathered a significant urban working class. Throughout Scotland church leaders were faced with an alien population that lived in visible squalor, in deepening ignorance of religion, and at greater physical, linguistic, cultural, and psychological distance from their social superiors. Their situation strengthened the barriers to their salvation and at the same time heightened uneasiness over the dislocation of traditional relationships. The nightmare of

3. D. J. Withrington, "Non-Church-Going, c. 1750–c. 1850: A Preliminary Survey," *Records of the Scottish Church History Society*, XVII (1973), 133–48; F. Engels, *Condition of the Working Class in England*, ed. W. O. Henderson and W. O. Challoner (Oxford, 1958), 41–43; A. A. Maclaren, "Presbyterianism and the Working Class in a Mid-Nineteenth Century City," *SHR*, XLVI (1967), 115–39.

a mechanistic society freed from paternalistic restraints—a nightmare both secular and religious—was becoming a reality.

It would be a mistake, however, to ascribe the benevolent work that resulted to pure fear of a faceless proletariat or even to a wish to control them for class ends, though there were doubtless some upon whom such motives had an effect. The poor themselves were worrying, but they also gave rival denominations opportunities to make converts and strengthen their following. All the Scottish churches feared Popery, but not as much as they feared each other. The established Old Kirk, in particular, had good reason to fear the advance of voluntary or dissenting denominations opposed to religious establishments, especially in Glasgow and the other cities of the Southwest. For many ministers, too, the unconverted poor gave fine opportunities for evangelism, a field in which the intense psychological strains of the personal conversion experience could be relieved by the drive into lifting the barriers to universal salvation. It was quite possible for the convert to see Arminianism as "the essence of rebellion," but still be impelled to express his intense gratitude for the gift of grace through good works.[4] No such expression of gratitude and no proof of revulsion from personal sinfulness could be more acceptable than to try to bring others to the state of personal purification where they too could receive grace. The result was a determination to remove the shackles of indolence, ignorance, and intemperance—in short, to inculcate the "ethic of respectability." It was for this purpose that each Scottish city, in the twenties and thirties, developed its complex of home missionary and tract societies, temperance organizations, and Bible societies.[5] At the same time that those institutions absorbed individual missionary energies, they soothed anxieties over the apparent breakdown of traditional religious and social bonds exemplified by the growing numbers of the unchurched poor.

4. R. Wardlaw, "The Nature and Uses of Good Works," Sermons (Edinburgh, 1829), 157–61.
5. L. C. Saunders, Scottish Democracy, 1815–1840 (London, 1950), 222–37; A. A. Maclaren, Religion and Social Class: The Disruption Years in Aberdeen (London, 1974), 167–207. On the social control controversy, see L. Banner, "Religious Benevolence as Social Control: A Critique of an Interpretation," JAH, LX (1973), 23–41.

The domestic response was only one campaign in the world war against the forces of sinfulness, though domestic problems themselves were terrifying illustrations of its urgency. Exactly the same returns could be gained by carrying the fight overseas. This too could absorb the energy released by individual conversion. Moreover, foreign work was equally potent in assuaging anxieties over the apparently unstable state of society at home. In two areas, the rewards for foreign benevolence were specially alluring. Missionary work not only represented a direct obedience to the injunctions of the Savior but also offered a psychologically attractive element of risk, even possible martyrdom. Antislavery work, too, was particularly comforting because it was a paradigm for total warfare against the spiritual enslavement of man prior to the gift of grace. It therefore represented a comprehensive statement against the forces of evil in all their manifestations, whether at home or abroad. At the same time, by reaffirming their distrust of the impersonal chattel relationship, the abolitionists were doubtless able to gain some confidence in their ability to handle the frightening qualities of their own society, which itself seemed headed towards a depersonalization of labor. Whether in a religious or a purely secular sense—though the two were seldom separated—the unchurched poor were the main contributors to the insecurity of the middle class. The new distance between employer and employed signalized the loss of an organic social unity that had been familiar and comforting, whether or not it had ever been real.

To that extent antislavery was an important symbolic response to both the social and spiritual shortcomings of early industrial Scotland. It actually gained in urgency as concern over the magnitude of these shortcomings deepened. It is no accident that Glasgow was one of the filthiest and most squalid cities in early Victorian Britain but that its contribution to American abolition was outstanding. There is no paradox behind the deep commitment to the benevolent ethic among its own close corporation town council. It is not a surprise that it was in Glasgow, an early slum city, that John Dunlop founded the first temperance societies in Britain and that Thomas Chalmers pioneered his Mechanics' Institutes, or that both men were also deeply interested in slavery. Glasgow charities were energetic but unostentatious, with "no colonnaded facade or florid minaret, reared rather to minister to the vanity of the giver than to the necessities of the recipient," for human vanity was the least pressing of benevolent motives.[6] Middle-class philanthropy was a response to signs that society had become irreligious and atomized, and it fulfilled exactly the same function whether it took a foreign or domestic direction. In Scotland, as in England and America, the home and overseas branches of the benevolent empire expressed the same concerns and were supported by the same men and women. There were few leaders in the Scottish abolition societies who did not also sit on the committees of one or more groups dedicated to domestic reform.[7]

This catholicity of reform enthusiasm makes the energy the Scots turned to helping the American abolitionists all the more striking. The Glasgow and Edinburgh emancipation societies, in particular, were working enthusiastically for universal emancipation only a few months after the West India Emancipation Act. They continued their activities for many years, and in the case of Glasgow until after the Civil War. At times of uncommon excitement they were able to raise audiences running into thousands.[8] At various points in these thirty years most Scottish cities, even little ones like Berwick-on-Tweed, were able to float antislavery societies, though none but those of Aberdeen, Edinburgh, and Glasgow had a continuous working existence. For obvious reasons, it was always the groups in the two largest cities that were most powerful and most important. They are especially interesting because many of their members developed loyalties different from those of their fellows in other parts of Britain. In 1841, when the schisms in the American movement spread to Britain, the London-based national organization—the British and Foreign Anti-Slavery Society—which was reluctant to associate abolition with other radical issues, took a conservative or "new organization" position opposed to the universal reform views of William Lloyd Garrison and his "old

6. Strang, *Glasgow and Its Clubs*, 512.
7. See Appendices B and D.
8. C. C. Burleigh (ed.), *The Reception of George Thompson in Great Britain, Compiled from Various British Publications* (Boston, 1836), 64; *Liberator*, August 28, 1840.

organization" followers. Many, though by no means all, of the Glasgow and Edinburgh abolitionists took the opposite, or Garrisonian, standpoint. With allies in Dublin, and later in Bristol, they remained the most important supporters of the American radicals until the Civil War, in spite of the more or less consistent conservatism of the national society. The early foundation of the two main Scottish groups is perhaps in itself a hint of their determination to lead an independent course.

The Edinburgh Emancipation Society was founded on October 27, 1833, five weeks before its Glasgow counterpart and indeed before any comparable English body. For the previous few weeks George Thompson, the former Agency Committee lecturer, whose Scottish following was already substantial, had been lecturing in town on the new cause of world emancipation. At the October 27 rally, the chair was taken by the Reverend Dr. John Ritchie of the Relief Secession Church, later a well-known political radical and the city's delegate to the Complete Suffrage Union. It was decided that the old Society for the Abolition of Negro Slavery should be reestablished as the Edinburgh Society for the Abolition of Slavery Throughout the World, thereafter normally referred to as the Edinburgh Emancipation Society. It was committed to the widened cause of abolition of slavery and the slave trade throughout the world. The whole purpose of Thompson's visit to Scotland was to raise money for an American trip he was then planning at Garrison's suggestion. No doubt he was satisfied that the new group came out strongly in his support.[9]

One of the Edinburgh Emancipation Society's main difficulties from the outset was the instability of its leadership. At its foundation, its treasurer was Alexander Cruickshank, a Quaker hosier. Its four secretaries were Dr. Andrew Macaulay, a physician and radical Whig town councilor; James Ogilvy, an accountant; Henry Tod, a Writer to the Signet; and the great botanist Dr. Robert K. Greville. By 1836, Greville and Macaulay had temporarily stopped

9. Minutes for December 6, 1833, in GESMB, I; *Edinburgh Emancipation Society for the Abolition of Slavery Throughout the World, No. 1* (Edinburgh, 1835), 1; G. Thompson, *A Voice to the United States of America from the Metropolis of Scotland: Being an Account of Various Meetings Held in Edinburgh on the Subject of American Slavery, upon the Return of Mr. George Thompson from His Mission to That Country* (Edinburgh, 1836), 3.

abolitionist work, while Cruickshank and Ogilvy had become ordinary committee members. Tod was still a secretary, along with
William Somerville, Jr., who was probably a stationer. A prominent evangelical bookseller, William Oliphant, Jr., had become
treasurer.[10] By 1840, Cruickshank and Greville were sharing most
of the secretarial work. The three other active leaders were John
Dunlop, later one of the most important Anti-Corn Law Leaguers
in Edinburgh; John Wigham, a prosperous Quaker manufacturer
of shawls, who was the friend and brother-in-law of William
Smeal, the secretary of the Glasgow Emancipation Society; and
Charles Ziegler, a Church of Scotland bookseller and publisher
who eventually became a member of the evangelical Free Church.
These were the officials in control of the men's society at the time
of the division of 1841. They resisted pressure to break from the
conservative leadership of the national society, though they were
unable to prevent the local ladies' society from doing so. In 1846
they still formed a caucus that could transmit representative Edinburgh abolitionist opinion to London.[11]

The Edinburgh Emancipation Society was a powerful body, but
it never had such consistent support as the Glasgow one. This and
the instability of the leadership were linked with peculiar conditions against which all the city's benevolent organizations had to
contend. Its philanthropic tradition was not insignificant, though it
had a practical tone. During the postwar depression, for instance,
Edinburgh had the unemployed poor earn their relief money by
cutting out the romantic paths round the Calton Hill, building the
carriage road across Holyrood Park, and leveling Bruntsfield Links
for the genteel golfing public. Yet it developed the same complex
of societies to promote good causes as other nineteenth-century
cities. Its local antislavery tradition, too, was a strong one. The
first abolitionist meeting of 1814, which organized ten thousand
signatures for a parliamentary petition, was a classic example of
the intertwining of Scotland's religious and political radicalism.
The *Edinburgh Review* group were vigorous antislavery men, es-

10. "Committee of the Edinburgh Society for the Abolition of Negro Slavery,"
in Oliver and Boyd's *Edinburgh Almanac or Universal Scots and Imperial Register
for 1835*, 453; Thompson, *Voice to the United States*, 8.
11. A. Cruickshank to J. Scoble, June 13, 1846, C15/130, A. Cruickshank to
J. Scoble, June 8, 1846, C15/130a, both in ASP.

pecially the volatile Brougham, whose enterprises towards the March of the Mind were bitterly satirized in Thomas Love Peacock's portrait of the Steam Intellect Society. Another of the Reviewers, the prominent Edinburgh journalist Thomas Pringle, became secretary of the London Anti-Slavery Society in 1827.[12] What gave the early Edinburgh movement its distinctiveness, however, was the work of the Old Kirk minister of Saint George's in Charlotte Square, Andrew Thomson. He changed the course of the British antislavery movement by taking an immediatist position in 1830. Most Edinburgh evangelicals were quick to follow Thomson's lead.[13] It was logical that the city which gave birth to the first immediatist society in Britain should, three years later, almost to the day, float the first group committed to world abolition.

This did not make it any easier to maintain enthusiasm in Edinburgh on a continuing basis. No one in his senses, or at least no one of means and in his senses, remained in the capital over the summer if it could be avoided. Edinburgh was not a commercial city in any sense of the word. When the courts and the university were out of term, there was very little of an elite left. There was a philanthropy season in Edinburgh, and like all seasons it carried with it a close season. Most of the interruptions in its antislavery work lead back to this kind of problem. Dr. Greville once had to write that an August rally was out of the question because "there is *Scarcely a Member of committee in Town.*" He suggested that Glasgow would be a much better prospect, "being a commercial place always in a state of activity."[14]

The Glasgow Emancipation Society was founded five weeks later than the Edinburgh one, and it was from the outset the

12. J. Anderson, *A History of Edinburgh from the Earliest Period to the Completion of the Half Century 1850* (Edinburgh, 1856), 329; Saunders, *Scottish Democracy,* 222–37; W. Ferguson, *Scotland, 1689 to the Present* (Edinburgh, 1968), 275; Anderson, *History of Edinburgh,* 442–43; T. Pringle, *Narrative of a Residence in South Africa,* ed. A. M. Lewin Robinson (Cape Town, 1966), ix, xxvii, xxx.

13. Anderson, *History of Edinburgh,* 405–06; Thomson, *Substance of the Speech Delivered at the Edinburgh Society for the Abolition of Slavery, on October 19, 1830* (Edinburgh, 1830); *idem, Slavery Not Sanctioned, But Condemned by Christianity* (London, n.d.); Edinburgh Female Anti-Slavery Association, Resolution and Rules, report adopted November 29, 1830, copy in John Rylands' Library, Manchester.

14. R. Greville to J. Tredgold, August 2, 1840, C7/72, in ASP; E. Wigham to M. Estlin, July 27, 1853, in BPL-G.

stronger of the two bodies. A group first met to discuss its formation on December 6, 1833.[15] They had been summoned by a circular from John Murray, a modest landowner and placeman, the col-
lector of customs at Bowling Bay, one of the small Clyde ports.
Murray came from a good family. He was distantly related to the
Oswalds of Shieldhall, a branch of a substantial West Indian family of the eighteenth century. As a child he had had serious pul-
monary trouble, and he had been sent out to Saint Kitts for a cure
in his early twenties. He worked there for ten years, passed
through a conversion experience, and returned to the West of
Scotland a convinced evangelical and abolitionist. He was heavily
committed to organizational radicalism in religion, and he eventually left the prestigious Tron Church to join the Relief Secession,
specifically over the issue of patronage. In person, as his friend
James McCune Smith put it, he was "tall and gaunt, and would
strongly remind one of Henry Clay." The resemblance stopped
there—"he never made a speech of one minute long"—but he was
a tireless and talented administrator, and a man of extraordinary
dedication.[16] He was apparently convinced, like so many of the
Scots abolitionists, that both patronage and slaveholding were
forms of property ownership distorted to a point that made them
the symbolic antithesis of vital Christianity.

At the preliminary meeting in Glasgow, Murray was able to
read an anticolonizationist circular from the New England Anti-
Slavery Society, as well as Garrison's 1833 *Appeal to the Friends
of Negro Emancipation Throughout Great Britain*. Although Garrison did not visit Scotland on his 1833 trip, Scots had already been
exposed to the controversy with the American Colonization Society by Murray's eccentric evangelical friend Charles Stuart, who
had been lecturing round the country against Eliot Cresson before
Garrison had even left America. Before they heard Stuart's critique, they had given enough money to the society to be promised
that one of the villages in Liberia would be called Edina.[17] The

15. Minute for December 6, 1833, in GESMB, I.
16. J. Smith, "John Murray," in J. Griffiths (ed.), *Autographs for Freedom* (Boston, 1853), 62–67. See also Resolutions of the New England Anti-Slavery Convention, Ms. 3925 f.206, in Small Collections, SNL.
17. C. Stuart, *Liberia; or, the American Colonization Scheme Exposed: A Full
and Authentic Report of a Lecture Delivered . . . at a Public Meeting in the Rev.
Mr. Anderson's Chapel, Glasgow, 1st April, 1833* (Glasgow, 1833); cf. W. Innes,

meeting was also encouraged by an enthusiastic letter from Dr. Ralph Wardlaw, the leading Congregationalist and pillar of the voluntary churches, who had just drawn an explicit parallel between emancipation and the atonement in his "jubilee sermon." It also heard the resolutions already adopted by the Edinburgh Society. The meeting was chaired by Anthony Wigham, a Quaker ironmonger who moved soon afterwards to Aberdeen, where he formed another small but active abolition group. Eventually the Glasgow reformers chose Murray as interim secretary and agreed to call a meeting to launch a Glasgow society similar to the Edinburgh one.[18]

The first full meeting was held in Wardlaw's Congregationalist chapel in West George Street. To the voluntaries or Scottish dissenters, who were opposed to the established Old Kirk and at that time included the most influential evangelicals in the west of Scotland, this was a prestigious venue. It was also a hint of the strength the society hoped to draw from the dissenting denominations, whether from historically antiestablishment groups like the Congregationalists, or from the Presbyterian Secession Churches, which had only moved to a voluntary position, partly under American influence, in the twenties. The meeting was highly successful. The new association was entitled "the Glasgow Emancipation Society, having for its Object the Abolition of Slavery throughout the World," and its subscription was set at the large sum of five shillings. Robert Grahame of Whitehill, an old ally of Thomas Clarkson's, sent word that he would be prepared to become president. The new society resolved that it too would support George Thompson's mission to the United States.[19]

The officials of the GES were able to build on a strong local tradition of benevolence as well as one of antislavery commitment. Glasgow had begun to turn against slavery before its West India involvement was forcibly ended by the Act of 1833. One of the

---

Liberia: or the Early History of the American Colony of Free Negroes on the Coast of Africa, Compiled from American Documents (Edinburgh, 1831); R. Cresson to R. Gurley, January 28, 1833, in Letters Received, American Colonization Society Papers, LC, cited in B. Fladeland, *Men and Brothers: Anglo-American Antislavery Cooperation* (Urbana, Ill., 1972), 211.

18. Circular of December 7, 1833, in GESMB, I, in flyleaf.

19. Minutes for December 12, 1833, in GESMB, I. For a list of Scottish denominations, see Appendix A.

secretaries of the new society was William Smeal, a Quaker tea merchant who does not seem to have been a leader in the earlier movement. His colleague John Murray, however, had been much involved in the campaign for West India emancipation. The local abolition society had been founded in 1823, but it was Ralph Wardlaw who persuaded it to take an immediatist position, only a few weeks after Andrew Thomson did the same for the Edinburgh group.[20] Wardlaw now became senior vice-president of the new society. It would have been surprising if Glasgow had made major contributions to the movement before 1833, but it had at least made respectable ones upon which the GES was able to build. In practical terms, however, it was more important that the new society was blessed with a stable leadership throughout its life.

Both the Edinburgh and Glasgow Emancipation Societies had two or more secretaries and a treasurer. Their institutional structure gave these officials disproportionate power. Beneath them was an unwieldy committee decorated by city reformers prominent in other good causes, and sometimes by pious gentry from the surrounding countryside. This was the usual system for a Victorian benevolent society. Since committee attendance was full only at times of extraordinary excitement, they operated in practice through a handful of active leaders working over the heads of officials and rank-and-file members who lacked the time for, or interest in, day-to-day administration. The Glasgow society allowed itself three or four vice-presidents, but their function, like that of the presidents, was largely ornamental.[21]

It would have been difficult to devise a system that concentrated more power in the hands of the secretaries. Committees were theoretically elected at anniversaries, and general policy was sometimes discussed by meetings of all the society's members and friends. The resolutions that went before such gatherings were checked by members active enough to serve on and attend committee meetings, but they were drafted by the secretaries and

20. W. L. Alexander, *Memoirs of the Life and Writings of Ralph Wardlaw, D.D.* (Edinburgh, 1846), 297–300.
21. GESR, 1834–1851, give printed committee lists showing the structure of the committee. New committees were only listed in GESMB until 1836. The Edinburgh society seems to have abandoned its honorary officials after 1835.

seldom challenged unless highly controversial. The same was true of most of the pamphlets and broadsheets published by the society. Again, the secretaries carried on the bulk of the correspondence and often decided on their own initiative to whom they should write and who should be invited to speak in their city. At the same time, communications from other societies and the stream of pamphlets and papers sent from America all passed through their hands. Though none of the Scots officials ever acquired the same encyclopaedic knowledge as someone like Richard Davis Webb of Dublin, they too steeped themselves in antislavery literature. Smeal eventually came to edit the *British Friend*, a paper that was at first devoted to abolition, and Dunlop and Greville both produced important pamphlets. Their specialist knowledge of events in America was at least enough to discourage challenges from rank-and-file members or even committee colleagues. None of these men was ever paid, but the power of Smeal and Murray, Dunlop and Greville, was very real. This was all the more evident at times of controversy, when they could judiciously weight their societies' attitudes in the direction they found personally most appealing.

When the Scottish societies responded to the schisms in the American movement in 1841, the opinions and temperaments of their officials took on a special importance. In Glasgow, events were turned by the aggressive radicalism of Smeal and Murray, and their personal loyalty to Garrison. In Edinburgh, however, Dunlop, Greville, and Cruickshank stopped short of the social iconoclasm of the British and American Garrisonians. One of their important allies in the EES was John Wigham. But within the Edinburgh Ladies' Emancipation Society, which had been formed as an auxiliary of the EES, they were staunchly opposed by its secretary, Jane Wigham, who was John Wigham's second wife and William Smeal's sister. She cooperated closely with Eliza Wigham, John Wigham's daughter by his first marriage. After 1841, the two of them made their small society one of the country's most effective Garrisonian organizations. Indeed the American schisms were reflected in microcosm in the Wigham household at 5 South Gray Street. While the old man was supporting the conservative leaders of the male Edinburgh society, the rest of the family were using the secretaryship of the ELES to radicalize it in the same way as Murray and Smeal in the Glasgow group.[22]

Both the Wigham and Smeal families were North Country immigrants to Scotland, and both had a great role to play in this later phase of the country's antislavery movement. Both had arrived in the 1780s, paradoxically when the Society of Friends was losing Scottish membership. Both had originally lived in Edinburgh as members of Edinburgh Two Monthly Meeting. William Smeal was born in Leith in 1793, but moved to Glasgow as a child. Later he became a modestly successful grocer and teaman in the Gallowgate. In spite of his extreme views on slavery, he remained a deeply traditional Friend, whose "Quaker simplicity" William Lloyd Garrison praised rather patronizingly.[23] One of his family friends was Anthony Wigham, who was a founding vice-president of the GES. When he moved to Aberdeen, he set up a smaller society there. It was to his cousin John Wigham of Edinburgh, called John Tertius, that Smeal's sister Jane became married in 1840. Prior to this she had been secretary of the Glasgow Ladies' Emancipation Society, which had been formed at the same time as the men's society as its auxiliary. His daughter Eliza never married, and she is the Eliza Wigham who was still very much a force in Edinburgh philanthropy in the seventies. Her father was in partnership with Anthony's brother John, usually referred to as John Wigham, Jr., an important Edinburgh radical and an associate of Duncan Maclaren. His family lived at 10 Salisbury Road, five minutes away from John Wigham Tertius, and all were "on terms of closest love and friendly intimacy."[24]

22. M. Estlin to M. W. Chapman, October 27, 1855, in BPL-G.
23. G. B. Burnett and W. H. Marwick, *The Story of Quakerism in Scotland* (London, 1952), 164; W. L. Garrison to J. Nichol, October 9, 1865, Ms. 3925, in Small Collections. Family information here and elsewhere is taken from the typescript *Biographical Dictionary*, in Friends' House, London. Business information is from the Glasgow post office directories, 1834–1841. There is a condensed family tree of the Wighams, showing their relationships with the Smeals and Richardsons, in G. C. Taylor (ed.), *British and American Abolitionists: An Episode in Transatlantic Understanding* (Edinburgh, 1975), 547.
24. "Address to Prudence Crandall," in GESR, 1835, 42; J. Smeal to E. Pease, December 21, 1836, in WLG-G; *Eliza Wigham: A Brief Memorial, Reprinted and Revised from the "Annual Monitor"* (London, 1901), 10–16; J. B. Mackie, *Life of Duncan Maclaren* (2 vols.; Edinburgh, 1888), I, 122–23, 232, 236, 249, and II, 14; London *Patriot*, January 9, 1840; *League*, January 20, 1844; Jane Wigham to M. W. Chapman, January 4, 1847, in BPL-W.

The wider relationships of the Wighams were as interesting as their intimate ones. John Wigham Tertius' first wife had been Jane Richardson of Whitehaven. This and the marriage of John Wigham Jr.'s daughter Jane to Edward Richardson of Newcastle tied them to the leading family in the English free produce movement, and incidentally gave rise to some suspicion among the most radical abolitionists. Again, John Wigham Tertius' daughter Mary married into the Edmundson family of Dublin, thus connecting them by marriage to Richard Davis Webb's wife Hannah. Eliza Wigham spent most of her summers with her sister, among the Dublin "anti-everythingarians," and indeed most of her relations moved permanently to Ireland later in the century. The connections of the Scottish Quakers became all the more elaborate in the fifties, when they were joined by two able former Friends who had been disowned for their marriages. One was Priscilla Bright Maclaren, daughter of John Bright and wife of the radical Lord Provost of Edinburgh. The other, even more important, was Elizabeth Pease Nichol, the Darlington Garrisonian leader who moved to Glasgow after marrying the professor of astronomy there, a man much her inferior, as the abolitionists thought. After his death she moved to Edinburgh to live with Eliza Wigham. Their house was still a gathering place for Edinburgh radicals long after the Civil War, and it was after long conversations there that John Hyslop Bell set about writing his *British Folks and British India*.[25] The Wighams and Smeals moved in a cohesive world of reformers. Their Quakerism apart, however, they were typical of the leaders of the Glasgow and Edinburgh emancipation societies. All came from a background of solid but unspectacular prosperity, and most were voluntaries or other types of dissenting Christians outside the established Church of Scotland.[26]

25. A. Paton to W. L. Garrison, February 7, 1851, in BPL-G; *Eliza Wigham: A Brief Memorial*, 6; D. Riach, "Ireland and the Campaign Against American Slavery, 1830–1860" (Ph.D. dissertation, University of Edinburgh, 1975), 111; Mackie, *Life of Duncan Maclaren*, I, 52–53; R. D. Webb to M. W. Chapman, July 24, 1857, in BPL-W; J. H. Bell, *British Folks and British India Fifty Years Ago* (London, 1891), 2.

26. The Glasgow committee lists on which the following section is based are taken from GESR, prior to the division of the society in 1841. The Edinburgh committee has been reconstructed more imperfectly, by taking names that appear in one or both of the lists in Oliver and Boyd's *Edinburgh Almanac or Universal Scots and Imperial Register for 1835*, p. 453, and Thompson, *Voice to the United*

The Glasgow committee included only one landed gentleman, Robert Grahame of Whitehill. He was Provost of the city and, incidentally, the brother of the author of "The Sabbath." Of the two permanent secretaries, one was a grocer and tea merchant, and the other a West Indiaman who had retired to become a senior customs official, though Murray's work was done for part of 1834 by Smeal's brother James, who was a surgeon. Until his emigration to Canada, the treasurer was James Johnston, who was probably a provision merchant or wholesale grocer. He was succeeded by James Beith, an umbrella manufacturer.[27] The vice-presidents during most of the period prior to 1841 were Anthony Wigham, the Quaker ironmonger, and the Reverend Drs. Ralph Wardlaw, James Heugh, and Alexander Kidston, all voluntary ministers much given to denouncing the Old Kirk. In 1839 they were joined by Baillie William P. Paton, a future leader of the anti-Garrison party in Glasgow, who was a commission merchant, or broker, and the equivalent of an alderman.

Of the lay committee members of the Glasgow society, thirty-nine were appointed and served between 1833 and 1841. There is some difficulty in identifying all of them, due to duplication of commonplace names, but only three definitely do not appear in the post office directories and can therefore be assumed to have had no business or professional interests. It is significant, however, that only seven of the seventeen members added during the society's alliance with the Chartists in 1839 had interests substantial enough for their names to appear in the directory for that year.[28] Prior to 1841, however, almost all of them owned or managed professional or commercial enterprises, though none of them was rich enough to be nationally famous in the same way as men like Joseph Sturge or Samuel Gurney in England. For good tactical reasons, members included one newspaper editor and four booksellers

States, 8. Unless otherwise stated, information on occupations comes from the post office directories for Glasgow, and from titles next to names on the Edinburgh lists. The analysis in the text is based on _all_ the names appearing on both the Edinburgh lists, and _all_ the Glasgow ones prior to 1841. For the sake of brevity, Appendices B to E are more selective.

27. J. R. Anderson (ed.), _The Burgesses and Guild Brethren of Glasgow, 1751–1846_ (Edinburgh, 1935), 316.

28. GESR, 1841. See also Appendix E.

or publishers, among them George Gallie, who handled most of the society's pamphlets and reports. There were only six other men in professional occupations—two "writers," or lawyers, one teacher, one accountant, one doctor, and James McCune Smith, the future black American leader who was then a medical student at Glasgow University. Apart from Smith, no college student or teacher ever served on the committee, a matter for considerable astonishment in a Scottish city. The bulk of the group were in substantial business occupations, ranging from shipping agents and spirit dealers to the most interesting of all, Robert Kettle, who was a national temperance leader and a cotton yarn merchant. With the single exception of William Smeal himself, all the lay members of committee who were neither professional nor landed were prosperous enough to have become burgesses, in most cases by purchase.[29]

The religious bias of the committee is also of some interest. There is no convenient way of finding out the affiliations of the lay committee members. However, the ministers on the committee were presumably there because their fellow members belonged to the same denominations. The identification of the twenty-two ministers who served on the committee at one time or another before 1841 provides a rough guide to the religious composition of the society at large. Only three, James McTear, Edward Campbell, and Robert Thompson, do not appear in the ecclesiastical lists of Oliver and Boyd's *Edinburgh Almanac and National Repository*. This implies either that they were very young clergymen who were never given a parish, or, more probably, that they were Baptists, Methodists, or Unitarians, who are not included in this work. In either case, the rest were overwhelmingly from the voluntary denominations. Only four were ministers in the established Church of Scotland, and one of these was Patrick Brewster, a moral force Chartist from Paisley, whose brother was the Principal of Edinburgh University. Four were Congregationalists, one a Baptist, and one a Wesleyan Methodist. Four came from the United Secession Church, five from the Relief Secession, and two from the Original Secession. All these men were voluntaries, but half of them came from the old Secession Churches. Though they

29. Anderson (ed.), *Burgesses and Guild Brethren*.

had long been outside the established Old Kirk, and bitterly hostile to it, they had recently sharpened their antagonism, at the outset of the Voluntary Controversy, by adopting the true voluntary position of opposition to religious establishments in general.[30] In conclusion, the Glasgow antislavery movement was dominated, after 1833, by a prosperous sector of the middle class. But it was a sector belonging not to the strengthening evangelical wing of the established Old Kirk, but to the full range of voluntary or dissenting denominations. Though their theological liberalism varied drastically, they were equally hostile to an Erastian establishment, including the party within it that would eventually become the Free Church at the Disruption of 1843. More emancipation society committee members also served on the committee of the Glasgow Voluntary Church Society than on any of the city's other benevolent organizations.

The relative weakness of religious dissent in Edinburgh and the relative strength of the business community in Glasgow account for most of the differences between the leadership of the two societies. In Edinburgh, there are two surviving lists of the committee, the first of them in the *Edinburgh Almanac* for 1835, where the society is still described under its old name of the Edinburgh Society for the Abolition of Slavery. It allowed itself a little gentility among its honorary officials. Its president was Lord Moncrieff, a law lord who was also ninth baronet of Moncrieff, and son of the evangelical churchman Sir Harry Moncrieff. One of the three vice-presidents was Henry Lord Cockburn, the Lord of Session, friend and schoolfellow of the Reviewers, and great raconteur. Another was the Reverend Dr. Robert Gordon, another evangelical, who went to the Free Church at the Disruption. The third was the Reverend Edward Craig, a leading Episcopalian. The same list showed Alexander Cruickshank, the Quaker hosier, as treasurer, and Robert Greville, the Episcopalian botanist, as one secretary. Dr. Andrew Macaulay, another secretary, was also an

30. Clerical members have been traced through the ecclesiastical lists in Oliver and Boyd's *Edinburgh Almanac and National Repository*, 1834–1841; *Fasti Ecclesiae Scotticanae*; occasional references in GESMB. W. Ewing (ed.), *Annals of the Free Church of Scotland, 1843–1900* (2 vols.; Edinburgh, 1914), II, 76–363, provides a *fasti* for those ministers who were in the Old Kirk but joined the Free Kirk at the Disruption in 1843.

Episcopalian. The denominations of the other two secretaries are not known, but they were respectively an accountant and a lawyer. On the next list available, which is published in one of George Thompson's pamphlets in 1836, all these senior officials except Henry Tod, the lawyer, had dropped out. Tod had been joined by William Somerville, a stationer, as cosecretary, and Cruickshank had been replaced as treasurer by a bookseller named Somerville. Cruickshank and Greville reappeared as leaders of the society later in the decade, along with their friends John Dunlop, the Congregationalist "manufacturer," William Ziegler, the Free Church bookseller, and John Wigham, the shawl maker.

Thirty-three of the society's lay committee members appear on one or both of the lists available, excluding men like Cruickshank, who served at one time or another as executive officials. Three of these are given titles identifying them as substantial gentlemen. One, Captain Hugh Rose, was an ex-soldier. Ten came from various branches of the Edinburgh legal establishment. One of them, incidentally a Baptist, was an accountant, one of them was an agent, and three were doctors. One is described as an engineer, and eight were in commercial businesses of one kind or another. Four are unidentified. There were also eight ministers on the ordinary committee. They suggest the voluntary character of the movement even more clearly than it is suggested in Glasgow, in spite of the fact that the overwhelming strength of the voluntaries was in the west of Scotland. Two were from the Cameronian or Reformed Presbyterian Church, and one came from the Associate Synod of Original Seceders. The four others who have been identified—the Reverend Drs. Peddie and John Ritchie, William Peddie, and Edward Halley of Leith—were all leaders of the United Secession Church.[31] All of them appear only on the second committee list, from which Dr. Gordon of the Old Kirk, as well as Cockburn and Moncrieff, had disappeared. These loyalties tell a very clear story. After the first few years of its life, the Edinburgh Emancipation Society was dominated by voluntaries from the Presbyterian Secession Churches. Though the secessionists later played a lesser part in antislavery in Edinburgh than men like

31. Information from titles in committee lists, and C. B. Watson (ed.), *Roll of Edinburgh Burgesses and Guild Brethren* (Edinburgh, 1833).

Wigham, Greville, and Dunlop, the society never drew much support from either wing of the established church, though the latter's
evangelicals had played a major part in the fight against slavery
in the West Indies.

It is no surprise to find the Edinburgh society with more lawyers
and doctors than the Glasgow one. Edinburgh, then as now, was a
city ruled by the professional classes. In both cases, voluntarism
and prosperity were the main characteristics of the abolitionist
leadership. This also appears to have been the case in the little
society in Aberdeen, which included the moral philosopher Principal Daniel Dewar of Marischal College but was otherwise thoroughly voluntary in tone. Dewar is the only university professor
who appears in the Scottish antislavery movement at this stage,
in spite of the high social status of academics in Scotland. The
reason for this is that there was no such thing as a voluntary professor, since acceptance of a chair implied loyalty to the Old Kirk.
Dewar himself was an evangelical and antipatronage man, but he
could not follow those who seceded from the establishment at the
Disruption of 1843, since this would have involved demitting office.[32] Along with Dr. Gordon of the Edinburgh society, and Patrick Brewster of Paisley, he was the only prominent minister of
the Church of Scotland who worked energetically for universal
abolition after 1833 .

Of the fashionable form of evangelicalism that Andrew Thomson had harnessed to the movement there was no longer a trace.
All the establishment ministers who had served on the 1823 committee of the Edinburgh Abolition Society had withdrawn.[33] Perhaps this was because the evangelicals in the Old Kirk were now
so heavily involved in the first stages of the Ten Years' Conflict
against the moderate or propatronage party. They were also fighting a rearguard action of their own against the voluntary onslaught
on the principle of religious establishments. The new universal
abolition societies, in either case, were led by those very voluntaries who were at odds with both parties in the Old Kirk. They

32. Rice, "Abolitionists and Abolitionism in Aberdeen," 83–85; G. Martin, *Emi-
nent Divines in Aberdeen and the North* (Aberdeen, 1888), 223–26.
33. *First Annual Report of the Edinburgh Society for Promoting the Mitigation
and Ultimate Abolition of Slavery* (Edinburgh, 1823), where the committee list
has five ministers of whom three came from the Church of Scotland.

were prosperous and professionally successful. In general their politics were Whig or radical. If, however, they occasionally found their role in British politics frustrating, their religion also denied them the surrogate political life of the national church. This may explain the zest with which they carried on their interdenominational feuds, in particular the long vendettas against the establishment itself. In this context, antislavery must have been all the more attractive to them after 1833, because it was a good cause that their Old Kirk rivals had abandoned at the crucial point where it could be argued that the real worldwide struggle was beginning.

These church loyalties are the major distinctive characteristic of the Scottish abolitionists. Their leadership was not as prosperous as that of the later BFASS. There was no one in the Scottish societies to rival the merchant princes of the national society. The Friends had a strong grip on it, and among them were some of the wealthiest men in Britain.[34] To take two examples, Joseph Sturge was the richest corn merchant in the country, and Joseph Gurney's fortune laid the foundation of the modern Barclay's Bank. These men were very far removed from little provincial Quakers like Smeal and Cruickshank and the other men who served with them on the two main Scottish committees. However, the later schisms in the British movement do not appear to lead back to a crude economic division between local and national leaders. The difference in wealth was one of degree. Their rivalries less often reflected a lateral division within British society as a whole than a vertical division between one part of the country and another, though it is also true that all such lines were blurred. The Scottish leaders, in purely Scottish terms, were fairly well off, even if they were seldom people of real public consequence. There were certainly gradations of wealth between different British leaders, and the poorer ones may occasionally have felt socially inferior to the richer ones. In general, however, their class interests and system of values were similar.

The American theory that the abolitionists were led by a dis-

---

34. H. R. Temperley, *British Anti-Slavery, 1833–1870* (London, 1972), 69–70; *idem*, "The British and Foreign Anti-Slavery Society" (Ph.D. dissertation, Yale University, 1960), 49–53.

placed elite has no application in Scotland.[35] Probably those who led the West India campaign were more a part of the Scottish social and political establishment than their successors, but neither group was in any sense in decline. In Glasgow, after 1833, the dominant element were middling or upper middling manufacturers or merchants, not necessarily first generation ones, profiting from the city's phenomenal growth during the period. In Edinburgh, too, the leaders were substantial dissenters or voluntaries in business or the professions, a self-confident and successful group whose religion was a partial hindrance to their social mobility. Yet their sense of belonging to their churches was strong, for Scottish dissent was expansive in the early part of the century, and the history of secession was a long one. The groups from which the Scottish abolitionists drew their strength were not distinguished from other Christian reformers by circumstances of wealth or status, but by their loyalty to a separate religious tradition.

Their aspirations and day-to-day lives were not markedly different from those of comparable groups in England. It is true that they all spoke Scots. Though the old regional dialects were breaking down among the educated classes, who were already gravitating towards the lingua franca of "educated Scots" spoken by the modern bourgeoisie, their speech would still have been too broad to be readily understood by a modern Englishman or American. This was not yet something that gave them a sense of inferiority, though they had recognized the value of speaking standard king's English since the previous century. With the conspicuous exception of Principal Dewar of Marischal College, who was active in the Aberdeen Anti-Slavery Society, none of them spoke Gaelic. They would have regarded the wearing of the kilt as ridiculous. Like all Lowland Scots prior to Queen Victoria's obsession with Balmoral, they considered the Highlands a desert and the Highlanders a pack of savages, tinged only intangibly with nobility. They themselves were intensely urban. They were beginning to gather in emerging suburban communities, for instance, on the fringes of the second New Town in Edinburgh, or Hillhead in

35. *Cf.* D. Donald (ed.), *Lincoln Reconsidered: Essays on the Civil War Era* (New York, 1961), 19–36; J. Gusfield, *Symbolic Crusade: Status Politics and the Temperance Movement* (Urbana, Ill., 1963).

Glasgow. Perhaps they were using antislavery and other benevolent work to offset the relative loneliness and absence of community ties in the new environment they were creating for themselves.[36] William Smeal, who still lived above his shop in the
Gallowgate, as generations of Scottish shopkeepers had done before him, was an exception. John Murray, who kept a small estate
outside town, and held a patronage civil service post, was even
more unusual. None of them, however, would have been without
two or three domestic servants. Most of the ministers lived in the
kind of modest manse environment described earlier in the century in J. G. Lockhart's *Adam Blair*.

All the leading abolitionists hovered close to a line that divides
the Victorian middle class—the line between those who could
keep their own carriage and those who could not. Only a very few
of them, like Baillie Paton or Duncan Maclaren, rose above it. The
clergymen were equally unlikely to possess a luxury vehicle, though
some did keep the characteristic trap or gig of the country minister. When Dr. Wardlaw sent his own brougham to fetch Mrs. Stowe
during her 1853 Glasgow visit, and was recorded in the papers
as having done so, he must have been the envy of most British
dissenting clergy and many establishment ones too. On the whole
the Scots abolitionists were appealing people. They were fond
of visiting one another, very affectionate, and often extremely wit-
ty. Carriages aside, they are best exemplified by Duncan Maclaren,
"The living voice of Scottish middle-class dissenting radicalism."[37]
Whatever else may be said about the quality of that radicalism, it
is clear that he and his antislavery friends were not consciously
using abolition as a means of diverting attention from abuses at
home. As far as they were concerned, domestic and foreign good
works were all one enterprise, and both were attractive for similar
reasons.

This social background is not distinctive enough to explain the
broad difference between Scottish and English behavior when the

36. In Glasgow, for instance, where information is full, I have taken a city map
and used the post office directories to plot addresses of GES committee members.
They are heavily clustered in Hillhead.
37. Ferguson, *Scotland, 1689 to the Present*, 306.

movement divided in 1841. This difference was always blurred, but it is clear that the radical Garrisonian abolitionists found disproportionate sympathy north of the border. One hypothetical explanation is that their tradition of cultural independence made the Scots in particular respond negatively to London attempts to impose a national uniformity on abolitionists. Perhaps, indeed, the BFASS might have run into just as much difficulty in Scotland if it had taken a radical rather than a conservative position on the American schisms.

Some of the distinctiveness of the Scottish movement also leads back to the strong voluntary loyalties of its leaders. It was natural that they should be attracted to the beleaguered American abolitionists in general. Those who visited Scotland must have seemed an elite of talents, piety, and to some extent wealth, who were excluded from their rightful positions as leaders of their society by having taken the most extreme possible position on slavery. The Scottish voluntaries saw themselves in the same light and felt excluded from their rightful position as leaders of their society by having taken the most extreme possible position on patronage and church establishments. At the same time, the failure of the Old Kirk to carry on the fight for world emancipation could consciously or subconsciously be cast as another backsliding among the persecutors.

In some ways, too, voluntary Christians were more likely than others to adopt the root-and-branch testament of the Garrisonians. This does not mean that all the voluntary abolitionists, or even a majority of them, took Garrison's side in the divisions of 1841. In general, they were socially and theologically conservative men and women to whom his views, objectively considered, were repellent. A few, like John Murray or Andrew Paton of Glasgow, thought through the Garrisonian critique and accepted it on its own ideological merits. But most of those who came to support Garrison and his followers probably did so because they did not perfectly understand their socially radical views on issues other than slavery, or because they were prepared to condone it temporarily for nonideological reasons. For the voluntaries, American radicals, who were relatively harmless because their substantive concerns were foreign, raised comforting and romantic echoes of their own revolutionary religious past. Garrison's group, superficially considered, had special attractions, even more of the alluring quality of being an embattled band of saints, persecuted for the sheer rigor of their testimony on slavery. Their views on nonresistance, on women, and on the Sabbath, heresies that would normally have horrified conservative reformers, and did indeed horrify them once they absorbed their full import, could become tolerable under certain circumstances simply because of their unpopularity, precisely because they were another mark of distinctiveness for seceders who had long been accustomed to think of themselves as a saving remnant. The Secession Churches had always cultivated an inward and outward image as a persecuted minority, in much the same way as the Garrisonians. It is now hard to envisage William Lloyd Garrison as Old Mortality, Samuel Gurney as Bloody Claverhouse, and the World's Convention as Bothwell Brig, but in 1840 and 1841 the parallels may have seemed less arcane. In 1846, it was easy for the voluntaries to respond to the Old Kirk's intolerance of the Garrisonians as another and only too predictable lapse among the Erastians. Most British Christians found the religious and social views of the Garrisonians repulsive, insofar as they understood them, and the Scottish voluntaries at large were no exception. It is still true that in 1841 the American radicals had a better chance of making converts among them, a people steeped in the history of their own distinctiveness, than anywhere else.

Speculation of this sort apart, the Scottish antislavery experience was much affected by the character of the man who founded the Glasgow and Edinburgh emancipation societies. This was George Thompson, who had more influence on the American antislavery movement than any Briton except Richard Davis Webb of Dublin —and Webb is *sui generis*. Many of the Scots who took a radical position in 1840 and 1841 must have done so out of personal loyalty to Thompson. He was a friend and protégé of Dr. Wardlaw, and he was already well known in Scotland when he came north to gain support for his American trip at the end of September, 1833. He had attracted a good deal of attention when he visited Glasgow as an Agency Committee lecturer earlier in the year. The Scots had also followed his debates with the West Indian agent Peter Borthwick, who was himself a member of a prominent Border family.[38] As for the new GES, its loyalty to Thompson was to be a factor in its policy for the next thirty years.

Thompson's career as a professional reformer was an extraordinary one, and it brought his friends into many strange byways of radicalism. Politically he was typical of his constituency: " 'On questions related to manufactures and buying and selling, I am a *free trader*; on subjects related to . . . religion and education, I am a *voluntary*; and on purely political subjects I am a *radical*' (great cheering)." A superlative orator with somewhat vulgar good looks, he had very much of his friend Garrison's gift of inspiring intense personal devotion, especially among women. Perhaps the secret of his success, especially in Scotland, Ireland, and the provinces in general, is that he was sufficiently unpolished to avoid making other provincials feel insecure. Moreover, as the son of a Wesleyan bank clerk from Liverpool, with no higher education beyond a short and abortive enrollment at the Inns of Court, he was never quite socially acceptable to the magnates of the national society. This may have stemmed less from class distrust than from suspicion of a man of brilliant talents who became so professional a reformer that he seemed little more than a sort of rhetorical hired gun. The genteel Edward S. Abdy, for instance, found it hard to sympathize with a man who was pleading a cause simply because someone had put a fee in his pocket. "He is looked on," remarked the Bristol ophthalmologist John Bishop Estlin, "as a sort of *Adventurer*, trading by his wits in any cause open to him." Poorer reformers further removed from the establishment of wealthy piety found a quicker sympathy for a man who clearly found it hard to make ends meet and whose marriage to a social superior had brought nothing but deprivation and childbearing for her, and bitterness for him. Certainly there was never a trace of hypocrisy about Thompson. He was a sort of street Arab of reform, a man who had been raised in a hard and shattering school. There is something deeply attractive about his ready but unpolished gifts,

38. G. Thompson, *Substance of an Address to the Ladies of Glasgow and Its Vicinity, upon the Present Aspect of the Great Question of Negro Emancipation . . . Also, Some Account of the Formation of the Glasgow Ladies' Emancipation Society* (Glasgow, 1833); *A Full Report of the Proceedings at the Meeting of Messrs. Thompson and Borthwick, at Dalkeith . . . Taken from the Glasgow Chronicle* (Glasgow, 1833).

his constant haste, his cheeerful sloppiness, his athletic endurance, his absolute willingness to do the job he had been paid for and do it well. Even Sam Weller, Sr., in spite of his distrust of the Brick Lane branch of the United Grand Junction Ebenezer Society, would have warmed to a temperance lecturer who could write gleefully about a Staten Island Christmas when he and Sidney Gay had conspired to send out for liquor behind the back of Lizzy Neal Gay.[39] Much to Garrison's dismay, too, Thompson held steadfastly to the view that it was not immoral to take snuff. His life had few happy moments, and across the passage of the years it is hard to grudge him either of these impieties.

The sutras of Thompson's reform incarnations would have made a great Victorian novel. He was twenty-nine in 1833, and it was logical to turn the expertise he had acquired working for the Agency Committee to the world attack on slavery, especially since this was also the year in which his lifelong friendship with Garrison began. His first American trip came after the foundation of the Glasgow and Edinburgh Emancipation Societies, over the winter of 1834–1835. Antislavery remained one of his most consistent interests even after his return. He visited America again in 1851, largely to recoup his losses from a short but financially disastrous spell as radical M.P. for Tower Hamlets. On a third American trip, in 1865, he was able to join Garrison in watching the Union flag go up over Fort Sumter. For thirty years Thompson was the most important radical abolitionist in Britain—the only one not tied to the regional movement of a particular city, the only genuinely national figure among the Garrisonian group, and as such accepted as a leader by them all, including the Scots.[40]

Thompson was much more important to the antislavery move-

39. G. Thompson, *Address . . . to the Electors of Tower Hamlets* (London, 1847), 14; entry for May 28, 1835, fragment, in Deborah Weston Diary, BPL-W; G. Stephen, *Anti-Slavery Recollections* (London, 1854), 149–52; E. S. Abdy to [?], n.d., fragment, in BPL-W; J. B. Estlin to S. May, n.d., in BPL-M; G. Thompson to S. H. Gay, May 24, 1859, in Gay Papers, Columbia University Library.

40. C. D. Rice, "The Anti-Slavery Mission of George Thompson to the United States, 1834–1835," *Journal of American Studies*, II (1968), 13–31; W. L. Garrison (ed.), *Lectures of George Thompson, with . . . a Brief History of His Connection with the Anti-Slavery Cause in England* (Boston, 1836), v–x; *Biographical Sketch and Portrait of George Thompson, Esq.*, (rpr. from *India Review*, January, 1843, pp. 1–3; offprint from Norwich *Advertiser*, 1846, copy in BPL; T. Farmer, "Life of George Thompson," *Liberator*, February 26, 1864, only two installments printed; "The Late George Thompson," obituary, n.d., in BM.

ment than it was to him, for it was only one in the gamut of good causes through which he played his life. He spoke frequently for the peace and temperance movements. He became famous for his work as a lecturer for the Anti-Corn Law League. Later he flirted with the Complete Suffrage Union.[41] In 1839 and 1840 he worked as an agent for the Aborigines' Protection Society, and thereafter as a lecturer for the British India Society. He was also editor of its paper, the *British India Advocate*. His visit to India in 1843 was widely publicized in Britain, especially among abolitionists who were quick to see the danger free Indian cotton would pose to the South.[42] In due course he became the agent of the Rajah of Sattarah, a corrupt princeling who described himself as a reforming landlord, in his claim against the British. At one point he had a seat on the Court of East India Proprietors. After his return from his 1851 trip to America, and his failure to be reelected as M.P. for Tower Hamlets, he joined his son-in-law Frederick W. Chesson as coeditor of their own reform paper, the *Empire*. It failed, and Thompson desperately took a job in India as a commercial agent. He returned shattered in health, partly paralyzed. He was a prominent figure in the British Freedmen's Aid movement, and his trip to Fort Sumter with Garrison is one of the major symbolic events in the history of the antislavery movement.[43] He had an extraordinary life, this prizefighter of Victorian reform, but its consistent themes are India, America, the British provinces, and slavery. The last three were also the main themes of the Scottish movement for universal emancipation.

Since Thompson and the Scots had all this in common, it is not

41. For example, see Thompson, *Voice to the United States*, 33–34; *The Speeches Delivered at the Soiree in Honour of George Thompson, Esq.* (Paisley, 1837), 5–13; C. C. Burleigh (ed.), *The Reception of George Thompson in Great Britain: Compiled from Various British Publications* (Boston, 1836), 108 17; London *Patriot*, January 13, 1840; G. Thompson, *Paradise Regained by Sir James Graham, Bart.* (Carlisle, 1842); *National Reform Tracts, No. 1* (London, 1850); *National Reform Tracts, Nos. 2 & 3: The Fifty Shilling Freehold Franchise* (London, 1850).

42. Minute for September 6, 1838, in GESMB, I; GESR, 1839, 26; ASR, February 26, 1840; G. Thompson to R. Allen, December 22, 1840, C154/204, October 19, 1841, C154/205, both in ASP; *Biographical Sketch and Portrait of George Thompson, Esq.*, 11; GESR, 1843, 42ff.; *British Friend*, October 31, 1843, May 31, 1843.

43. C. U. Aitchison (ed.), *A Collection of Treaties, Engagements, and Sanads Relating to India and Neighbouring Countries* (14 vols.; Rev. ed.; Calcutta, 1931), VIII, 361–63; *Anti-Slavery Advocate*, February, 1855; WLG, IV, 97–152.

surprising that so many of them followed him in his loyalty to
Garrison and the American radicals. This is a personal factor, but
it is an important one. It might have been less important if the
Scottish movement had not already had special characteristics of
its own. First, many of its members were voluntaries, men and
women who, though they were conservative in many respects, had
a deep sense of their own distinctiveness from other Christians.
Second, the Scottish societies quickly developed traditions of autonomy that predisposed them against all hints of outside interference. These traditions of autonomy drew strength from the
events of the thirties. Not the least important was George Thompson's visit to the United States.

CHAPTER 3

Portents of Idiosyncrasy
George Thompson
and the Mid-Thirties

During the years from 1833 to 1838, the British antislavery movement presented an outward picture of purposeful unity. The memory of the Emancipation Act was still fresh. Morale never dropped
low enough for the destruction of the apprenticeship system to
seem anything but a foregone conclusion. Condemnation of slavery
was now a part of the churchgoing public's credo that could be
taken for granted. Apart from a few isolated pockets of colonial
high Toryism, the abolitionists were preaching to the converted.
The bitter infighting of the forties and fifties lay in a distant and
inconceivable future. Even north of the border, these were fat and
placid times for the abolitionists. Both the Edinburgh and Glasgow
societies issued pamphlets and drummed up public meetings with
a regularity unmatched at that time in other British cities. For the
discussion of specially interesting subjects, they could draw audiences of two or three thousand. Even when the GES met to present an address to Daniel O'Connell, an action which split the
committee because it implied a standpoint on the Irish repeal
movement, it filled the Trades Hall with three thousand sympathizers.[1] Apart from the quasi-evangelical Anti-Corn Law League,
and the temperance movement in its later phases, no other non-
political cause was ever able to draw support of this order in Scotland. In the whole British context, too, the support of the Scottish
groups, relative to the size of the two cities, was unsurpassed.

Perhaps the Scottish societies would have been less independent
if any national antislavery organization had been continuously

1. Minutes for September 19, 1835, September 23, 1835, in GESMB, I; GESR,
1836, 13–16; *A Full and Correct Account of the Meeting Held in Hope Street
Baptist Chapel, to Present the Emancipation Society's Address to Daniel O'Connell*
(Glasgow, 1835).

active during the thirties. At times when the focus of British abolitionists was on the United States, when there were few opportunities for concrete action, there was no immediate need to maintain a national society to channel such action. In the thirties one could flourish only when the current object of interest did give an opportunity for work coordinated by some form of national institutional structure—in 1833, in the years of the fight against apprenticeship, and after late 1839. By the end of the decade enthusiasm for world abolition was high enough to require a permanent vehicle through which pressure could be brought to bear on the governments concerned, either through lobbying at Whitehall, or memorializing diplomats from guilty foreign nations. The result was the formation of the British and Foreign Anti-Slavery Society. It was kept alive in the forties by the continuing urgency of imperial concerns and by a changing American situation that gave the British new scope for diplomatic activity, for instance, over the Texas question. After 1839, one of the principal concerns of the Scots was to define the way in which they should respond to the national leadership of the BFASS.

In the thirties, however, there was no such continuous national leadership for them to respond to. Early in 1834 the young radicals of the Agency Committee had launched the British and Foreign Society for the Universal Abolition of Slavery and the Slave Trade. In spite of its dynamic leadership, the new group prospered ill, for there was at this time no specific issue over which provincial abolitionists had anything to gain by channeling their efforts through London. The situation changed only when the atrocities of the apprenticeship system were revealed by Joseph Sturge's Caribbean visit in 1836–1837. Sturge, a Quaker corn merchant from Birmingham, a man of great piety and considerable wealth, founded a new Central Negro Emancipation Committee on his return. From November, 1837, coexisting with the now dormant Anti-Slavery Society of 1833, it did the same kind of coordinating work in the fight against apprenticeship as the old Agency Committee had done against slavery. With the overthrow of the apprenticeship and the liberation of the West Indian slaves from the last remnant of their old chattel relationship, the British evangelical public shed its implication in the sins of the planters. There would be important imperial controversies in the future, but none would have the force of West India slavery and apprenticeship. For the moment universal emancipation was the main antislavery interest. It was at this wider problem that the British and Foreign Anti-Slavery Society was aimed.[2]

The BFASS inherited eight of the committee members of the old Universal Abolition Society of 1834. It has survived until the present day. Though it never raised the national enthusiasm of 1833 and 1838, it was vigorous in the forties and fifties, in part because of unwillingness to allow the West Indians to escape public vigilance a second time, but more centrally because of the depth of British interest in world emancipation. Like the provincial societies, it was specially interested in the American situation. Like them, too, it was committed to pacifist methods. Soon after its formation, both the old Anti-Slavery Society and the Central Negro Emancipation Committee dissolved. Its only remaining rival, though it was a formidable one, was Buxton's short-lived African Civilization Society, which proposed to end the slave trade by exposing the West African hinterland to peaceful commerce through opening the Niger.[3] In the next two decades, at the national level at least, there was none of the chopping and changing of the thirties. The BFASS was the only real national vehicle for abolitionist efforts. It was frequently to find itself at loggerheads with its less conservative provincial colleagues.

Although there were several portents of these sorry schisms in the thirties, the movement was still superficially united. Such disagreements as there were were not unfriendly. The thirties were the brief era of good feelings in the American movement, and the British abolitionists were not encouraged in their internal squabbles by their overseas allies. Again, two of the major growth points for future dissidence were still dormant. The Hibernian Anti-Slavery Society was only formed in 1837, at first in close contact with

2. H. Richard, *Memoirs of Joseph Sturge* (London, 1864), 133ff.; J. Sturge and T. Harvey, *The West Indies in 1837* (London, 1838); H. R. Temperley, *British Anti-Slavery, 1833–1870* (London, 1972), 24–27, 29–41; B. Fladeland, *Men and Brothers: Anglo-American Anti-Slavery Cooperation* (Urbana, Ill., 1972), 243–51.
3. BFASS, *Sixty Years Against Slavery* (London, 1900); Temperley, *British Antislavery*; P. D. Curtin, *The Image of Africa: British Ideas and Action, 1780–1850* (Madison, Wis., 1964), 289–317.

London and under the guidance of Sturge's personal friend Richard Allen. The Bristol and Clifton Ladies' Anti-Slavery Society, later a center of ferocious Garrisonianism, was founded in 1840, initially as a formal auxiliary of the national body. Even George Thompson, though he was always thought a little vulgar in some circles, still had enough status for his growing interest in American universal reform to pass unnoticed even by the most respected and conservative national leaders.[4] As went Thompson, so went Scotland. Both the major societies did what they could to support the national leadership.

In the attack on apprenticeship in particular, the future Scottish renegades lined up firmly in support of their more conservative colleagues in England. The job of the Central Negro Emancipation Committee was to coordinate the all-important petitions and pressure on M.P.'s which the provinces alone could provide. In 1837 and 1838 the Glasgow and Edinburgh societies passed repeated resolutions against the West Indians, sent deputations to reason with northern politicians, and drew up mammoth petitions to be presented by their friends in London. The GES petition of April 16, 1838, by itself had 102,200 signatures.[5] In the final stages they sent their own delegates to London, to attend mass meetings in Exeter Hall and march through the city streets, in solemn procession, bearing copies of their resolutions, remonstrances, and petitions against the apprenticeship clause. The Scots who traveled south came not only from Glasgow and Edinburgh but also from smaller regional centers like Paisley and Aberdeen. All Scotland was roused over the apprenticeship. George Thompson found it worthwhile to lecture on it in towns as obscure as Saltcoats and Irvine and even, indeed, Gaelic-speaking Ballater. "Give me the battering ram of opinion," he exhorted British abolitionists at large, "and let me bring the prison house for ever to the ground." The Scots needed little convincing. Even in 1835 John Murray had

4. E. Baldwin to H. Stokes, July 17, 1837, C2/13, July 29, 1837, C2/14; both in ASP; H. M. Wigham, *A Christian Philanthropist of Dublin: A Memoir of Richard Allen* (London, 1886), 13–14, 235, 256; *BCR*, 5 and *passim*; G. Thompson to GES Committee, February 18, 1834, April 17, 1834, August 6, 1834, in GESMB, I.
5. Minutes for March 13, 1837, June 9, 1837, April 16, 1838, in GESMB, II; GESR, 1838, 14; J. Murray to E. Wright, July 20, 1837, in Elizur Wright Papers, LC; W. Smeal to H. Stokes, September 15, 1837, C3/62, R. Greville to H. Stokes, June 15, 1835, C2/102, J. Ogilvy to H. Stokes, August 2, 1837, C3/47, all in ASP.

pointedly remarked that, unlike the Universal Abolition Society, the GES had always known that "nothing but full and complete abolition would answer." In 1837, 1838, and at other times when they thought cooperation worthwhile, the Scots were quite prepared to help their colleagues in the national movement.[6]

This does not mean that there were no signs of future independence. From the outset, both the Glasgow and Edinburgh Emancipation Societies refused to become auxiliaries of the new Universal Abolition Society. At the same time, the Glasgow group announced that they would send funds to the London Anti-Slavery Society only for purposes which they themselves stipulated, specifically to support their agent George Thompson's trip to the United States. Four years later, under Thompson's influence, they merged temporarily with the Aborigines' Protection Society, a move entirely outside the policy of the national leaders. Again, if there is a single theme which runs through the whole of this period, it is George Thompson's influence among abolitionists north of the border.

When the Universal Abolition Society was formed, it immediately set about forming auxiliaries in the provinces. Their job was to be the humble one of collecting what money they could to send to London, as well as whipping up support for petitions organized nationally. This had great appeal for struggling local groups without the means to organize their own propaganda. It had none for the two main Scottish societies, for whom a London affiliation would have meant a real sacrifice of independence and prestige. It may well have rankled, too, that the national group had apparently pirated the worldwide reform idea which they thought of themselves as having pioneered. But even if this was not a factor,

6. Minutes for December 18, 1837, March 14, 1838, March 19, 1838, April 16, 1838, May 17, 1838, in GESMB, II; G. Thompson to W. Oliphant, March 28, 1838, in Gen. Mss., EUL; R. Wardlaw to Miss Wardlaw, April 2, 1838, in W. L. Alexander, *Memoirs of the Life and Writings of Ralph Wardlaw, D.D.* (Edinburgh, 1846), 274–75; Richard, *Memoirs of Joseph Sturge*, 163ff; Aberdeen *Herald*, April 22, 1837; Ms. list of lecture appointments, in Thompson's hand, in Scrapbooks Collected by George Thompson and F. W. Chesson, IV, in LC, hereinafter cited as Thompson Scrapbooks; G. Thompson, *Speech . . . at the Great Anti-Slavery Meeting Held in Hood Street Chapel, Newcastle* (Gateshead, 1838), 10; J. Murray to J. Scoble, June 12, 1835, C20/29, in ASP.

they had funds and members quite adequate for their propaganda
needs, and indeed superior to anything the Universal Abolition
Society itself could then boast.

At its foundation, the Glasgow Emancipation Society's secretary, John Murray, had pointed out with unmistakable satisfaction
that it was turning the normal pattern upside down for the Scots
to lead the nation towards universal abolition. When the society
was asked to become an auxiliary of the London group, it did at
least agree to act "in concert" with that group's proceedings. They
would only send funds to London on the condition that they
should be "applied exclusively to the support of George Thompson's Mission to the United States." The London committee had
hopefully enclosed an "Address to the President" with its circular
to potential auxiliaries, but the Glasgow group refused to accept
some of its expressions, and in some cases to sign it. Murray was
instructed to write off asking for clarification and for an explanation of the suspicious absence of some of the great leaders of the
past from the committee list. The reply was evasive and unsatis-
factory, not least because it was humiliatingly sent out over the
signature of the secretary's clerk.[7] The Glasgow society went on
its independent way.

In Edinburgh also the Universal Abolition Society was unsuccessful in bringing the local emancipation society under its aegis.
It too had been formed by Thompson, and its early efforts went
towards supporting his American trip. Perhaps what prevented it
from becoming an auxiliary of the London group in 1834 was the
same consideration upon which it later maintained its independence from the BFASS—a distrust of the unquestioning pacifist
position of the London leadership. For most of the Edinburgh
members the Guinea Coast was a special case, which set it outside
the canons of the Christian testimony on war. "The law," concluded the Edinburgh secretary Dr. Greville, "must be made a
terror to evildoers."[8] Though this was a position at odds with radical Christian pacifism, it was probably a perfectly logical one, and

7. Minutes for December 12, 1833, March 20, 1834, and J. Crisp to J. Murray,
March 29, 1834, in GESMB, I.
8. R. Greville to J. Tredgold, April 12, 1839, C7/70, in ASP.

indeed it anticipates the response of many American abolitionists to the Civil War. In either case, the Edinburgh leadership, like that of Glasgow, maintained its independence both from the Universal Abolition Society and its successor the BFASS.

The GES was also charting a special course for itself when it merged temporarily with the Aborigines' Protection Society in 1838. It had been founded two years before to keep benevolent opinion alive to the plight of defenseless or uncivilized populations of British possessions outside the slaveholding Caribbean. Its paid agent, predictably, was George Thompson. He continued working for it until the following year, when the new British India Society founded by Joseph Pease decided to employ him.[9] For the Aborigines' Protection Society, his job, as usual, was to travel around the country, in an endless and grueling series of one-night stands. In each city, he would appeal individually for the support of prominent local philanthropists, hold public meetings, and stirringly lecture existing antislavery societies on the miseries and irreligion of Africa and the Orient. In Glasgow he had more confidence than usual in his influence. He presented his Irish colleague Montgomery Martin to the GES with a view to absorbing it into the Aborigines' Protection Society, for which Martin worked. At his public meetings, he managed to whip up a great deal of sympathy, especially for the peoples of British India, in whom he was becoming increasingly interested. The local group was duly reconstituted as the Glasgow Emancipation and Aborigines' Protection Society.[10]

In fact these unions had no practical effect. The last time the GES minutes mention Thompson's group is October of the following year, when Sir Culling Eardley Smith appeared at a meeting to memorialize Lord Melbourne, of all unlikely people, on the plight of the slaves rescued from the Baltimore schooner *Amistad* in 1839. By this time those Glasgow abolitionists who had an im-

9. G. R. Mellor, *British Imperial Trusteeship, 1783–1850* (London, 1951), 257; offprint from *India Review*, January, 1843, p. 7, copy in BPL; Minute for May 13, 1839, in GESMB, II. Cuttings on Thompson's work in this area have been preserved in Thompson Scrapbooks, V.

10. Minute for September 6, 1838, in GESMB, II; GESR, 1838, p. 52ff.; *Public Meeting: Junction Between the Glasgow Emancipation Society, and the Aborigines' Protection Society, from the Glasgow Argus, of Sept. 16, 1838* (Glasgow, 1838); M. Wigham to M. W. Chapman, April 1, 1839, in BPL-W.

perial bent, and they were always in a minority, were absorbed, like George Thompson, by the specific problems of British India. They were perhaps diverted, too, by swelling rumors of dissent within the American movement. Nevertheless, the flirtation with the Aborigines' Protection Society does have some significance. The only other British group to show this interest was the one in Newcastle, which later developed along lines of its own to become the British center of the free-produce movement.[11] In Newcastle as in Scotland, this little incident of the thirties is a pointer to future independence.

It is difficult to imagine the Scottish antislavery movement in the thirties without the continuing influence of George Thompson. Amid all the chaos of his extraordinary career, during which he was at one time professionally employed in almost every area of mid-Victorian reform, one of the few consistent threads is the strength of his following in Scotland. He had not been born in Scotland, but in Liverpool, though he lived for a time in a little cottage in the Edinburgh suburb of Newington, close to the various branches of Wighams. Nevertheless, as he moved from one employment to another, he would always move quickly to interest his Scottish friends in whatever cause he was working for. With some exceptions, they loved him. His easy witticisms, his presence, his fluent moralizations, his knack of hinting deliciously at the shocking without overt obscenity, were not lost on any Victorian audience. To the Scots, however, the professionalism that made him distasteful to the establishment may have been an asset. It opened a chink in his moral armor that prevented him from taking on the threatening quality of an ideal. Moreover, his making a living from reform and the honorable poverty that drove him to do so had much the same effect as being a Scot—the effect of unjustly excluding him from the national benevolent establishment. What brought the Scots close to Thompson may have been their inchoate sense that he shared their membership in a permanent out group. It could only become an in group by changing the frame

11. Minute for October 15, 1839, in GESMB, II; GESR, 1839, p. 82ff; Minute of Committee of Newcastle Emancipation Society, April 8, 1839, with resolutions passed at a public meeting to hear George Thompson, February 2, 1839, C7/20, in ASP.

of reference entirely, which is exactly what Thompson and his radical Scottish followers did when they chose to remain loyal to Garrison in 1841. In either case, Thompson's influence in Scottish reforming circles was a spectacular one indeed.

Thompson's mission of 1834, at the time, was a bold attempt to change the course of the American movement. The Scots abolitionists supported it, and they were quick to convince themselves that they alone had initiated it. What they conceived as its success therefore gave them a high sense of their local achievements, which made them doubly reluctant to accept external guidance, from London or anywhere else. Actually Thompson's mission was only possible because it came at a particular point in time. Given the intense religious anxieties behind the concern over slavery, it became a matter of psychological urgency for British abolitionists to do something personal and concrete over American slavery, as soon as the work of Charles Stuart, Nathaniel Paul, and Garrison himself destroyed the comforting illusion that the African Colonization Society had the problem in hand. In fact, Thompson was supported not only by the Glasgow and Edinburgh groups but also by the Universal Abolition Society, which actually saw his mission as the first of a series of similar ones. Moreover, as Garrison was quick to point out, it was he who had made the whole enterprise possible by suggesting it to Thompson during his 1833 visit, when the two of them had several joint lecturing engagements. The friendship between these erratic and brilliant men was still a close one when Thompson died in Leeds, in poverty, in 1878. Their relationship was a most significant one in Scotland, where so many abolitionists would in effect do what Thompson told them. The mission of 1834 strengthened his friendship with Garrison, buttressed the Scottish tradition of local antislavery achievement, and increased Scottish admiration for Thompson himself. It is doubtful whether it did much to help American abolitionists, but it had a real effect on the future behavior of Scottish ones.[12]

12. "A Staffordshire Gentleman" to J. Coffin, June 21, 1833, N. Paul to W. L. Garrison, April 10, 1833, and June 22, 1833, all in *Liberator*; J. Phillips to W. L. Garrison, June 6, 1832, in BPL-G; B. Fladeland, *Men and Brothers: Anglo-American Antislavery Cooperation* (Urbana, Ill., 1972), 209–18; Temperley, *British Anti-Slavery*, 25–26; W. L. Garrison (ed.), *Lectures of George Thompson, with . . . a*

There is one other sense in which Thompson's mission was extraordinary. He was the only one of all the abolitionist visitors to the United States who was delegated and financed as the agent of the *members* of a British antislavery society. Even John Scoble's trip in 1842 was ordered by a committee much criticized for its distance from grassroots sentiment. Some visitors, like Sturge or Gurney, came from income brackets high enough to pay their own way. Others, like Abdy or the Reverend James Cox, were combining abolitionism with other business. Thompson's visit, on the other hand, was a response to a genuinely popular demand for British action on a foreign problem. He was supported by men and women of relatively modest means, who collected the substantial sums needed for his expenses and stipend. Such rank-and-file efforts, however, were confined almost wholly to Scotland. He had founded the Glasgow and Edinburgh societies with such ease partly because of the attraction of their doing something so concrete as sending him to America. Even when he accepted some funds from the new national society, he was careful to reassure the Scots that he would always think of himself as "peculiarly your representative." They followed his plans with great interest, and specially instructed him to carry goodwill presentations of plate and books to Prudence Crandall of Canterbury, who had been victimized by her neighbors for accepting black children at her school. Thompson's credentials were presented to him at a series of mass farewell meetings, drawing audiences of two thousand and upwards.[13]

Thompson left on August 15, 1834, and after a five-week passage went safely through customs with Miss Crandall's silver salver. The other guests in his New York hotel promptly had him ejected after passing resolutions deploring the presence of "foreign incendiaries" in the house—a response that perhaps typifies what the American in the street thought about all British attempts to inter-

Brief History of His Connection with the Anti-Slavery Cause in England (Boston, 1836), xii-xx; *WLG*, IV, 335; S. J. May, *Some Recollections of Our Anti-Slavery Conflict* (Boston, 1869), 115–25; O. Johnson, *William Lloyd Garrison and His Times* (Boston, 1880), 133–38; *WLG*, I, 434–67; C. D. Rice, "The Anti-Slavery Mission of George Thompson to the United States, 1834–1835," *Journal of American Studies*, II (1968), 13–31. The following passage is a condensation of this paper.
13. M. Estlin to S. H. Gay, July 23, 1853, in Gay Papers, Columbia University Library; G. Thompson to GES Committee, February 13, 1834, in GESMB, I; *Liberator*, September 13, 1834; Minute for January 24, 1834, in GESMB, I.

fere in the private life of the republic. Indeed 1834 saw a great deal of violence against abolitionists, and Thompson was lucky that he arrived late in the summer, when the excitement over the New York riots against the wealthy philanthropists Arthur and Lewis Tappan had died down. When the *United States* packet took up her pilot at that time, he immediately told her captain that to allow Thompson to go ashore, had he been on board, would have been to take responsibility for his lynching. In antislavery circles, on the other hand, Garrison had already made sure that Thompson's reception would be a warm one.[14] Until his midnight departure across Massachusetts Bay in the following November, he met with nothing but adulation from those who were already loyal to the abolitionist cause, and nothing but bitter resentment of foreign interference from those who were already convinced supporters of slavery. No single incident illustrates this twin American effect of the British agitation more clearly than Thompson's first antislavery mission.

Thompson began with a lecture at Lowell, Massachusetts. He spent October touring Maine uneventfully and with some success. In early December, however, when he lectured again in Lowell, a crowd of "mobocrats" hurled a brick through the window, so close to his head that "a slight change of its direction would have silenced the eloquence of our friend forever." Thereafter he remained for some time in Boston. He lectured on a weekly basis to sympathetic audiences, particularly on the defects of a Congregationalist-inspired attempt to unite colonizationists and abolitionists. He made a number of short trips to other major American cities. In one Philadelphia church the press of people to hear him was so great that the galleries partly collapsed. On his way to the American Anti-Slavery Society anniversary in May, he also toured through upstate New York.[15] Thereafter he remained in Boston,

14. G. Thompson to R. Purvis, August 9, 1834, G. Thompson to W. L. Garrison, September 24, 1834, both in BPL-G; M. W. Chapman (ed.), *Harriet Martineau's Autobiography* (2 vols.; Boston, 1877), I, 337; *Liberator*, August 10, 1833, January 11, 1834, March 22, 1834, April 12, 1834, September 3, 1834, September 27, 1834.

15. A. Rand to W. L. Garrison, December 3, 1834, in *Liberator*, December 6, 1834; G. Thompson to E. Wright, in Ms. Collections, NYHS; G. Thompson to R. Purvis, February 24, 1835, in BPL-W; H. Benson to G. Benson, February 22, 1835, March 27, 1835, in BPL-G; A. Buffum to W. L. Garrison, 1835, in *Liberator*, March 21, 1835, April 4, 1835; W. L. Garrison (ed.), *Letters and Addresses of George Thompson.*

making short excursions into New England. Among them was a ten-day visit to Andover Seminary, where he tried to persuade the students to follow the example of the group led by Theodore Weld at Lane Seminary in Ohio and secede from their college on anti-slavery grounds. Feeling against him continued to rise as the summer lengthened and warmed up, and violent hostility to abolitionists in general gathered force. One of his meetings was again broken up in September, in Abington, and by the following month Boston itself was unsafe for him.[16] A series of demonstrations culminated in the great riot of October 20, 1835, when Garrison narrowly escaped being martyred. He was only saved by a discreet shout of "He is an American!" from the crowd. In fact it was the "infamous foreign scoundrel" who was intended for the tar kettle, and by this time most Boston abolitionists were convinced that they were not justified in risking Thompson's valuable life any longer. He himself later recorded that "my life was sought . . . I could not go abroad without the almost certain prospect of death." He did not appear in Boston after the riot, and he had to be secretly rowed out to the New Brunswick packet on November 8. He left his family to visit relatives in the South, presumably incognito.[17]

The tragedy of the British efforts to aid the American movement is condensed in the responses to Thompson's visit. They fall into two clear groups, for there was no middle ground of opinion on the "mad missionary."[18] Convinced abolitionists were already accustomed to look to Britain for encouragement and guidance. From a basis of prior agreement with Thompson, they were quick to eulogize his powers of persuasion. The conservative black abolitionist James Forten was just as convinced as energetic female reformers like the Weston sisters that their guest could not fail to silence scoffers and even win over the unregenerate. In fact the

16. *Liberator*, July 18, 1835, July 25, 1835, August 1, 1835, August 8, 1835, October 10, 1835, October 17, 1835.

17. *WLG*, II, 9, 21; J. L. Thomas, *The Liberator: William Lloyd Garrison* (Boston, 1966), 200–206; D. Weston to M. Weston, October 22, 1835, A. Weston to M. Weston, October 30, 1835, both in BPL-W; G. Thompson to H. C. Wright, November 25, 1835, W. L. Garrison to H. B. Garrison, November 7, 1835, November 9, 1835, all in BPL-G.

18. Extract from New York *Courier and Inquirer*, May 11, 1835, in *Liberator*, May 30, 1835.

issue was already too emotive for thinking in these terms to be realistic. Abolitionists were being mobbed throughout the country in these months, and poor Thompson had the gratuitous disadvantage of being a foreigner. If he made any converts at all, they were already biased towards abolition if not committed to it, or else young enough to be in a sense moral tabulae rasae, like the Andover youngsters he led to secede from their seminary.[19] The second response to Thompson, the proslavery one, was just as predictable, for his presence confirmed every suspicion of a British-financed conspiracy to overthrow the young republic by dividing it over slavery. Like other responses to subversion, the attack on Thompson enabled American defenders of the status quo to present themselves both consciously and subconsciously as guardians of egalitarianism and progress.[20] Thompson's arrival simply gave further support for existing prejudices against the abolitionists. The Glasgow and Edinburgh ladies who sent Thompson on his way, though they could hardly be expected to have known it, could not have found a less suitable way of helping their friends in America. Quite apart from his foreign origins, there were some moral lapses in Thompson's own past that could conveniently be pilloried. At the same time, his own enthusiasm often led him into tactlessness that could have been avoided and that was ultimately damaging.

When a moderate paper received the news of Thompson's attack on the faculty at Andover, it prophesied gloomily that he would go on to subvert the colleges at Amherst and Cambridge. It bewailed the hard times on which a movement so intrinsically good had fallen: *"It is now all I, I, and no attempt is made to enlist the good and wise men of the land.* ALL IS AIMED AT THE RABBLE."[21]

19. Entries for May 28, 1835, August 1, 1835, November 8, 1835, fragment, in Deborah Weston Diary, BPL-W; J. Forten to J. M. Smith, September 8, 1835, in BPL-C; G. L. L. Row to W. L. Garrison, October 27, 1834, H. Benson to G. W. Benson, February 25, 1835, S. J. May to Garrison, November 24, 1835, all in BPL-G; R. Reed to W. L. Garrison, July 15, 1835, in *Liberator*, July 18, 1835; ms. draft of Philadelphia Anti-Slavery Society Report for 1835, at American Antiquarian Society, Worcester, Mass.; G. L. L. Row to A. Phelps, November 21, 1834, A. Phelps to C. Phelps, July 18, 1835, both in BPL-P.

20. L. L. Richards, *"Gentlemen of Property and Standing": Anti-Abolition Mobs in Jacksonian America* (New York, 1970), 62–71; D. B. Davis, "Some Themes of Counter-Subversion: An Analysis of Anti-Masonic, Anti-Catholic, and Anti-Mormon Literature," MVHR, XLVII (1960), 205–24; idem, *The Slave Power Conspiracy and the Paranoid Style* (Baton Rouge, 1969).

21. Extract from Boston *Courier*, n.d., in *Liberator*, August 1, 1835.

Whatever Thompson's reasons for his attacks on the good and
the wise, it was more often he than they who lost stature from
them, at least in the eyes of those Americans who were not already
committed to antislavery. Paradoxically he launched his most injudicious attack on another British abolitionist who was visiting
America at the same time. This was the Reverend Dr. F. A. Cox,
a London Baptist minister who was also a committee member of
the Universal Abolition Society.

Cox refused to attend the 1835 anniversary meeting of the
American Anti-Slavery Society. He wished to maintain a position
of neutrality, not, as he put it, over the "great principles" involved,
but "with regard solely to the political bearings of the question,
with which as a stranger, a foreigner, and a visitor, I could not
attempt to intermeddle." His southern colleague Dr. George Bethune had actually warned him that "he wd. not answer for his
life" if he spoke at the meeting, and in the climate of mid-1835 he
may well have been right. It is intriguing to imagine the spectacular diplomatic incident that would have ensued if Cox had indeed
been lynched. Certainly he cannot have been anxious to court
martyrdom, but it is also possible that he was genuinely diffident
about taking a public role while overseas. In either case, he was
dismissed by Garrison as "this servile and timorous man." Thompson's comments were so scathing that even Garrison later felt it
best to expurgate them from his edition of his friend's American
speeches. In Britain Thompson's exposure of Cox was well received
in some quarters, though this may have been because there were
few abolitionists who were not biased against the Baptists, against
the leadership of the Universal Abolition Society, or against both.
The British Baptists themselves were conscious enough of the slur
to which Cox's caution had exposed them to begin the ostentatious publication of their monthly periodical *Slavery in America*.[22]
Among uncommitted Americans, however, it can only have seemed

22. *Liberator*, May 16, 1835, May 23, 1835, May 30, 1835; J. Rankin to G.
Thompson, May 28, 1835, and cutting from New York *Observer*, n.d., both in
Thompson Scrapbooks, I, LC. *Cf*. Garrison (ed.) *Letters and Addresses of George
Thompson*, 74; Glasgow *Chronicle*, March 6, 1836; extract from Birmingham *Re-
former*, n.d., in *Liberator*, September 5, 1835; London *Patriot*, June 1, 1836; Min-
ute for March 1, 1836, in GESMB, I; GESR, 1836, 23; Fladeland, *Men and
Brothers*, 230–32.

that Thompson had attacked the Baptist minister because he did not share his gentlemanly reluctance to interfere in the private affairs of his hosts. The alternative and more damning explanation of Thompson's vehemence was that he was a paid agent in a sinister British conspiracy from which the purer Cox had remained aloof.

Thompson's denunciations of men generally considered to be real moral leaders might have been better received if his own past had been impeccable. When the Glasgow and Edinburgh abolitionists sent him abroad, they had been unaware of something the committee of the Universal Abolition Society knew but chose not to tell them. Thompson later admitted that in 1829, before he took up his post with the Agency Committee, he had embezzled fifty pounds on leaving his employer. By 1839, he had paid back a hundred and fifty, which included generous interest, and he could write to Weld that he considered the master he had cheated a close friend.[23] In fact he was most fortunate that he was allowed to atone for his crime by paying interest instead of going to jail, as the American press was quick to point out when the embezzlement was brought to its attention. The London committee had known of Thompson's past and took a calculated risk in endorsing his mission. Even some abolitionists came to have their doubts about him once the proslavery papers published affidavits on the incident—doubts that increased when both he and the American Anti-Slavery Society refused either to deny or excuse the accusations. Their only response was to state that unspecified charges had been made against Thompson and to republish his credentials, references and antislavery biography.[24] The situation remained as obscure as ever, and it left the opposition with ample scope to denounce Thompson as an English felon who had chosen to visit Boston instead of the new Australian penal settlement at Botany Bay.

23. G. Thompson to A. G. Weld, June 15, 1839, in G. H. Barnes and D. L. Dumond (eds.), *Letters of Theodore Dwight Weld, Angelina Grimké Weld, and Sarah Grimké, 1822–1844* (2 vols.; New York, 1934), II, 774–77.
24. E. Wright to T. Weld, November 18, 1835, in *ibid.*, I, 246; *WLG*, II, 4; [?] to C. Weston, November 3, 1835, in BPL-W; S. E. Sewall to W. L. Garrison, October 27, 1835, W. L. Garrison to T. Knapp, November 19, 1835, both in BPL-G; Liberator, December 5, 1835; Burleigh (ed.), *Reception of George Thompson in Great Britain*, iii–v.

Thompson's doubtful past would have been less important if he had not been a foreigner. In a country with strong nativist tendencies, it was telling for critics to present his mission, and indeed all British attempts to promote American emancipation, as part of a foreign plot against the liberties of the republic. This had two important functions: first, the tactical one of discrediting the abolitionists in general and, second, the psychological one of resolving conscious or subconscious tensions between the ideal of freedom and the reality of black slavery. The American abolitionists themselves were not blind to the way in which they were cast as allies of foreign tyrants. In the popular mind, an abolitionist missionary from overseas was by definition interfering in domestic politics, as the handbills circulated against Thompson in Salem and Boston indicate. In theory it was possible to differentiate between foreign "moral influence" and "an improper and unconstitutional interference."[25] In practice this distinction was too subtle to have any relevance. It seemed all the more likely that Thompson's aim was "to subvert our settled institutions," since his Scottish colleague Captain Charles Stuart had spent the summer of 1834 campaigning in the West.[26] The legacy of anti-British sentiment was also exploited in two letters by the Reverend Dr. D. D. Whedon, a Congregationalist scholar from Wesleyan College in Connecticut who was himself later dismissed from the University of Michigan for preaching the higher law doctrine against slavery. "England," he pointed out, "has been, and still is, a GIGANTIC SLAVER." He also drew an explicit parallel between Thompson and the Catholic priests then laboring in America. Slavery, he concluded in a second letter, had in any case been foisted on the republic only by British tyrants. Anxieties over British plots were not confined to the uneducated. Peleg Sprague, not a professional scholar like Whedon but a highly sophisticated Massachusetts lawyer, could also denounce Thompson as "an avowed *emissary*, sustained by foreign funds, a *professed agitator*, upon questions deeply, profoundly political, which lay at the very foundation of our Union.

25. *Liberator*, July 31, 1840, November 20, 1840; Chapman (ed.), *Harriet Martineau's Autobiography*, II, 294; S. J. May to M. Carpenter, December 29, 1843, in BPL-M; W. L. Garrison to R. D. Webb, March 1, 1845, in BPL-G.
26. Extract from New York *Courier and Inquirer*, September 13, 1834, in *Liberator*, October 11, 1834.

... He comes here from the dark and corrupt institutions of Europe to enlighten *us* upon the rights of man and the moral duties of our own condition."[27] It must have been a real comfort for many perfectly decent and literate Americans to deduce that opposing the enemies of slavery was fighting on the side of progress.

Thompson could be more particularly denounced because of his Scottish connections. The Scots had been predominantly loyalist at the Revolution, and figures like John Witherspoon, James Wilson, and Alexander Hamilton are atypical of the immigrant group as a whole.[28] Indeed it may even be true that the Revolution was fought against the Scottish mafia in the colonies and at Whitehall, and that the English were driven out as a mere incidental. A Scottish background, whatever its advantages in intellectual circles, was no union card for a lecturer on inflammatory public issues. Thompson's trip, too, gave splendid opportunities for satire. It was a rich spectacle, this group of harebrained old Scotswomen sending a pious embezzler across the Atlantic to bring American society down in ruins. To the New York *Courier and Inquirer*, the main organ of the conspiracy interpretation of Thompson's visit, his backers were "canting old women," and "the old pussy cats of Glasgow." The abolitionist missionary, it warned, "represents Miss Lucretia McTabb and a bevy of old maids at Glasgow, who pay his board, wages, and travelling expenses, to lecture the citizens of the United States on their domestic duties, one of the most urgent of which is, to lodge him in Bridewell, until he give security to keep the peace—after which, he ought to be packed up like a quintal of codfish, and sent back to the Caledonian damsels who exported him." Garrison's saying that Thompson's Scottish support was "honorable to all parties" did not make it any less Scottish.[29]

At the same time, Thompson's tribulations only encouraged those who believed in him to persevere. They closed ranks behind him as the proslavery critique became more vicious. Indeed they tended to accept the rising tide of nativist violence as conclusive

27. *Liberator*, February 25, 1835; *WLG*, I, 497.
28. I. C. G. Graham, *Colonists from Scotland: Emigration to North America* (Ithaca, N.Y., 1956), 128ff. *Cf.* the persistence of the legend of general Scottish contributions to the revolutionary fight, as expressed, for instance, in *Scottish Field*, November, 1975, p. 33–34.
29. Garrison (ed.), *Lectures of George Thompson*, xxi–xxii, xxv.

evidence that the monster was in its death throes.[30] None of his American friends seems to have registered that the response to Thompson the conspirator was an ideal mechanism for avoiding the tensions created by the response to Thompson the abolitionist. Thompson himself, in a sense rightly, saw the mob violence against him as a symptom of the moral cancer produced in democracy by slavery, and called for a greater effort against it as the only way of *saving* the republic.[31] Few committed abolitionists would have disagreed with him, but none perceived that all he could hope to do on his mission was encourage the converted and repel the unregenerate. If his work had a real impact in America, it was that, like all radical antislavery activity, it helped accelerate the process of polarization between proslavery and antislavery camps. He did little to strengthen the cause, and he did not change the existing situation, though he may have helped harden it.

Where Thompson's exertions did have a real influence on the strength and nature of the movement was in Britain. In 1839 Theodore Weld's *Slavery As It Is* became available as a universally used source of information, some of it pornographic, on the American situation. Four years earlier nothing of the sort was available. The 2,400 items of newspapers and three volumes of placards and cuttings Thompson brought back with him had a very real function. The facts he drew from these materials were lurid and sometimes distorted, but they gave him the wherewithal to attract large crowds and encourage them to form local societies. This seems to have been most true in Scotland, where his mission had already received such great publicity. During the first half of 1836, he held one or more enthusiastic meetings in Greenock, Dumbarton, Bonhill, Stirling, Edinburgh, Glasgow, Dundee, Montrose, Aberdeen, Ballater, Airdrie, Kilmarnock, Saltcoats, Irvine, and Falkirk.[32] In all of them, a new society was formed, or an old

30. *Liberator*, October 17, 1835, October 24, 1835, October 31, 1835. S. T. Pritchard, *Life and Letters of John Greenleaf Whittier* (2 vols.; London, 1895), I, 145–54.

31. G. Thompson to W. L. Garrison, October 22, 1835, in Glasgow *Chronicle*, January 19, 1836; Garrison (ed.), *Letters and Addresses by George Thompson*, 106–16; and J. A. Collins, *The Anti-Slavery Picknick* (Boston, 1842), 12–15.

32. G. Thompson to W. L. Garrison, November 27, 1835, in Garrison (ed.), *Letters and Addresses of George Thompson*, 117–18. C. C. Burleigh (ed.), *The Reception of George Thompson in Great Britain: Compiled from Various British*

one goaded into action. In some towns, too, remonstrances were later adopted to send to America.[33] It is inconceivable that Thompson would have been so successful without the publicity he had attracted during his trip, and the interest aroused by the new information he had brought back with him.

For the future, however, the real importance of the Thompson mission was that it confirmed him in his personal loyalty to William Lloyd Garrison. This would be the most significant in areas where his personal influence was strong. It was nowhere stronger than in Scotland, where local leaders still regarded him as "their" agent when they were called upon to choose their loyalties in a divided movement. When the schisms began in 1840 and 1841, Thompson's taking the radical or Garrisonian position had a real impact in Scotland. Exactly the same was true of Ireland, where Richard Davis Webb, the most interesting of all British Garrisonians, had originally been converted to universal abolition by Thompson.[34] Throughout the forties and fifties, indeed, the friendships Thompson had formed on his 1834 mission continued to influence his loyalties within the American movement and therefore those of his own British followers. Fortified in his radicalism by Garrison's visits in 1840 and 1846, and by his own second mission in 1850, he became a more or less constant British voice in favor of the radical or old organization view.

Thompson was behind all the later attempts to form a national British Garrisonian society. None came even close to success, but all were aimed at breaking the British and Foreign Anti-Slavery Society's claimed monopoly of antislavery orthodoxy. The short-

---

Publications (Boston, 1836), *passim*; Thompson, *Voice to the United States*, *Report of the Discussion on American Slavery, in Dr. Wardlaw's Chapel, Between Mr. George Thompson and the Rev. R. J. Breckenridge* (Glasgow and Boston, 1836); cuttings and ms. memoranda, in Thompson Scrapbooks, VI.

33. See, for example, Thompson *Voice to the United States; Remonstrance on the Subject of American Slavery by the Inhabitants of Dumbarton and the Vale of Leven* (Glasgow, 1837); *Letter on American Slavery: The Association of Congregational Churches in Aberdeen and Banff Shires, to Their Congregational Brethren in the United States of America* (Aberdeen, 1837), rpr. in Aberdeen *Herald*, April 15, 1837; *The Earnest Expostulation of Christians of All Denominations in Montrose and Its Vicinity, with the Christians of the United States of America*, broadsheet, 1837; J. R. Campbell to E. Wright, August 4, 1837, in Elizur Wright Papers.

34. R. D. Webb, *The National Anti-Slavery Societies in England and the United States* (Dublin, 1852), 5.

lived Anti-Slavery League of 1846, the Manchester Anti-Slavery League, the Manchester Union Anti-Slavery Society which seceded from it in 1854, and the Emancipation Committee of 1859 were all formed wholly or partly at his instigation and looked up to him as their major British leader.[35] Again, the Dublin group's *Anti-Slavery Advocate* and the Glasgow group's *British Friend* both saw him as the main foil to the conservatives of the London society and the heretical new free-produce societies based in Newcastle. Frederick Chesson's ephemeral little *Anti-Slavery Watchman* signified its loyalty to the editor's father-in-law by decorating its masthead with one of his most famous quotations: "The American slave is an animated hoeing-machine in the fields; a pampered, or a scourged hound in the house; a dumb Chattel in the Court of Justice; a leper in the house of prayer; an Outcast even in the Christian Churchyard."[36] Perhaps, indeed, it was because Thompson's followers felt that they themselves were still outcasts from the dominant elements in British society, and even British reform, that their sympathy for the slave and their loyalty to him were equally deep.

Though their loyalty to Thompson was to have a profound significance for the Scots abolitionists, it was only one of a number of signs of future dissidence they showed in the thirties. Their very foundation as autonomous bodies, and Glasgow's idiosyncratic course in amalgamating with the Aborigines' Protection Society, also looked forward to an uneasy relationship with any form of national leadership. It may be, in fact, that the peculiar intricacy of Scottish church life, and the specially high literacy of even the most modest levels of the Scottish middle class, would have molded the northern movement along lines of its own even if it had not been presented with the problems of the American division in 1840 and 1841. In either case, when the movement broke up, many of the Scots, though by no means all of them, took a radical or Garrisonian standpoint at odds with that of the BFASS.

35. *ASR*, September 24, 1846; GESR, 1846, 8; *Anti-Slavery Advocate*, September, November, 1854; *Anti-Slavery Watchman*, January, 1854; G. Thompson to L. A. Chamerovzow, July 25, 1859, C37/7, July 28, 1859, C37/8, both in ASP.
36. *Anti-Slavery Watchman*, January, 1854.

It is not likely that they were impelled to do so by an economic or class distrust of the London leadership. What some of them did show was a kind of regional arrogance about London dictation. They were influenced, too, by the accident of Thompson's personal loyalty to Garrison and by a long tradition of religious distinctiveness that made the embattled quality of radical antislavery attractive, independent of its ideological content. More simply, in the thirties, the heyday of Scottish abolitionism, they had been accustomed to hear nothing but adulation of Garrison. With their own traditions of nonconformity, they were ill disposed to follow the lead of a clique of London businessmen who suddenly told them they should change their views. There is a Buchan adjective, *swiert*, which combines reluctance, stubbornness, general nastiness, and an unwillingness to cooperate. This well describes their frame of mind, but perhaps such nuances of sentiment are unimportant. What matters is that by the time the Scots were presented with the bewildering American story of schism and counterschism, at the World's Anti-Slavery Convention of 1840, they were well prepared to take a different course from the conservatives of the London committee.

CHAPTER 4

The World's Anti-Slavery
Convention and the
Mission of John Collins

In 1840 the British and Foreign Anti-Slavery Society organized one of the most extraordinary events in the history of Atlantic reform, the World's Anti-Slavery Convention. After Karl Marx, the second best known nineteenth-century visitors to the British Museum are two of its delegates, Lucretia Mott and Elizabeth Cady Stanton. It was their talk on the museum steps, among other London conversations, which ultimately led to the summoning of the Seneca Falls Convention and the launching of the women's movement in America.[1] The antislavery significance of the world's convention was equally great. It was there that the horrifying tale of the feuds in the American movement was first told to the British abolitionist public. Its response was passionate. In the following year, during the visit of the radical American abolitionist John Anderson Collins, every British antislavery society became involved in the controversy. The national movement as a whole split up along lines directly reflecting the fragmentation in America. In Ireland, the Hibernian Anti-Slavery Society cut off official relations with the BFASS. In Edinburgh, the men's emancipation society remained silently loyal to the conservative London group, while the ladies' society broke away from it. The Glasgow Emancipation Society itself split up amid bitter recriminations, after the dominant element had stopped cooperating with the national body. Its ladies' auxiliary, which was a weaker body, simply lapsed, and Collins converted it into a Glasgow Female Anti-Slavery Society, though it did not go through the same spectacular controversy as

1. F. B. Tolles (ed.), "Slavery and the 'Woman Question': Lucretia Mott's Diary of Her Visit to Great Britain to Attend the World's Anti-Slavery Convention of 1840," *Journal of the Friends' Historical Society* Supplement No. 23 (1952), 1; E. C. Stanton, *Eighty Years or More: Reminiscences, 1815–1897* (New York, 1898), 82–83.

the men's group. In the future the Scots would often be able to give a strong pull for antislavery, but it would never again be a pull all together.

British observers must have been puzzled by the breaking up of the American movement. In 1840 the American conservatives or "new organization" group split away from the more radical "old organization." The most influential leaders in the former were the New York businessmen Arthur and Lewis Tappan, while the latter was generally loyal to William Lloyd Garrison of Boston, now a nonresistant who was suspicious of all human agencies based on force. It is difficult to generalize on the issues that divided the two factions, partly because each included a wide range of individuals, partly because their ideology was dynamic rather than stable, and partly because, in consequence, both found it impossible to maintain a working unity. By the fifties, neither had a clear identity. Repeated subdivision had left the Garrisonian group undistinguishable, while any shared goals the new organization had originally possessed had fallen casualties to the different forms of political and quasi-political loyalty chosen by its members. It was only for a very short time, if ever, that the Tappanite new organization and the Garrisonian old organization were organizations in anything but the most tenuous sense. Even in the fifties, however, they retained their broad ideological importance as a focus for emotional loyalty within the movement.

The persistence of this rivalry, long after the institutional split behind it had become irrelevant, does suggest a genuine though imprecise ideological disagreement. By the later thirties, the American movement was suffering from personal rivalries and possibly also from regional resentment of centralization in a national society based in New York. But it became impossible to work in harmony as the two groups of abolitionists developed fundamentally different views on the nature of a good society and on the objectives and tactics of reform.[2]

2. A. Kraditor, *Means and Ends in American Abolitionism: Garrison and His Critics on Strategy and Tactics, 1834–1850* (New York: 1969), 8–9 and *passim*; L. Perry, *Radical Abolitionism: Anarchy and the Government of God in Anti-Slavery Thought* (Ithaca, N.Y., 1973); M. L. Dillon, *The Abolitionists: The Growth of a Dissenting Minority* (DeKalb, Ill., 1974), 113–39; J. B. Stewart, *Holy Warriors: The Abolitionists and American Slavery* (New York, 1976), 89–96.

This is not to say that all reasons for antislavery infighting were ideological or tactical; it is not to say that all or even many Britons fully understood the philosophical basis of the American divisions upon which they took sides; and it is not to say that feuds that were originally ideological could not come to perform nonideological functions. Like all political or quasi-political movements with an idealistic base, antislavery developed a leftward momentum that set its most radical supporters at odds with less bold men and women they had left further back along the continuum. It is not being uncharitable, either, to say that the movement's moral intensity was so great that it tended to produce a sort of anarchical individualism in benevolence. The personal involvement of the evangelical reformer was so deep that he felt entitled to his own moral autonomy, an expectation that did not promote the efficiency of group efforts. "They defied each other," wrote Ralph Waldo Emerson, "like a congress of kings ... the fertile forms of antinomianism among the elder puritans, seemed to have their match in the plenty of the new harvest of reform."[3] They frequently used their antislavery arguments as a means of expressing distastes and rivalries of other sorts. In Britain, indeed, this was a major function of the schisms between the abolitionists. Nevertheless, in 1841 the regular leadership of the British societies soon developed a grasp of the issues at stake. Their real error was that, even in the fifties, they tended to assume that the old and new organizations were more united and more coherent than they actually were, which meant that the central division in the movement retained an organizational vitality in Britain when it had become an emotional relic in America. Before 1841, on the other hand, British abolitionists do not seem to have understood how deeply their American allies were split over ideology and tactics.

The American disputes originated in the early thirties, and the rancor deepened as the decade went on. There was always a difference of style between the evangelical but genteel group centered round the Tappan brothers, and those leaders who were less concerned over long-term expediency. Arthur Tappan, as early as 1831, was pointedly writing to Garrison that "you would do more

3. "New England Reformers" (1844), in *Essays, First and Second Series* (London, 1906), 338–39.

good, if you would . . . have more argument and less invective." By 1835 his brother Lewis could dismiss the language of the *Liberator* as "unchristian."[4] Unfortunately, however, the disagreements went beyond the problem of when it was and was not ethical to be frank in print.

To the Tappan group that eventually became the new organization, it seemed tactically unsound to mix abolition with other issues. James Gillespie Birney, for instance, was sure that bringing up women's rights and nonresistance would be "enough to frustrate the whole concern, no matter how strong it may be."[5] It was not, in fact, very strong at all. The catholic approach of the Garrisonians was like showing a red rag to a bull who had already had a burr put under his tail. Heterodoxy was likely to repel more potential converts than it could ever attract, and there were plenty proslavery slip fielders to snap up whatever tactical chances the abolitionists gave them. To men like Henry C. Wright, John Anderson Collins, and Garrison himself, however, it was only natural to discuss slavery along with other abuses. Their assumptions were entirely different. The antislavery campaign was only one front in a millenial war, where it was mere tactical common sense to integrate efforts with those on other fronts. In any case, it was not logically possible to handle slavery as a single issue, since it was only a symptom of a disorder that threatened every organ of society.

Behind the disagreements on tactics, there lay irreconcilable differences over the objectives of the antislavery reform. To the conservative new organization, slavery was the most horrifying of a number of flaws in a polity that was fundamentally sound. They attacked it as the atrocity it was, and indeed they worked energetically against other social abuses. But their interest was in the fine tuning required to create a "respectable" society based on the values of the evangelical elite. They had no intention of restructuring political and religious institutions. Indeed the failure of their earlier attempts at individual moral suasion had led many of

4. A. Tappan to W. L. Garrison, October 12, 1831, copy, L. Tappan to G. Thompson, January 2, 1835, both in BPL-G.
5. J. G. Birney to L. Tappan, August 23, 1837, in D. L. Dumond (ed.), *Letters of James Gillespie Birney, 1831–1857* (2 vols.: New York, 1938), I, 418.

them to work against slavery through the churches or the electoral system, even if this involved them in organizing antislavery parties, as they ultimately did. To most of the Garrisonians, party work was unacceptable, for they had moved to the radical position that slavery and other social imbalances were much more than correctable aberrations. They were evidence that a corrupt society should be rebuilt *de novo*, by separating from all institutions that sanctioned force or ultimately relied on it. Many of the Garrisonians had become Christian anarchists whose views clearly threatened the traditional-minded businessmen and ministers who had hitherto dominated the movement and who were the leaders of the Tappanite group. Slavery was crucially important for the Garrisonians, since they shared the religious background from which it drew its peculiarly compelling symbolic significance. But they saw it as illogical to separate the antislavery cause from the "extraneous issues." All tended equally to the end of subverting corrupt institutions and replacing them with the unimpeded rule of God.

For the Garrisonians, then, it was irrelevant that the catholicity of their enthusiasms lost supporters for the antislavery movement. The 1839 Peace Convention, at which the New England Nonresistance Society was founded, resolved that "whatever the gospel is intended to destroy at any period of the world, being contrary to it, ought now to be abandoned."[6] No Garrisonian would have rejected this view. No Tappanite could possibly have accepted it. The objectives of the two groups were not merely different, they were mutually exclusive.

Much of the early disagreement in the American movement was expressed in terms of a debate over the role of church institutions and their leaders. In 1836, Garrison caused considerable consternation in clerical circles by denouncing William Ellery Channing's conciliatory *Essay on Slavery* and ridiculing Lyman Beecher's orthodox views on the Sabbath. By the following year few clergymen were comfortable over his support of Sarah and Angelina Grimké. They were alarming not only as feminists but also as a symbol of the new breed of professional lecturers who were presenting themselves as moral arbiters without the sanction of the trained clergy. Moreover, they gained special publicity because of their view that

6. *WLG*, II, 233.

the American churches had been and were derelict in their duty over slavery. To northern ministers, as a group either with a professional vested interest or with considered moral priorities of its own, the work of the Grimkés was evidence that society was in revolt against their ethical guidance. In July, the General Association of Congregationalists in Massachusetts issued a Pastoral Letter that decried the raising of issues calculated to "disturb the work of those ministers who think that the promotion of personal religion among their people ... is the proper object of their ministry."[7] Garrison's response to this view, not unnaturally, was scathing.

Garrison was in any case becoming more alarming, as the influence of John Humphrey Noyes drew him towards the nonresistant position that all governments based ultimately on force are unscriptural and therefore intolerable.[8] The corollary of this view was that it was a matter of duty not to participate in the workings of any existing political institutions. Its ultimate thrust was a nihilist one, and Garrison's conservative contemporaries recognized it as such, however much they agreed that slavery itself represented a moral anarchy. The issues at stake between the two groups of reformers were much more fundamental than the position of women, the value of the Sabbath, the literal authority of Scripture, or the proper level of politeness to be preserved in the attack on the South. One of them held that all reform, including antislavery, should be promoted in such a way as to avoid harm to existing religious and political institutions. The other was convinced that all reforms, especially antislavery, should be advanced precisely because they would work towards the overthrow of such institutions, and their replacement by noncoercive communities headed by Christ and voluntarily under His law. By 1838 it had become clear that men and women whose views were thus diametrically opposed could not continue working much longer in the same antislavery groups.

The process of division began in Massachusetts. In 1838 the rad-

7. WLG, II, 73–98; G. Lerner, The Grimké Sisters from South Carolina (Boston, 1967), 165–89; Liberator, February 27, 1836, July 23, 1836, July 30, 1836, August 6, 1836, August 13, 1836, August 11, 1837.

8. P. Brock, Radical Pacifists in Ante-Bellum America (Princeton, 1968), 139–69; Perry, Radical Abolitionism, 55–91; WLG, II, 221–57.

icals won a symbolic victory by having Abby Kelley elected to one
of the standing committees of the Massachusetts Anti-Slavery Society. What was much worse in conservative eyes was their growing tendency to conflate the aims of the movement with those of
the nonresistant pacifists, the views of whom were expounded at
length in the *Liberator*. Probably a number of conservative abolitionists simply withdrew in disgust over these developments, but
a small group of them made a desperate attempt to put the movement back on an acceptable course. Many of them were Congregationalist ministers, but they were also men whose commitment
to antislavery was just as sincere as that of the Garrisonians—like
Charles Torrey, who later died in a southern prison, or the abolitionist pioneer Amos Phelps. At the 1839 annual meeting of the
Massachusetts society, they were crushingly defeated in an attempt to commit the society to the standpoint that abolitionism
and nonresistance were incompatible. Later in the year Phelps and
his group withdrew to form a new body that admitted the viability
of political action against slavery.[9]

In the same month of May, the radicals came very close to gaining control of the national movement. At the American Anti-Slavery Society's annual meeting, they almost defeated James Birney's
resolution in favor of conscientious political action, close enough
to alarm the conservatives on the Executive Committee into wind-
ing it up. By the time of its 1840 annual meeting, they had carefully brought its affairs to a standstill. They had, for instance,
transferred the ownership of its paper, the *Emancipator*, to the
New York Young Men's Anti-Slavery Society, a conservative group
still under conservative control. It was therefore all but irrelevant
when the splendid management of John Anderson Collins ensured
the election of a new and radicalized Executive Committee, complete with women members. The hollowness of the victory did not
spoil Garrison's satisfaction. "We have made clean work of everything" he assured his wife Helen, "adopted the most thorough-
going resolutions, and taken the strongest ground, with *crashing*
unanimity."[10]

9. J. A. Collins, *Right and Wrong Among the Abolitionists of the United States,
or, the Objects, Principles, and Measures of the Original American Anti-Slavery
Society Unchanged* (Glasgow, 1841), 29–38; WLG, II, 233–308.
10. W. L. Garrison to H. B. Garrison, May 15, 1840, in *WLG*, II, 355.

The American conservatives may or may not have been realistic in their efforts to separate abolition from further-reaching reforms. In either case, they seceded to form a national body of their own, the American and Foreign Anti-Slavery Society. It consciously chose the London BFASS as its model but always remained much inferior to it in assets and strength. So did the rump of the old organization, the American Anti-Slavery Society. The center of gravity had shifted from the nation to the counties and towns. Nevertheless, the national division had symbolized a series of disagreements that split the American movement from top to bottom.

The complexity of the issues involved was not always understood in Britain. The most obvious explanation of the schisms was that they revolved around the role of women or the extent to which moral reformers should become embroiled in politics. It was easy to sneer that the conservatives had let the cause degenerate "from a holy warfare into a struggle for place and power," and just as easy to point out that "the worldly and corrupt would desire nothing more than that the good should retire in fear and disgust from the sphere of politics."[11] The constitutions of the new organization groups in America all left loopholes for political action, and their leaders were active in the formation of the first political parties aimed at working against slavery. Doubtless, British reformers considered the advantages and disadvantages of single-issue reform, and they can hardly have missed the frequency with which the role of women became a symbol of division. The simplest issue for them to understand, however, was the one of political participation. It was partly because of this, no doubt, that Lewis Tappan's conservative group found their main British allies in the national society, which had already built up working lines of political influence at Westminster. Garrison's old organization party, on the other hand, was only well received in the provinces, especially in Scotland and Ireland, where provincial, middle-class reformers were less directly involved in the national political process. It is probably not accidental that those Britons who appear to have

11. *Right and Wrong in the Anti-Slavery Societies: The Seventh Annual Report of the Boston Female Anti-Slavery Society* (Boston, 1840), 18; E. G. Loring to W. E. Channing, March 17, 1838, in Channing Papers, Massachusetts Historical Society.

understood and accepted the full implications of the nonresistant critique, men like Richard Webb of Dublin, or Andrew Paton of Glasgow, lived in areas where the sense of alienation from national institutions was deepest. This pattern of preference, so to speak, became clear as soon as the British were presented with information on the American controversy.

In general they did not have access to such information until the World's Anti-Slavery Convention of 1840.[12] Even then, the American delegates might have preserved a veneer of harmony in front of their London hosts if it had not been for the insoluble "woman question." Having first invited "delegates" of unspecified sex, the BFASS subsequently sent out a circular pointedly referring to them as "gentlemen," much to Garrison's chagrin. He insisted that his friends should *fail not to have the women recognised as equal beings*," although Sarah Grimké herself was by this time convinced, on tactical grounds, that any discussion of the issue was "greatly to be deprecated." In any event, the Philadelphia and Massachusetts radicals forced the issue by sending female delegates. Many later became prominent in the early stages of American feminism—Sarah Pugh, Abby Kimber, Lucretia Mott, Lizzy Neal Gay, Emily Winton, Mary Grew, and Abby Southwick. Elizabeth Cady Stanton, who had just married the conservative abolitionist Henry Stanton, was also there. "I hope," wrote Gamaliel Bailey to the presidential candidate for the Liberty party, that "unfavourable winds may delay them until the Convention is over."[13]

The winds blew fair, but the women delegates were confined to a sort of railed gallery set aside for their convenience. They were later joined there by Garrison, who had been becalmed off Sandy Hook by a providential misinterpretation of Bailey's malevolent prayer. He had not been present during the violent argument over

12. Tolles (ed.), "Slavery and the 'Woman Question'"; *ASR*, June 17, 1840, July 1, 1840, July 15, 1840; London *Patriot*, June 7, 1840, June 24, 1840; *WLG*, II, 366–420.
13. Minutes for June 14, 1839, May 15, 1840, BFASS Minute Books, I; *Liberator*, May 8, 1840, May 29, 1840; W. L. Garrison to G. Bradburn, April 24, 1840, S. H. Grimké to E. Pease, May, 1840, both in BPL-G; C. C. Catt and N. R. Shuler, *Woman Suffrage and Politics* (New York, 1923), 17; Stanton, *Eighty Years and More*, 71–91; G. Bailey to J. G. Birney, April 18, 1840, in Dumond (ed.), *Letters of James Gillespie Birney*, I, 557.

the women, which broke out as soon as Thomas Clarkson, feeble but still venerated, opened the proceedings and left the hall. Wendell Phillips, spurred on by his wife's memorable "Don't shilly-shally, Wendell!" proposed that the women be admitted. The Reverend Nathaniel Colver, surely the most spiteful of the Massachusetts conservatives, promptly jumped up in support of the BFASS decision. The most ominous portent was the way in which the British delegates rushed to join in the argument. Though Birney later outlined the dangers of nonresistance and no-government for their benefit, they seem at the outset to have treated the question of admitting the women on its own merits. For instance, the Reverend George Harvey, a Glasgow minister from the Relief Secession, flatly announced that seating the women would be "acting in opposition to the plain teaching of the word of God." The most revealing speech came from George Thompson. Perhaps with an eye to his livelihood as a professional lecturer, he urged that the movement should not divide over the issue. He did insist, however, that a refusal to accept the women would be a refusal to put them "on a footing of equality," and indeed an insult to the American group that had sent them.[14]

In any event Phillips' resolution was heavily defeated. The American women had come three thousand miles to watch the convention from the gallery, and they were disposed to feel, with Garrison, that "dear Thompson has not been strengthened to do battle for us." In this they were not quite correct. Although the rest of the proceedings were more or less peaceful, what Thompson had done was bring it home that the refusal to seat the women was effectively a gesture of noncooperation with the Garrisonian societies across the Atlantic. Again, it was not only Garrison but also the black abolitionist Charles Remond and the New Hampshire leader Nathaniel Peabody Rogers who had joined the women in their philanthropic purdah. The controversy was endlessly discussed in the convention hotel rooms. It was just plausible that the women had been excluded because the great London Quakers wished to strike at Hicksite Friends like Lucretia Mott and Sarah

14. *Proceedings of the General Anti-Slavery Convention Called by the Committee of the British and Foreign Anti-Slavery Society and Held in London, from Friday, June 12th, to Tuesday, June 23rd, 1840,* 23–35, 38; ASR, June 6, 1840.

Pugh.[15] Few can have believed that the issue was as simple as that. As the provincial delegates left London, their thoughts turned less upon the slave than upon the feuds among his champions.

Nevertheless, it took some time to become clear that the controversy had been serious enough to split the movement apart. Before the convention, the evangelical press had followed the lead of the *British and Foreign Anti-Slavery Reporter* in suppressing all references to the bitter divisions in the American movement. The Scots, for instance, had only had occasional hints of dissension, like the publication of one of Angelina Grimké's pamphlets in Peterhead in the previous year, or the reprinting of her *Appeal to the Christian Women of the South* in 1837, with an introduction by George Thompson. Afterwards, reform newspapers like the *Scotsman* published edited accounts from which the embarrassing discussion of the woman question was missing. Even a Tory paper like the *Scottish Guardian* lost sight of the issue in its description of the convention as a faceless rabble of infidels, Jews, and females. Most British abolitionists, however, must have known enough to sympathize with one side or another, though few fully understood what the sides stood for. In 1840 Richard Davis Webb was almost alone in his comprehension of the Garrisonian position. In the world he looked forward to, he noted, "There would be no slaves, no kings, no beggars, no lawyers, no doctors, no soldiers, no palaces, no prisons, no creeds, no clergy, no sects, no war, no grinding labour, no luxurious idleness, no peculiar Sabbath or Temple, but every day and every place 'holiness unto the Lord,' no restraints but mutual restraints, no constraining power but love."[16] This was very

15. W. L. Garrison to H. B. Garrison, June 29, 1840, in BPL-G; entry for June 12, 1840, in Tolles (ed.), "Slavery and the 'Woman Question'"; D. Weston to A. W. Weston, August 22, 1840, in BPL-W; E. C. Stanton to T. Weld and S. Grimké, June 25, 1840, in G. H. Barnes and D. L. Dumond (eds.), *Letters of Theodore Dwight Weld, Angelina Grimké Weld, and Sarah Grimké, 1822–1844* (2 vols.; New York, 1934), II, 845–47; W. Howitt to L. Mott, June 27, 1840, in *Ninth Annual Report of the Board of Managers of the Massachusetts Anti-Slavery Society* (Boston, 1841), appendices, vii–x.
16. A. Grimké, *Slavery in America: A Reprint of an Appeal to the Christian Women of the Slave States of America* (Edinburgh, 1837); *idem, The Spiritual Rights of Christian Females, Advocated in a Letter by an American Lady, with Notes Appended by a Lady in This Country* (Peterhead, 1839); *Scotsman*, June 20, 1840, June 24, 1840, June 27, 1840; *Scottish Guardian*, June 26, 1840; R. D. Webb to S. Poole, August 3, 1840, copy, in BPL-G.

strong meat indeed, much too strong to be digested by British abolitionists during their short exposure to the Garrisonians at the convention. For another year they remained in a state of uneasy unity, aware that there were different factions in the American movement but still willing to cooperate with both. Perhaps there might have been no division in the British societies, at least along American lines, if they had not had to absorb further external influences in the months following the convention.

On the other hand, distrust of the decision to exclude the women was deepest in those areas where abolitionists already had traditions of local independence and where they would eventually split away from the BFASS. Individuals like Daniel O'Connell or the temperance leader Father Mathew, and an isolated paper like the Leicestershire *Mercury*, had openly opposed it. Among the regular membership of the antislavery societies, however, dissent was loudest in Glasgow, Edinburgh, and Dublin. Considering the distance between Scotland and London in prerailway terms, the Scots were well represented at the convention. Some of their delegates would have been in London in any case—for instance, O'Connell himself, who was there as the representative of the GES. Altogether Glasgow sent twenty-four delegates, including Smeal, Murray, and the two M.P.'s for the city. Edinburgh sent eight, among them John Dunlop and James Greville. Aberdeen had two—the home missions leader Edward Kennedy and the highly suspect Baptist Dr. James Hoby, whom Thompson had attacked along with Cox on his American mission. Paisley had one delegate, along with a half-share in William Smeal. The tiny society at Berwick could only share the services of the Reverend John Clarke with Kingston, Jamaica. A number of other Scots, the Reverend George Harvey of the Relief Synod among them, went to London as delegates of their churches or denominations rather than their antislavery societies.[17] By no means all of these men came out in favor of including the women. Later, too, many of them developed strong bonds with Garrison's enemies. John Dun-

17. *Proceedings of the General Anti-Slavery Convention . . . 1840*, 117; D. O'Connell to L. Mott, June 20, 1840, in *Ninth Annual Report . . . of the Massachusetts Anti-Slavery Society*, appendices, vi–vii; R. Allen to W. L. Garrison, September 1, 1840, in BPL-W; in *Liberator*: September 25, 1840, and extract from Leicestershire *Mercury*, n.d., July 31, 1840. Lists of delegates are printed in *Proceedings of the General Anti-Slavery Convention . . . 1840*, and in ASR, June 17, 1840.

lop, for instance, led the Edinburgh Society into support for the BFASS, and in due course he became the author of a pamphlet on the importance of political antislavery parties. After the convention, however, the aggressive majority of the Glasgow delegates, with their Dublin allies and a minority of the Edinburgh ones, became the core of provincial opposition to the conservative policy of the national society.

Their Dublin colleagues were a fascinating group, whose cooperation with American abolitionists suggests a pattern of provincial alienation similar to that of the Scots. The figure around whom all their activities revolved was Richard Davis Webb. Like several of the Scottish abolitionists, he was a moderately successful printer and publisher. After 1840, his life and that of his circle can be traced through his massive output of delightful but nearly illegible letters to the American radicals he met during and after the world's convention. Though he was fascinated by the whole range of radical reform, slavery was at the center of his millennial vision. "The welfare of liberty, humanity & civilization throughout the world," he wrote, "is identified with the success of this enterprise." Eventually, as editor of the *Anti-Slavery Advocate* and a principal correspondent for the American *Anti-Slavery Standard*, he reached a point where he was practically monitoring the whole exchange of men and ideas between the British and American Garrisonians. Webb stood alone among British radical abolitionists in having a first-rate mind, a powerful intellect capable of grasping and adapting concepts that, perhaps fortunately, were beyond the wit of many of his contemporaries. He was a Friend, but not an orthodox one, "only a very middling sectarian of any kind whatever." Webb was a delightful man, and it is easy to see how his friends—the Unitarian convert James Haughton, Eliza Wigham's sister Mary Edmundson, the beautiful and forthright Maria Waring—were persuaded to adopt his views on universal reform, or, like the rich Quaker draper Richard Allen, at least to tolerate them. Even the children were affected and themselves tried to preach to their dolls—"Now thee's going to a slavery meeting; now thee's going to a temperance meeting." Nathaniel Peabody Rogers, an Ishmael of reform whose canon of radical integrity was a refined one indeed, once noted wistfully that "I never experienced such a *liberty* as I *could not help feeling*, in a single day among these Irish hearts."[18]

Webb's group of Dublin "anti-everythingarians" was a law unto itself, but it is not surprising that its response to the world's convention was not dissimilar from that of the Scots. Webb himself had been converted to universal abolition by George Thompson. The group was connected to the Scots by family ties: Eliza Wigham's long visits to Mary Edmundson made her a regular summer member of the Dublin circle. The Hibernian Anti-Slavery Society had not been founded until 1837, and at first it worked in close cooperation with the old London Universal Abolition Society.[19] Its leaders, however, were in rather the same position as the Scots abolitionists, especially the voluntaries who were at odds with the national church establishment. As Irishmen, they never had an entirely satisfactory position in British political life. As Quakers, or other nonconformists, their position vis-à-vis the Protestant ascendancy was also insecure and ambivalent. At the same time, they had strong traditions of local autonomy, cultural and benevolent. They too often tended to oppose national centralization in quasi-political reform causes.

This quickly became apparent when the Hibernian society's delegates appeared at the world's convention. The party included Haughton, Maria Waring, the Allens, and the Webbs, together wtih Webb's brother, sister-in-law, and father. They were personally and intellectually overwhelmed by the American radicals. "They are strong and fine, and firm," wrote Maria Waring. "They are American abolitionists, a new race of being. . . . They regard women not as dolls but as human beings." Almost all the contacts the Irish delegation made were with American radicals clearly dis-

18. D. Riach, "Ireland and the Campaign Against American Slavery, 1830–1860" (Ph.D. dissertation, University of Edinburgh, 1975); R. D. Webb to G. Combe, October 4, 1848, Ms. 7298 f.92, in Combe Papers, SNL; R. D. Webb to C. M. McKim, September 10, 1860, in May Collection, CUL; H. M. Wigham, *A Christian Philanthropist of Dublin: A Memoir of Richard Allen* (London, 1886), 13–14; J. A. Collins, "Irish Reformers," in *Liberty Bell* (Boston, 1843), 170–74; *Herald of Freedom*, March 24, 1843, rpr. in *A Collection from the Miscellaneous Works of Nathaniel Peabody Rogers*, (2nd ed.; Boston, 1849).

19. R. D. Webb, *The National Anti-Slavery Societies in England and the United States* (Dublin, 1852), 5; E. Baldwin to H. Stokes, July 17, 1837, C2/13, July 29, 1837, C2/14, both in ASP.

trusted by the British national leaders. To these Dublin nonconformists, such new friendships made up for lifetimes of political
and religious exclusion. Eighteen months later, Webb could still
gloat that if the BFASS had been sane, they would have kept the
Americans "enclosed in their own exclusive circles, and only allowed provincials like myself to look at them from a distance, like
the cat and the King." Their response to the exclusion of the wom-
en was similar to that of Smeal and Murray. Webb might have
been speaking for all the Scottish and Irish radicals when he wrote
from the convention that "I could have the most dependence upon
the old or Garrison party."[20] The exclusion of the women, building
on the past tensions of the thirties, had given the future British
extremists a strong bias towards the Garrisonians. In itself, however, the convention had not made a breach with the national
society inevitable. Good motives were still admitted on both sides,
and the main point made as a rider to all disagreements was that
continuing united action was desirable.

The proof that the Scots had not lost faith in cooperation was
the welcome they gave the American delegates of entirely different views who toured Britain after the convention. There were
three separate groups of them. First came Lucretia and James
Mott, along with Sarah Pugh and Abby Kimber, two other Hicksite Friends from Pennsylvania who were later to have great influence among the British Garrisonians in Leeds, Manchester, and
Bristol. The second group, led by Garrison himself, included his
future archenemy Nathaniel Peabody Rogers, editor of the *Herald
of Freedom*; the sophisticated black leader Charles Remond; and
the lapsed Scottish Quaker from Pawtucket, William Adam. The
last group to visit the Scots and Irish included James Gillespie
Birney, then the Liberty party presidential candidate, and the future women's rights pioneer Elizabeth Cady Stanton, and her husband Henry, another of the Lane rebels. With them they took
John Scoble, the secretary of the BFASS, a devious man universally and deservedly hated by the provincial abolitionists. Even
he, together with this cross section of American antislavery leaders, could still be heartily welcomed and politely listened to in

20. M. Waring to S. and L. Poole, June, 1840, "Jottings for Maria Weston
Chapman" [R. D. Webb to M. W. Chapman, February 22, 1842], and R. D. Webb
to S. and L. Poole, June, 1840, copy, all in BPL-G.

Glasgow and Edinburgh in the months following the convention.

Mrs. Mott, as a Hicksite, had already been insulted in London, where she was not invited to the lavish parties at the Backhouses' and the Gurneys'. "Where there were young people," she was told, "they were afraid of our principles." In late July, however, she was warmly received in Dublin, where she noticed that the Webbs still had portraits of Birney and Gerrit Smith in their drawing room, as well as of Clarkson and Garrison. She and her party only arrived in Scotland in August, hugely delighted to find they had followed the gooseberry season north. The highlight of their Scottish visit was a trip to Abbotsford and Dryburgh Abbey, in the improbable company of a Georgia slaveholder. It seems that one of the few things that still united the sections was their romantic enthusiasm for Scott. They were also able to visit both Glasgow and Edinburgh twice. In Edinburgh they stayed first with George Thompson, and then with the phrenologist George Combe, later a conservative abolitionist. It was still not thought strange that Abby Kimber and Sarah Pugh should be entertained jointly by John Dunlop, later the leader of the new organization in Edinburgh, and Patrick Brewster, the moral force Chartist and future Garrisonian who was visiting from Paisley.[21] In Glasgow, such distrust as the Motts encountered came from Quakers worried about the Hicksite heresy, and William Smeal was among them. Nevertheless, they were made personally welcome by Smeal, and they attended an important GES annual meeting at which they heard speeches from Charles Remond, and from two Oberlin College fund raisers. The meeting was later taken over by highly articulate moral force Chartists, for whom Mrs. Mott felt some sympathy. She made no attempt to speak, though Smeal would probably have supported her if she had. She did give a public lecture of two hours, at a separate Sunday meeting, without any recorded opposition.[22] As the Hicksites posted south to Tynemouth to visit Har-

21. Entries for June 13, July 25, August 3, August 4, and August 13, 1840, in Tolles (ed.), "Slavery and the 'Woman Question'"; J. Mott, *Three Months in Great Britain* (Philadelphia, 1841), 15–16.

22. Entries for August 7 and August 10, 1840, in Tolles (ed.), "Slavery and the 'Woman Question'"; Minutes for August 7, 1840, August 10, 1840, in GESMB, II; Mott, *Three Months in Great Britain*, 65–69; extract from Glasgow *Argus*, n.d., in *Liberator*, October 9, 1840; W. Smeal to W. L. Garrison, August 1, 1840, in BPL-G; A. D. Hallowell, *James and Lucretia Mott* (Boston, 1884), 171–72.

riet Martineau, it can hardly have seemed to them that the old or new organization question had been an issue in their Scottish reception.

By and large the same was true of Garrison's own visit to Scotland. As she considered the whole British episode, Elizabeth Cady Stanton concluded that Garrison had made a fool of himself every time he opened his mouth inside or outside the convention. In fact he was working from the perfectly coherent intention of winning as many Britons as possible over to his own interpretation of universal reform. At one point he wrote proudly to Henry Clarke Wright, the Young Turk of nonresistance:

> We "sifted into" the minds of those with whom we came in contact, all sorts of "heresies" and "extraneous topics," in relation to Temperance, Non-Resistance, Moral Reform, Human Rights, Holiness, etc. etc. . . . On the subject of non-resistance, I had very much to say in England, Scotland, and the Emerald Isle; especially in view of the monuments and statues erected in honour of naval and military warriors, and of the numerous castles, and forts, and arsenals, and armed troops, which were everywhere to be seen. I carried out with me six bound volumes of the Non-Resistant, six copies of the engraved Declaration of Sentiments, and a bundle of non-resistant tracts, all of which I distributed in the most judicious manner, and to a great acceptance. . . . In short, I did what I could for the redemption of the human race.

He and his friends ensured that the Irish were well supplied with writings on Christian anarchy, while Thompson was made responsible for delivering a file of the *Non-Resistant* to Smeal and the Glasgow radicals.[23] Even if many British reformers failed to understand the implications of Garrison's position, it is striking that there was no sign of an attempt to refuse him either social acceptance or a full hearing.

In Scotland, even conservative Edinburgh gave Garrison and his friends a warm reception. On the evening of their arrival, they spoke at a temperance rally from seven till two in the morning. They rose heroically for a state breakfast at which Dr. Greville,

23. E. C. Stanton to A. G. Weld, June 25, 1840, in Barnes and Dumond (eds.), *Letters to Theodore Dwight Weld*, II, 845–46; W. L. Garrison to H. C. Wright, 1840, R. D. Webb to S. and L. Poole, June, 1840, G. Thompson to W. L. Garrison, August 9, 1840, all in BPL-G.

later a firm Broad Street or Tappanite man, announced that "it would be little better than a mockery" to describe their work for the slave. The evangelical Edinburgh *Witness*, which in a few years would be filling countless hundreds of column inches with attacks on the radicals, wrote cheerfully about Garrison's "mildness, gentleness, and firmness"; announced that Rogers, in spite of being an American journalist, was *not* "ignorant, impudent, and vulgar"; and pointed out that Remond, though an American Negro, had an accent "quite as good as that of most well-educated Scotchmen."[24] In Glasgow the radicals were received even more warmly, without dissent even from conservatives like George Harvey. Their principal rally, on August 27, was actually held in Dr. Wardlaw's Congregationalist chapel. Wardlaw, later one of the leading anti-Garrisonian Glaswegians, introduced Rogers with the felicitous remark that he was "not from Harmony—(cheers)—not from the misnamed cradle of misnamed socialism—(cheers)—but from Concord." This did not deter Garrison from printing the proceedings of the meeting in the *Liberator* as a personal triumph, or from eulogizing Wardlaw as one of the saving remnant of "faithful" abolitionists left in Britain. Certainly the disagreements had not been forgotten. At the Glasgow meeting Thompson was able to secure a resolution in favor of the female abolitionists of America, and Smeal later penciled enthusiastic lines of approval opposite the text of Garrison's remarks criticizing the London committee.[25] It was still clear, however, that the Garrisonians could be welcomed in Edinburgh and Glasgow without outraging conservative abolitionists. A short visit made it clear that the same was true of Dublin.

Rogers and Garrison sailed home on August 4, on the same ship as a group of new organizationists that included the Reverend Nathaniel Colver. The two radicals traveled steerage, somewhat consoled for their "second table condition" by their insulation from the "wine and brandy drinkers" in the after cabin. They were

24. Extract from *Scottish Pilot*, n.d., in *Liberator*, August 21, 1840; *Witness*, July 23, 1840.
25. *Report of the Speeches and Reception of the American Delegates at the Great Public Meeting of the Glasgow Emancipation Society* (Glasgow, 1840), 3; *Liberator*, August 28, 1840, September 4, 1840; *Report of the Speeches and Reception of the American Delegates*, 23, 9. Smeal's copy is in the Smeal Donation, Mitchell Library.

also much comforted by the recollection of their warm provincial reception. Rogers in particular was greatly taken by Scotland, to the point of drawing parallels between conservative abolitionist conspiracies in New Hampshire, and the time when King Edward, the Hammer of the Scots, "came down to these glens and mountains to 'new organise' Scottish independence."[26]

The welcome given to Garrison and his group would have been less striking if his conservative opponents in Birney's group had not been equally well received only a few weeks later. In Edinburgh, they all stayed at John Wigham's house in South Gray Street. They were apparently not ill treated by their hostesses Eliza Wigham and Jane Smeal Wigham, who were the later leaders of the Edinburgh Garrisonian group. John Wigham had already warned them that they should not allude to the woman question and that they could expect to encounter much local feeling that George Thompson had been badly served by the London BFASS committee. Mrs. Stanton herself had developed a loathing for Scoble at an early stage in the trip. Their hosts, however, were polite even to him, and they were all feted at a public meeting on October 14 and a mass breakfast two days later. What is more surprising is that they had an even finer reception in Glasgow. Scoble was pessimistic about the visit, since he had heard that Smeal was "excessively sore about the woman's question," and in fact Thompson had written guardedly to Webb that they expected to be "favoured(?)" with a visit from Birney and Stanton.[27] In any event they too were given a mass meeting in Dr. Wardlaw's chapel, on October 20, with supporting speeches not only from Thompson, but from Charles Remond, whom an attack of lung inflammation had detained in Murray's house at Bowling Bay. Scoble was so pleased by this that he concluded mistakenly that "Garrisonism has made but little way in Scotland."[28] In Dublin,

26. N. P. Rogers to R. D. Webb, August 3, 1840, in BPL-G; N. P. Rogers to P. Pillsbury, July 22, 1840, in *Liberator*, August 21, 1840.

27. John Wigham to J. Tredgold, October 6, 1840, C/10, 178, in ASP; Stanton, *Eighty Years and More*, 104; J. G. Birney to J. Tredgold, October 16, 1840, C5/36, J. Scoble to J. Tredgold, October 15, 1840, C10/27, both in ASP; J. Scoble to J. Tredgold, October 14, 1840, C10/28; G. Thompson to R. D. Webb, August 9, 1840, in BPL-G.

28. W. Smeal to W. L. Garrison, July 30, 1840, in BPL-G; J. Scoble to J. Tredgold, October 30, 1840, C23/117, in ASP; Minute for October 20, 1840, in GESMB, II; extracts from Glasgow *Argus*, October 22, 1840, in *Liberator*, November 27, 1840, December 4, 1840.

too, Webb had noted gloomily that "we won't be so much at our ease with [Birney and Stanton]," but this did not prevent their appearance along with O'Connell and him at two tempestuous meetings in the Rotunda.[29] However bitter the feelings at the convention, they had not made it impossible for British old organization sympathizers to listen to the new organization, or vice versa.

What the convention had done was create strong preferences. By the end of the following year, however, they had become deep enough to divide the British societies in exactly the same way as the American ones. The reason for this was not purely a British one, and it is perfectly possible that the societies would have returned to their usual rather inefficient level of cooperation if they had not had to absorb new influences from overseas. By the end of 1840, indeed, the *Anti-Slavery Reporter* was still ignoring the divisions. Only two of the Garrisonian visitors remained in Britain over the winter. Professor Adam, however, had returned to his interest in the problems of British India, while Charles Remond was still convalescing from his lung condition at Bowling Bay, with John Murray as his host and William Smeal's brother Robert as his doctor.[30] The arguments of June were fading into the past, when they were given new values by the visit of John Anderson Collins. At this point the precarious unity of the British movement collapsed once and for all.

The decision to send Collins was a response to the equally precarious solvency of the American movement. After they drove their opponents from the national antislavery society, the American Garrisonians quickly discovered that they had taken over a cipher. By the time of their secession, the conservatives had all but wound up the affairs of the American Anti-Slavery Society, which had already been weakened by the financial crash of 1837 and the inability of the Tappan brothers and other stricken busi-

29. R. D. Webb to W. L. Garrison, September 2, 1840, R. D. Webb to E. Pease, November 4, 1840, both in BPL-G; extracts from Dublin *Freeman's Journal*, n.d., in *Liberator*, November 27, 1840; extracts from Dublin *Monitor*, October 29, 1840, in *Liberator*, December 4, 1840.

30. W. Adam to J. Tredgold, March 19, 1841, C4/6, May 12, 1841, C4/8, C. Remond to R. Allen, January 7, 1841, C154/202, all in ASP; W. Smeal to W. L. Garrison, July 30, 1840, in BPL-G. Adam was the author of *The Law and Custom of Slavery in British India, in a Series of Letters to T. F. Buxton, Esq.* (London, 1840).

nessmen to keep their financial pledges. In a very real sense, this
posed the question of budgetary and therefore institutional survival. The Tappan brothers and the conservative Executive Committee, rich though they were, could hardly have been expected to
continue underwriting the society's staggering debts at a time
when their control of its affairs was problematic and their own
financial position was fragile. It was only logical to start liquidat-
ing such assets as the society had. In April, for instance, before
he could marry Elizabeth Cady and take his honeymoon at the
world's convention, Henry Stanton had to accept part of a substantial arrears of salary in virtually unnegotiable tracts from the
society's stocks. In general, however, debts could not be paid in
this way, for though the society owned some fifteen thousand dollars' worth of publications, it was not possible to create a magical
bull market in abolitionist literature overnight. The *Emancipator*
itself was losing money hand over fist. The only way to pay off its
debts, for which the conservative and *nouveau pauvre* Executive
Committee was personally liable, was to continue producing it,
and the only way to continue producing it in a form that had an
outside chance of making money was to keep it out of the hands
of the "interloping committee." As Stanton wrote to Amos Phelps,
whom he had no reason to deceive, "There is no trick, ruse, or plot
about this matter. *We have, & can get, no means.*"[31]

It was only after Garrison returned from the convention that
the shocking truth dawned on him. The American Anti-Slavery
Society he and his friends now controlled lacked money, pamphlet
stock, and above all a newspaper. What the new organization had
done as an act of budgetary self-defense was a specially horrifying
swindle to their opponents, and it rankled for years.[32] At one level
the *Emancipator* transfer symbolized the corruption of the system
that the conservative abolitionists, whose only interest was in the
narrow question of slavery, were still committed to support. In
crude practical terms what it meant was that the national society

31. H. Stanton to A. Phelps, April 17, 1840, in BPL-P; undated cutting, probably written by Joshua Leavitt, in scrapbook entitled in A. Tappan's hand "Relating to the Division of the Abolition Body," in Tappan Papers, LC.
32. *Liberator*, September 4, 1840, *et seq. Cf.* L. Tappan to M. Waring, May 14,
1847, in BPL-G; E. Quincy, *An Examination of the Charges of Mr. John Scoble
and Mr. Lewis Tappan Against the American Anti-Slavery Society* (Dublin, 1852),
21–23; *Liberator*, March 5, 1841.

was without a newspaper, except the new *Anti-Slavery Standard*, which was already in imminent danger of going under. With no funds to save it, Garrison naturally thought of sending Collins to raise money from the British friends who had so recently been feting him and his group. Unfortunately the whole sordid business of the *Emancipator* had one other level of meaning for those abolitionists who were not equipped to understand its more subtle ideological implications. It could be presented as an act of theft, a matter of right or wrong. It therefore presented a simply polarized issue upon which British abolitionists could project their existing rivalries. Its practical effect was to exclude cooperation between men and women who were impelled to take different sides on the problem.

The impact of Collins' mission was disastrous. His credentials presented the *Emancipator* transfer as a genuinely felonious act, even to the extent of denouncing poor penniless Stanton for his sybaritic trip to the world's convention on the proceeds of his stolen tracts.[33] Collins himself was a somber and driven man, a rigid anticlerical from Vermont, who had become general agent of the Massachusetts society after exposing the "clerical plot" against Garrison when he was a student at Andover. He was specially popular among the uncompromising women abolitionists in Massachusetts, and it was he who chartered the steamer *Rhode Island* to take the "boatload of ultraism" from Providence to New York for the rout of the conservatives at the 1840 national annual meeting. A man of considerable intellectual power, he eventually went beyond the Christian anarchism of the other Garrisonians to a form of communitarian socialism of his own. His hegira from anarchism to socialism was stimulated partly by his meetings while in Britain with Robert Owen. By the end of his trip he was writing that the slavery of the industrial working class had risen "out of the system of exchange, by which one class of men can secure the fruits of the poor labourer without returning him an equivalent."[34]

33. C. Marriott and J. Gibbons, for the American Anti-Slavery Society, to the abolitionists of Great Britain, September 25, 1840, in BPL-G, rpr. in *Liberator*, March 5, 1841.

34. J. L. Thomas, *William Lloyd Garrison: The Liberator* (Boston, 1973), 290, 312; A. W. Weston to D. Weston, March 8, 1839, D. Weston to A. W. Weston, March 17, 1839, May 3, 1839, all in BPL-W; J. A. Collins to E. Pease, July 4, 1841, in BPL-G.

A few years later Collins became the leader of the Owenite community at Skaneateles, in upstate New York, and successively the editor of the *Social Pioneer and Herald of Progress* and the *Communitist*. After the failure of the Skaneateles experiment, he became totally disillusioned with reform and turned to Whiggery. He moved to Ohio, where he became editor of the *Daytonian*, before moving on to California in 1848 to make a fortune in real estate and become a member of its legislature. From 1860 to 1867 he lived in Nevada, speculating in mining its quartz deposits. He also took a prominent part in the constitutional conventions of 1863 and 1864. Ultimately he returned to some of his early interests, as president of San Francisco's Society of Progressive Spiritualists.[35] At the time of his departure for Britain, however, when he was thirty-one, he was a committed Garrisonian anarchist, to whom the polarization of the British antislavery movement was in itself desirable as a precondition for further universal reform. Garrison could hardly have found an agent better suited to presenting the *Emancipator* issue in a way that would make division in the British societies inevitable.

Even the most sympathetic British abolitionists had doubts about the wisdom of Collins' mission. The world's convention and the excitement it stirred up had been followed by a lapse into comparative apathy. The financial strain of the trips to London must in itself have been great, and much of what money was left over from them had been gleaned by Dawes and Keep of the Oberlin College fund-raising mission. A good deal of British energy was also being channeled into the novel and exciting campaign for British India reform. Thompson himself had little time to help Collins because of the demands of his new job as agent of the British India Society.[36] This was specially damaging because of

35. *Liberator*, August 28, 1846, October 1, 1847; J. H. Noyes, *A History of American Socialisms* (Philadelphia, 1870), 164–68; W. R. Cross, *The Burned-Over District: The Social and Intellectual History of Enthusiastic Religion in Western New York, 1800–1850* (Ithaca, 1950), 332; J. F. C. Harrison, *Quest for the New Moral World: Robert Owen and the Owenites in Britain and America* (New York, 1969), 174; J. Schlesinger, *Workers in the Vineyard: A Review of the Progress of Spiritualism* (San Francisco, 1896).

36. H. R. Temperley, *British Anti-Slavery, 1833–1870* (London, 1972), 93–110; E. Pease to J. A. Collins, December 24, 1840, G. Thompson to J. A. Collins, March 3, 1841, both in BPL-G.

his great influence among the provincial abolitionists who were most likely to help Garrison's group. Again, many reformers were absorbed with the problems of the Anti-Corn Law League or the Chartist movement. Collins could not have chosen a worse time to appeal for support. Even his American employers were doubtful about sending him. The decision to do so was made by the Executive Committee of the American Anti-Slavery Society, which itself was even divided by it, and was kept secret from the rank-and-file abolitionists until after his departure. Even Garrison saw the trip as being justified only by the special nature of the crisis: "Nothing but the extreme exigency of the case . . . would have reconciled me to his going to England for the purpose of procuring pecuniary aid."[37]

Though Collins' presentation of the *Emancipator* issue did in fact win him many allies in the provinces, especially in Scotland, it soon became clear that there was absolutely no encouragement for him in London. From October to February, apart from a short and discouraging visit to Edinburgh, he stayed with Charles Remond at a boardinghouse in Southwark, constantly irritated at his companion's "slothful temperament." There were few invitations for him, and perhaps because this enforced idleness was intolerable for a man of his disposition, Collins' attitude to British abolitionists soured quickly. "The abolitionists I have met with have been laced up in sectarian jackets, and screwed up like the bride in the ballroom, unable to dance to the music . . . negro slavery . . . must be abolished by the square and compass. It must be done . . . without removing the dead carcass of a Quaker, Methodist, Baptist, etc. if perchance they stand on freedom's track. The car must stop, or go round. . . . New Organisation is the panacea." This timidity about damaging established institutions can hardly have surprised him. As he languished in his cheap lodgings on the wrong side of London, he soon concluded that British society itself was "a vast and complicated system of slavery." His drift towards Owenite socialism, about which he made no attempt to remain silent, cannot have endeared him to the millionaire leaders of the national movement. While in London Collins only received one or

37. C. Burleigh to J. S. Gibbons, September 26, 1840, W. L. Garrison to E. Pease, December 1, 1840, September 30, 1840, all in BPL-G; C. Burleigh to M. W. Chapman, n.d., in BPL-W; *Liberator*, February 12, 1841.

two gifts, from philanthropists who had private grudges against the committee of the BFASS.[38]

In general his reception was bleak. By mid-December he had lost patience. He determined to force the issue first by asking the London committee point-blank for support, and thereafter demanding their reasons for refusing it. This he did on the advice of Thomas Sturge, a Southwark shipowner who was involved in the African Civilization Society and had a considerable distrust of the Broad Street leaders, including his cousin Joseph. After some correspondence, Collins forced the BFASS to close the interchange by stating that "the course recently pursued by the American Anti-Slavery Society had alienated their confidence." They also considered the cause as "more truly represented" by the American and Foreign, or new organization Anti-Slavery Society.[39] Collins had approached them on the basis that a crime had been committed in the transfer of the *Emancipator*. The issue he raised was therefore morally nonnegotiable. It was all the more dangerous in that the BFASS committee had meanwhile received alarming letters from Nathaniel Colver. He set out to discredit Collins by outlining the November events at the Chardon Street Convention in Boston. He explained that Garrison "identifies himself with every infidel fanaticism which floats . . . all in harmonious effort against the Bible as our standard of faith." The *Liberator* was quick to point out that the convention distrusted Garrison's leadership as much as anyone else's, which was objectively true.[40] But the damage was done, for unlike women's rights or even nonresistance, infidelity was a phenomenon which could only be perceived in terms of an ethical absolute.

Between them, Collins and Colver had put British abolitionists in a position where their preference had to be projected against

38. J. A. Collins to E. Pease, December 8, 1840, G. Thompson to R. D. Webb, February 8, 1841, J. A. Collins to R. D. Webb, January 28, 1841, J. A. Collins to W. L. Garrison, December 12, 1840, J. A. Collins to [?], November 26, 1840, J. A. Collins to E. Pease, December 4, 1840, all in BPL-G.

39. Collins, *Right and Wrong*, App. L, 56–59, rpr. in *Liberator*, March 5, 1841, March 12, 1841.

40. N. Colver to J. Sturge, November 3, 1840, December 1, 1840, extracts rpr. in Collins, *Right and Wrong*, App. A, 45–46; entry for January 1, 1841, BFASS Minute Books, I. *Cf.* R. W. Emerson, "The Chardon Street Convention," *Collected Works* (Boston, 1933), X, 371–77; *Liberator*, January 29, 1841.

a moral polarity. It did not require a full understanding of the Garrisonian position for British evangelicals to react to this kind of problem. Whether the guilt of the opposition lay in theft or infidelity, cooperation between the two sides was no longer viable. Collins' stay in London brought him little formal support. What it did do was force the BFASS to react to issues that translated the existing rivalries and tensions in the movement into open disunity.

In the provinces, at a purely material level, Collins was more successful. Even there, he was often badly received, especially on the short excursions he made from London in midwinter. He and Remond made one pioneering trip to Scotland to visit Thompson at his cottage in Duncan Street, in Newington. Collins hoped to inveigle Charles Stuart, whose distrust of women had now pushed him firmly into the new organization group, into a debate in front of the committee of the Edinburgh Emancipation Society. This plan failed, and they returned to London leaving the minds of the local leaders "poisoned" by the views of Birney and Stanton.[41] A pilgrimage to Playford Hall to see Thomas Clarkson yielded nothing but an entirely apposite harangue from the old man on "the dangerous influence of Owenism." Snubbed by all the other abolitionists in Ipswich, Collins became the star speaker at a meeting that was more a Chartist than an antislavery rally. In Darlington, too, Collins had poor luck. He was thwarted by a task force of the local abolitionists, who took over his meeting and adjourned it on the grounds that none of the "London Interest" was present.[42] The Darlington visit, however, had a deeper significance, for it brought him into personal contact with Elizabeth Pease. She had done, and would do, more than anyone else to organize what provincial help Collins eventually attracted.

Elizabeth Pease, a radical Darlington Quaker, was important for Collins, important for the Garrisonians, and ultimately impor-

41. Collins, *Right and Wrong*, 70–73; G. Thompson to R. D. Webb, November 2, 1841, J. A. Collins to C. Stuart, November 6, 1840, C. Stuart to J. A. Collins, November 8, 1840, J. A. Collins to M. W. Chapman, December 3, 1840, all in BPL-G.

42. J. A. Collins to W. L. Garrison, January 1, 1841, J. A. Collins to Mrs. Clarkson, December 28, 1840, J. A. Collins to R. D. Webb, January 28, 1841, all in BPL-G; Ipswich *Express*, January 5, 1841; *Liberator*, July 30, 1841, August 6, 1841; *Tenth Annual Report of the Board of Managers of the Massachusetts Anti-Slavery Society* (Boston, 1842), 47–50.

tant in a purely Scottish context. She helped Collins energetically
from the beginning of his trip, when even radicals like Harriet
Martineau, William Smeal, and Richard Davis Webb were being
most discouraging.[43] She had been exposed to radical antislavery
ideas since childhood. Her father spent most of his fortune on
philanthropy, and he had been active in both the 1833 and 1838
campaigns. Eventually he became the prime mover behind British
India reform, which was aimed indirectly at undercutting American slavery.[44] In all these efforts his daughter was a most faithful
colleague. The British India plan was much admired by radical
abolitionists in America, and they had also been impressed by
Miss Pease at the world's convention. At that time she was thirty-
three—two years younger than Webb, two years older than Collins. She had written an *Address to the Women of England* against
apprenticeship in 1836, and in 1840 she was editing a pamphlet
denouncing American Quakers for their silence over slavery.[45] Her
British India work had brought her very much under Thompson's
influence, and her lifelong friendship with Wendell and Ann Phillips began in 1839. Through them, and through her contacts with
Angelina Grimké Weld and the Boston radical leader Maria Weston Chapman, she was kept well posted on the early squabbles in
America. Mrs. Chapman had cautioned her that "the treachery
which it is important to the cause to expose *here*, should not be
noticed in England otherwise than by that natural coldness which
involuntarily comes over us when we meet one whom we know

43. H. Martineau to J. A. Collins, November 10, 1840, W. Smeal to J. A. Collins,
November 10, 1840, R. D. Webb to J. A. Collins, January 7, 1841, all in BPL-G.
44. On the Pease family, see J. H. Bell, *British Folks and British India Fifty
Years Ago* (London, 1891); P. H. Emden, *Quakers in Commerce: A Record of
Business Achievement* (London, 1939), 42–59; A. M. Stoddart, *Elizabeth Pease
Nichol* (London, 1899), *passim*. Edward Pease, the "father of the railways," was
Joseph's brother and Elizabeth's uncle, while the Joseph Pease who was the first
Quaker M. P. was Edward's son and therefore Elizabeth's cousin.
45. Entry for June 6, 1840, in Tolles (ed.), "Slavery and the 'Woman Ques-
tion'"; W. Phillips to G. Thompson, June, 1839, E. M. Davis to E. Pease, December 28, 1839, W. L. Garrison to E. Pease, September 1, 1840, all in BPL-G;
Liberator, September 4, 1840, September 25, 1840, November 13, 1840; *Eighth
Annual Report of the Massachusetts Anti-Slavery Society* (Boston, 1840), appendix,
xxi–xxii; Bell, *British Folks and British India*, 9; E. Pease, "Society of Friends in
the United States: Their Views on the Anti-Slavery Question, and Treatment of
the People of Colour, Compiled from Original Correspondence" (Darlington, not
published, 1840).

has betrayed principles & persons." She went away from the convention "quite in love with W.L.G."[46] Like Collins, in fact, she was quickly moving beyond the nonresistant position to a secular critique of English social structure. By 1842 she could write that "it is to class legislation that all the evils which affect Gt. Britain . . . is [sic] to be attributed."[47]

Miss Pease encountered Collins at the most active phase of her antislavery career, and also at a time when she was going through an intellectual transition similar to his. Her tireless correspondence on his behalf was invaluable. She was a brilliant, tense, and lonely woman, perhaps much constricted by her relationship with an able father. Her friendship with Collins, like her later relationship with Henry C. Wright, seems to have given her one of her rare spells of happiness. Soon afterwards, in 1846, she was prostrated by her father's death. She only reemerged as a force in the movement in the fifties, after her marriage to John Pringle Nichol, who had the chair of astronomy at Glasgow. Before meeting him, at a water cure, she had convalesced with the Wigham family in Edinburgh. After his death, she returned to help them as a leader of the radical Ladies' Emancipation Society. She became its president during Reconstruction, and indeed she and Eliza Wigham were still closely allied illuminati in the Edinburgh reform world of the seventies.[48]

It was in Scotland that Miss Pease's friend Collins had his most spectacular effect among abolitionists. He went north for a second time in February. Her heroic efforts to counteract the Colver letters circulated by the "Papish Click [sic]" in the national society

46. M. W. Chapman to E. Pease, March 16, 1840, G. Thompson to R. D. Webb, August 9, 1840, both in BPL-G; E. Pease to M. W. Chapman, July 17, 1840, A. Phillips to M. W. Chapman, July 30, 1839, both in BPL-W; Bell, *British Folks and British India*, 9; O. Sherwin, *Prophet of Liberty: The Life and Times of Wendell Phillips* (New York, 1958), 116.
47. E. Pease to W. Phillips, September 29, 1842, in BPL-W. See also E. Pease to A. W. Weston, December 30, 1841, in BPL-W; undated diary excerpt, in Stoddart, *Elizabeth Pease Nichol*, 157.
48. E. Pease to E. N. Gay, January 29, 1848, in Gay Papers, CUL; W. Phillips to R. D. Webb, June 1, 1853, in BPL-G; *Eliza Wigham: A Brief Memorial, Reprinted and Revised from the "Annual Monitor"* (London, 1901), 11; Bell, *British Folks and British India*, 2; *Annual Report of the Edinburgh Ladies' Emancipation Society, and Sketch of the Anti-Slavery Events and Condition of the Freedmen* (Edinburgh, 1867), *passim*.

had done nothing to soften their force.[49] The Scots therefore had to respond to him in terms of a polarity between infidelity and theft. This was specially damaging in Glasgow, where the enthusiasm of Smeal and Murray was already putting the unity of the local society under serious strain. The intrusion of the issues raised by the *Emancipator* transfer and the Chardon Street Convention destroyed it once and for all.

Although the various American delegations were equally well received in Glasgow after the convention, the appearance of continuing unity was deceptive. Smeal and Murray were in any case disposed to distrust the national society qua national society, and they had felt considerable sympathy for the women delegates. When they wrote their annual report, they set the cat among the clerical pigeons by expressing that sympathy and by denouncing the conduct of the BFASS in this and other respects as "illiberal, unauthorized, and overbearing." This was especially offensive, since it ignored an earlier committee directive that the draft of the report should be substantially revised.[50] It was even worse that the secretaries had added a series of appendices setting out the full case of the old organization against the new organization. It was worst of all that one of these appendices was a complete reprint of Maria Weston Chapman's *Right and Wrong in the Anti-Slavery Societies.* This denounced the American clergy as proslavery villains, commended the progress of women's rights, dismissed the BFASS, and took the nonresistant position that all political action against slavery was immoral. Smeal and Murray completely compromised the society, on their own initiative, by pointing out that Mrs. Chapman's work "contained sentiments in themselves so excellent, and the spirit which it displays is so thoroughly that of *Universal* freedom, that it is earnestly recommended to all, to READ WITH ATTENTION."[51] Smeal and Murray were already at odds

49. J. A. Collins to H. G. Chapman, January 2, 1841, in BPL-W; J. C. Fuller to E. Pease, February 20, 1841, J. C. Fuller to *ASR*, not printed, February 20, 1841, J. A. Collins to R. D. Webb, January 28, 1841, all in BPL-G; *Liberator*, February 5, 1841, February 12, 1841. The Fuller letters were reprinted as a broadsheet, and also used in Collins, *Right and Wrong*, 73.
50. GESR, 1840, pp. 17–18; Minutes for August 7, 1840, September 14, 1840. October 21, 1840, in GESMB, II; *Report of the Discussion at the First Meeting of the Members of the Glasgow Emancipation Society* (Glasgow, 1841), 5.
51. GESR, 1840, p. 35ff. The original was *Right and Wrong in the Anti-Slavery Societies*. Smeal's personal copy is still in the Mitchell Library.

with their more conservative colleagues when Collins first appeared before the committee on February 12.

By this time Dr. Wardlaw, at least, had been sent copies of the Colver letters. Captain Stuart, too, had released a new denunciation of the "rhapsodists." Miss Pease's writing furiously that the "poor man . . . needs a *jacket* as *strait* for his body as that which he wears on his mind," did not make him any less dangerous. He could not be discounted simply because he was, as Thomas Sturge noted, "a violent man . . . from some degree of weakness capable of a degree of inveteracy more befitting those bereft of reason than a peaceable Christian." The committee decided, with extraordinary optimism, that the best way to reach a decision would be to hear a debate between Collins and Stuart. At the same time, Smeal was instructed to write to London asking for an explanation of the report that the London Committee had been defaming Collins. Unfortunately Stuart refused flatly even to consider a discussion with Collins, "knowing the total and deplorable derangement of your views *in this matter, both as to facts and principles.*"[52] In a humiliating gesture John Tredgold, Scoble's predecessor as secretary of the BFASS, sent Smeal and Murray bald copies of the noncommital notes he had sent in response to similar inquiries from Dublin, and eventually ended the correspondence.[53] Meanwhile the atmosphere in Glasgow was further heated by Collins' publication of his *Right and Wrong Among the Abolitionists of the United States*, which was brought out by the GES committee member George Gallie. It was probably doubly suspect to conservatives because Harriet Martineau, a notorious Unitarian bluestocking, had provided a preface, but it also presented the Garrisonian indictment in terms of moral absolutes. On March 10

52. Minutes for February 11, 1841, March 3, 1841, in GESMB, III; C. Stuart to R. Wardlaw, circular, February 8, 1841, J. A. Collins to W. L. Garrison, March 2, 1841, E. Pease to J. A. Collins, February 12, 1841, all in BPL-G; T. Sturge to J. A. Collins, February 12, 1841, in BPL-W; C. Stuart to W. Smeal, March 8, 1841, in *Resolutions of the Public Meetings of the Members and Friends of the Glasgow Emancipation Society; Correspondence of the Secretaries . . . Since the Arrival in Glasgow of Mr. John A. Collins . . . in Reference to the Divisions Among the American Abolitionists* (Glasgow, 1841), 25.

53. W. Smeal to J. Tredgold, March 5, 1841, J. Tredgold to J. Haughton and R. Allen, March 12, 1841, J. Murray and W. Smeal to J. Tredgold, March 29, 1841, J. Tredgold to J. Haughton and R. Allen, April 17, 1841, rpr. in *Resolutions of the Public Meetings*, 26ff. Discussion of the letters is noted in Minute for March 12, 1841, BFASS Minute Books, I.

Collins drafted a letter specifically asking for support. On the same day an explosive committee meeting argued over the failure of Smeal and Murray to clean up the annual *Report*, which had just come out in print. It had already driven Joseph Sturge to resign his position as a corresponding member. A few days later, the disintegration of the society began with the resignation of Dr. Ralph Wardlaw, certainly Scotland's most highly respected Congregationalist.[54]

For the next few weeks, the two groups jockeyed backwards and forwards for advantage. For two meetings the radicals were in control, and they were able to adopt a circular supporting Collins. In mid-April, however, the conservatives returned in force, led by Dr. Wardlaw's fellow Congregationalist Dr. Heugh and by Dr. David King of the United Secession Church. By fourteen to nine, they adopted three resolutions that precluded an identification with either American side or any of their publications or agents, pending further information. In effect this was an exclusion of Collins, and it indicates the extent to which his views were considered frightening. The Garrisonian view was that the victory had been won by packing the committee with members who had previously been inactive. Their response was to resort to unorthodox means of their own. After a public meeting, about which they did not trouble to tell their opponents, they called the so-called bazaar meeting of April 27. They had adopted an entirely new tactic, and the chairman in the bazaar was the Reverend Patrick Brewster, brother of the scientist and principal of Edinburgh. He was also a leading moral force Chartist. A principal speaker was the Reverend Dr. John Ritchie of Edinburgh, a secession minister but also a Garrisonian and moderate Chartist. The radicals had held a "workingman's meeting" the day before, to ensure enough labor attendance at the meeting to pass resolutions favorable to Collins. They were duly passed, and seventeen new members added to the GES committee. The price was that the meeting also

54. J. A. Collins to GES Committee, March 10, 1841, draft in BPL-G; Minutes for March 10, 1841, March 16, 1841, in GESMB, III; *Resolutions of the Public Meetings*, 7–10.

had to commit itself to support for the Chartist movement.[55] The Garrisonians had won.

"They call it Yankeeism," wrote Collins. "Smeal says they may call it what they please."[56] But even Smeal and Murray can hardly have failed to see that they had won their victory by going outside all the normal canons of Scottish evangelical reform. It was not abnormal for Chartists to take over reform meetings and turn them into demonstrations for suffrage.[57] The Chartists followed the progress of the antislavery movement, and at least one Chartist paper was willing to make a clear distinction between the purity of Garrisonianism and the hypocrisy of the Wardlaw element in the movement. What was entirely new was the deliberate conciliation of the Chartists to gain advantage in infighting within a purely middle-class reform movement. This was a logical outgrowth of Collins' move towards the Owenites and of his tendency to see chattel slavery and wage relationships as allied elements in the same system of oppression. His tactic actually went beyond the Garrisonian position, for a true nonresistant would have had no interest in the specific objectives of the Chartists. In fact he had been flirting with them for some time before the "bazaar meeting."[58] What the new approach did was add yet another ideological dimension to the old grudges of the convention, to the pro and con of nonresistance, and even to the moral antithesis between theft and infidelity.

Nevertheless, though this new social issue increased the bitterness between the parties, it does not seem to have been the main or even the final reason for division. The conservative group grad-

55. Minutes for March 25, 1841, March 29, 1841, April 13, 1841, April 16, 1841, April 27, 1841, in GESMB, III; *Report of the Discussion at the First Meeting . . . of the Glasgow Emancipation Society,* 18; extract from Glasgow *Post,* n.d., in *Liberator,* May 28, 1841; *Resolutions of the Public Meetings,* 2–5.

56. J. A. Collins to W. L. Garrison, May 2, 1841, in BPL-G.

57. For example, see London *Patriot,* January 13, 1840; *Scottish Guardian,* March 16, 1841; *Scotsman,* May 12, 1841; L. C. Wright, *Scottish Chartism* (Edinburgh, 1953), 115–69.

58. *Chartist Circular,* May 29, 1841; J. Harvey to J. Tredgold, April 19, 1841, C7/95, in ASP; J. A. Collins to editor of Glasgow *Argus,* n.d., approx. April 20, 1841, broadsheet, and J. A. Collins to R. D. Webb, April 18, 1841, both in BPL-G; Glasgow *Post,* April 17, 1841, extract in *Liberator,* May 28, 1841.

ually resigned in the weeks following the bazaar meeting,[59] but
they do not appear to have done so as a class reaction against
social and political objectives of the Chartists. Those who resigned
were not distinctive along lines of class or occupation, whether
from those who remained or from the new members who were
added to the committee. The new leaders were marginally less
prosperous than the old ones, but all came from the comfortable
middle class. Nor is there any clear split along denominational
lines. The only identifiable group who resigned were the Congregationalist ministers, and this may merely have been a matter of
personal loyalty to Ralph Wardlaw.[60] The reasons for the choices
made were complex, but what seems certain is that they were
made on the basis of the internal ideological conflicts presented by
Collins, and not as a response to the external threat of Chartism,
though the latter can hardly have had a positive effect in maintaining unity. In either case, the GES was now rid of its new
organization lumber, and it remained fast in support of Garrison
for the next twenty years.

Collins had much less success in Edinburgh. The city's two most
active Garrisonians, George Thompson and Thomas Ritchie, were
more active in the Glasgow society than in their own. The Edinburgh society was led by men strongly disposed against the Garrison group, and it flatly refused to see Collins again after the
debacle of his attempted debate with Stuart. He had much more
success among women abolitionists. In Glasgow the Ladies' Emancipation Society had remained in the hands of the conservatives,
and it had been necessary to found a Glasgow Female Anti-Slavery Society as a replacement.[61] Collins had had modest encouragement from some of Thompson's female friends in Edinburgh while
he was still in London. If he had spent time in Edinburgh, which
his absorption in the affairs of Glasgow did not allow him to do,
the societies there might have divided in the same way. As it was,

59. Minutes for May 19, 1841, July 20, 1841, July 30, 1841, August 2, 1841, in
GESMB, III.
60. See Appendix E. The one clergyman added was the Reverend George Rose,
a Methodist.
61. J. Dunlop to J. A. Collins, April 29, 1841, in BPL-G; *An Appeal to the
Ladies of Great Britain in Behalf of the American Slave* (Glasgow, 1841), *passim*;
First Annual Report of the Glasgow Female Anti-Slavery Society (Glasgow,
1842), 6.

it seems that the conservative women simply dropped quietly out of the society, in response to the clear Garrisonian sympathies of Jane Smeal Wigham, Eliza Wigham, and Harriet Gairdner, the wife of a local physician.[62] Their little group eventually came to be one of the important British Garrisonian bodies, an automatic calling point for any American radical who happened to be in Scotland. The men's society, on the other hand, became known as one of the British bodies most receptive to new organization visitors.[63] The social and religious background of the two groups was identical.

In financial terms Collins' mission was a disaster. He had to borrow money for his passage home from Wendell Phillips, who sailed with him on the Fourth of July packet. By this time even Garrison was convinced his return was long overdue. In fact the *Standard* survived on its own merits. For Collins himself, the mission had a central significance, for the lessons he learned from British society primed his transition from evangelical reform to socialism. He could never forget "the oppressive incessant toil and drudgery [to] which 17/20ths of your entire population are subjected & . . . the luxury, prodigality, & idleness which is saddled upon the other 3/20ths." By 1843 even Abby Kelley was horrified by his insistence on dragging the attack on property in general into his antislavery work. He was under considerable pressure when he resigned that year to move on to the uncertain future of his experiments at Skaneateles.[64] It is difficult to imagine how this restless man's life would have unfolded if he had not made his visit to Britain in 1841.

In Britain itself, that visit's effect upon abolitionists was shattering. Collins spent his last six weeks in Dublin, arriving just at the

62. J. A. Collins to E. Pease, December 4, 1840, H. Gairdner to J. A. Collins, December 10, 1840, June 19, 1841, all in BPL-G.
63. A. Phelps to E. Wright, March 1, 1844, in Elizur Wright Papers, LC.
64. W. Phillips to J. A. Collins, June 29, 1841, J. A. Collins to E. Pease, July 4, 1841, W. and A. Phillips to R. D. Webb, July 27, 1841, W. L. Garrison to J. A. Collins, April 1, 1841, J. A. Collins to E. Pease, August 16, 1841, all in BPL-G; *Liberator*, July 27, 1841; A. Kelley to M. W. Chapman, June 28, 1843, August 2, 1843, E. M. Collins to M. W. Chapman, August 15, 1843, J. A. Collins to M. W. Chapman, August 23, 1843, F. Douglass to M. W. Chapman, September 10, 1843, all in BPL-W.

time when Webb's Hibernian Anti-Slavery Society was breaking
off from the BFASS because of its refusal to support him.[65] What he
eventually left behind was a British movement that in general still
accepted the leadership of a conservative national society based
in London and allied with the American and Foreign Anti-Slavery
Society. Even among Collins' sympathizers, it is likely that only a
talented minority shared Elizabeth Pease or Richard Webb's sophisticated understanding of the complex factors behind the divisions he had presented. On the other hand, the way in which he
had presented them made a British fragmentation inevitable.
There were now groups of abolitionists in Glasgow, Edinburgh,
and Dublin, who were loyal to Garrison and did not recognize
the leadership of the BFASS leaders at Broad Street. All three
were George Thompson strongholds, with traditions of provincial
autonomy and previous grudges against the national group. What
Collins' visit did was translate their preferences into principles.
He had obliged them to come out and be separate both from local
rivals and from their country's corrupt antislavery leaders. Until
after the American Civil War, Britain would never again have a
united antislavery movement. For the next twenty years the Scots
were to steer the most devious and most consistently independent
course of all—except, of course, for Richard Davis Webb and the
Irish.

65. R. Allen to H. Stokes, February 4, 1841, C4/47, February 20, 1841, C4/48,
J. Haughton and R. Allen to H. Stokes, March 31, 1841, C4/50, H. Stokes to R.
Allen, April 16, 1841, copy, C4/51, all in ASP.

CHAPTER 5

The Forties: The Scottish Churches
and the Southern Slave

The Scots abolitionists, in the forties, concentrated on different issues from their colleagues in England. This does not mean that they were unaware of anything that was happening in the world of Atlantic antislavery. But there were large sectors of abolitionist activity that left them unmoved. They seem to have felt consistently that the issues of British governmental policy, to which the BFASS paid such close attention, were less urgent than the genuinely foreign problems of the movement in the United States.[1] Perhaps, indeed, it was precisely because they were using their antislavery commitment as a supplement to the unsatisfying realities of London-focused politics that they shrank so far from those areas where the problem of slavery and the political process met.

The contributions of the Scots over diplomatic and imperial issues were modest. They did become somewhat concerned over the relationship between free trade in sugar and the expansion of the slave trade. John Murray of Glasgow even devised an improbable scheme of installing British inspectors on all Latin American plantations, busily stamping each bale or barrel of produce as free or slave grown. A proper differential duty could then be imposed, and the integrity of antislavery principles preserved. Happily this suggestion was not pursued at Whitehall, and the issue never really divided the Scots as seriously as it did the national movement. In Buxton's ill-fated scheme to open the Niger they showed little or no interest. Under Thompson's influence as they were, it was natural for them to be interested in Indian slavery and British Indian reform. Thompson made his first trip to India in 1843, as the guest of the reforming landlord Dwarkanauth Tagore, and as agent of the British India Society he made special efforts to win

1. H. R. Temperley, *British Anti-Slavery, 1833–1870* (London, 1972), 93–183.

over his Scottish friends.[2] Yet he never managed to draw them into a consistent campaign of the sort envisaged, for instance, by Elizabeth Pease's father. On the problem of West Indian labor supply, the Scots did not share the general hostility to free or not-so-free emigration from Africa to the British Caribbean. The Glasgow abolitionists who did turn their attention to this problem were actually champions of the shipowner McGregor Laird's "toll-free bridge" plan for ferrying black labor backwards and forwards across the Atlantic. Again, few Scots became primarily concerned about the efficiency and morality of the West Africa Squadron, or the best means of suppressing the still-vigorous slave trade to Cuba and Brazil.[3]

In general they were convinced, with the American radicals, that the only way of ending the trade was to eradicate slavery itself at the American end, beginning with the United States before progressing to Cuba and Brazil. They remained unshaken in this view, though Lord Palmerston himself tried to remind Murray that "the great secret in all matters public or private is to find out what one can do and what one cannot, so that one may make one's efforts with a chance of success."[4] The Scottish abolitionists nevertheless continued to concentrate on North America, in a decade when the principal concerns of the national society and its English auxiliaries were imperial and diplomatic. At the same time, their work in support of the Americans was to some extent specialized. It is startling to find that they showed little interest in the Texas question or the Mexican War, both of which were matters of deep

2. C. D. Rice, " 'Humanity Sold for Sugar!' British Abolitionist Response to Free Trade in Slave Grown Sugar," *Historical Journal*, XIII (1970), 402–18; GES circular, April 24, 1844, in C17/76, ASP; *Proceedings of the General Anti-Slavery Convention, Called by the Committee of the British and Foreign Anti-Slavery Society, and Held in London, from Tuesday, June 13th, to Tuesday, June 20th, 1843* (London, 1844), 127–73; *ASR*, June 21, 1843, April 3, 1844, May 1, 1844, May 29, 1844, June 12, 1844; GESR, 1839, pp. 60–67. On British Indian slavery and reform, see Temperley, *British Anti-Slavery*, 93–110; J. H. Bell, *British Folks and British India Fifty Years Ago* (London, 1891).

3. *British Friend*, May 31, 1843, September 30, 1843, March 30, 1844, April 30, 1844; J. Murray to J. Scoble, May 11, 1843, C20/34, in ASP; *Proceedings of the General Anti-Slavery Convention . . . 1843*, 238–62. Cf. *ASR*, May 31, 1843; J. Dunlop to J. Scoble, May 19, 1848, in C16/85, ASP; C. Lloyd, *The Navy and the Slave Trade* (London, 1949), 104–114; Temperley, *British Anti-Slavery*, 168–84.

4. Palmerston to J. Murray, April 7, 1844, Ms. 3925, f.202, in Small Collections, SNL.

concern to their counterparts in America and England. Perhaps they were heeding Lewis Tappan's warning to Thompson that Mexican annexation would follow automatically if it were known that British abolitionists were against it—or Maria Weston Chapman's stoical reassurance that "we bear it as an *old* calamity." Unlike the English leaders, they shunned involvement in the two controversies where the British government had a real political role to play in the fight against American slavery. They seem to have courted the experience of working without recourse to the kind of lobbying that was the daily business of the BFASS.[5] Throughout the forties, they channeled almost all their energies into two activities. One was defining the proper role of the churches in relation to American slavery. The other, which gained momentum from the first, was the perpetuation of the infighting of 1841. In both, they made eager use of the movement's troubles to act out tensions and disagreements of a deeper but more local sort.

It is not surprising that the principal concern of the Scots was with the churches. The controversies of nineteenth-century Scottish church history reached an extraordinary level of vehemence and attracted wide middle-class participation. This was not because Scots are genetically prone to a sort of spiritual litigiousness, though they often seem to be. It was not even because of their genuinely democratic religious tradition, or because of a specially alert lay comprehension of theological niceties. In fact it was not the purely religious aspects of Scottish history that maintained the conflicts of the churches at such an extravagant level of enthusiasm. There had been no Scottish court since the Union of the Crowns in 1603, and the Union of 1707 had destroyed the base for a national parliamentary life. Such opportunity as there was for a political outlet in London was narrowed by the Dundas family machine and the Scottish managers. Even in mid-Victorian Scotland, after the First Reform Act, political involvement in the Dreepdaily Burghs and other such communities was not enticing

5. L. Tappan to G. Thompson, December 2, 1844, in Tappan Papers, LC; M. W. Chapman to G. Combe, January 27, 1845, Ms. 7278, in Combe Papers, SNL; J. Ogilvy to H. Stokes, August 2, 1837, C3/47, in ASP; GESR, 1839, pp. 93–95; Aberdeen *Journal*, July 19, 1843; G. Thompson to J. Scoble, April 10, 1847, C18/7, in ASP.

to thinking men. In this situation, some Scots channeled their energy into the ongoing debate over the proper cultural role of their small, old nation, within the large, new state. But until constituency politics were revitalized with the Second and Third Reform Acts, many middle-class Scots found a complement to political life in the bewilderingly complex affairs of their churches.[6]

This was even more so in the mid-Victorian period than in the eighteenth century, for the young men entering the church then were more able than ever before. Scotland was still educationally committed to "a programme of democratic intellectuality," geared with fair precision to training talented boys from every walk of life.[7] Unfortunately the democratic intellect had far outgrown the society it served, and the Scottish schools and universities depended on having their pupils absorbed overseas or in London. In the new century, the fall of the Dundas interest had removed the delicate Scottish network of patronage in the government and the armed forces. Although the East Indies and Canada still had jobs to offer, these too were constricted by the failure of the Scottish Whigs to use their patronage in the interest of their countrymen. The sugar islands, which had been an important area of employment up to the abolitionist success of 1807, became unattractive in the period of confusion that followed. It was only the Trevelyan-Northcote reforms that again enabled the Scots, in a new situation of competitive examination, to put their superior education to good use and begin the second phase of their dominance in Her Majesty's Civil Service. In the first part of the century, this was still in the future, and the country was confronted more alarmingly than ever before with the problem of producing more able young men than it could ever hope to employ internally. To go further with William Aytoun's fiction, it is probably true that some did try to make their fortunes with improbable schemes

6. W. E. Aytoun, "How I Stood for the Dreepdaily Burghs," in *Stories and Verse*, ed. W. L. Renwick (Edinburgh, 1964), 40–110; H. J. Hanham, *Scottish Nationalism* (London, 1969), 73–90; *idem*, "Mid-Century Scottish Nationalism," in R. Robson (ed.), *Ideas and Institutions of Victorian Britain* (London, 1967), 143–79; G. E. Davie, *The Democratic Intellect: Scotland and Her Universities in the Nineteenth Century* (2nd ed.; Edinburgh, 1964); D. Daiches, *The Paradox of Scottish Culture: The Eighteenth-Century Experience* (London, 1964), 49, 51–52.
7. Davie, *The Democratic Intellect*, xvii and *passim*.

like the great Glenmutchkin Railway swindle.[8] A more obvious alternative was to enter the ministry.

The church had always been an acceptable career in Scotland. It became even more so as the nation passed through the same upsurge in evangelical religion and the same profound shift in values as England and America. The deep Scottish anxiety over patronage, which ultimately led to the Disruption of 1843 in the Church of Scotland, had a major ideological and class component. But it was also connected with a serious gap between the rise in the numbers of trained ministers and the expansion of the job openings available to them. The churchgoing population as a whole remained static, in spite of, or perhaps because of, the heightening piety of the middle class.[9] It had not been thus in the eighteenth century, when most able young clergymen, like Mr. Goldie in John Galt's *Annals of the Parish*, were quick to find heritors who would provide them with a parish. It is not surprising that the leading Scottish ministers of the 1840s, who had begun their education early in the century, as the country's career perspectives began to narrow and its evangelical horizons began to widen, were men of extraordinary ability, great public ambition, and spectacular forensic talent. Scotland's appetite for clerical controversy, always a sharp one, was thereby much gratified.

Though the arguments between these men and their denominations took many forms, they were sometimes expressed as disagreements over the problem of slavery. At one level this was a simple matter of tactical advantage, for the United States had a particular form of relationship between church and state. It was based on a voluntary principle, without patronage and without a religious establishment. The problem of voluntary organization versus church establishments was the most important bone of contention between Scottish evangelicals. On the other hand, one of the few things upon which they were all in agreement was their opposition to slavery, which they were stirred to attack by much the same kind of religious anxieties as their brethren in England and Amer-

8. W. E. Aytoun, "How We Got Up the Glenmutchkin Railway and How We Got Out Again," in *Stories and Verse*, 1–39.
9. D. J. Withrington, "Non-Church-Going, c.1750–c.1850: A Preliminary Survey," *Records of the Scottish Church History Society*, XVII (1973), 99–113.

ica. Both the United States and American slavery therefore took
on an important role in their arguments. This was a time when the
Scottish voluntary denominations—the old Presbyterian Secession
Churches and the Congregationalists and Baptists—were gaining
in strength, especially in Glasgow and the West of Scotland, at the
expense of the established Church of Scotland.[10] It was comforting
to the latter, which could assume a universal disapproval of slavery, to point to bondage and brutality in America as a logical outgrowth of voluntaryism. It was equally important for Scottish
voluntaries to help the fight against slavery in America, so that its
method of church government would still present an unblemished
mirror for their own ideal. Indeed the internal strains in Scottish
middle-class society, together with the intense commitment to
antislavery, meant that the whole tortured process could go one
step further. Once the movement divided, it was possible for the
different denominations to attack one another on the basis of the
particular alliance they had chosen. It was just as damning to
argue that enemies had become friends with nonresistants and
heretics as it was to argue that enemies had reneged on the slave's
most devoted champions. American antislavery, by the forties, had
become an integral part of the polemical life of the Scottish
churches.

The use of slavery as a lever in clerical controversies was not
novel, either in Scotland or England. Even in the eighteenth
century, there are examples of highfliers and common sense philosophers turning their views on slavery against moderates and
Humean idealists. For instance, James Beattie of Aberdeen, the
common sense moralist, loathed and feared the polished clerical
intellectuals who dominated the Church of Scotland until the
eighties. He once denounced them for "talking of the eternal
concerns of mankind, with a frigidity and languor which a good
economist would be ashamed of, in bargaining for half a dozen
haddocks." He was clearly aware that a challenge to Hume's
standpoint on slavery would discredit both him and his moderate
admirers. He therefore pounced on the famous Hume footnote,
"In JAMAICA indeed they talk of one negroe as a man of parts and

10. W. Ferguson, *Scotland, 1869 to the Present* (Edinburgh, 1968), 307–308.

learning; but 'tis likely he is admired for very slender accomplish-
ments, like a parrot, who speaks a few words plainly." Beattie was
able to gain great credit for his group by demolishing this view
in his *Essay on the Nature and Immutability of Truth* of 1769. The
same was true of Samuel Stanhope Smith, who was an offshoot of
the Scottish tradition in that he succeeded his teacher and father-
in-law, Dr. John Witherspoon, as president of Princeton. His *Essay on the Causes of Variety of Figure and Complexion in the
Human Species* was less a defense of the Negro's humanity than
an attack on the infidelity of Henry Home, Lord Kames, and those
who shared Kames's views on the plurality of creations.[11] Slavery
and race were already useful polemical weapons in the eighteenth
century.

By the 1830s and 1840s their use had become wider. This,
paradoxically, was because of the total agreement of the British
churches over the immorality of slavery and their duty to support
American abolitionists. Even the Free Church of Scotland, which
later came under so much fire for its alleged proslavery activities,
never made any attempt to step outside these canons, and its 1844
delegation to the American churches did all it could to remonstrate
privately over slavery. Here the agreement broke down. The ways
in which the churches could try to influence their American colleagues ranged from simple advice to the refusal of communion,
first to slaveholders and ultimately even to those Christians who
insisted on keeping up relations with them. The confusion was
worsened by Scripture's ambivalence over slavery. It became easy
to discredit rivals by denouncing the particular way in which they
chose to carry out their duty over slavery. In 1835, for instance,
an Old Kirk minister was able to imply that the voluntary churches
were not trying to influence the American churches they admired.
In a reprint of Albert Barnes' *Picture of Slavery in the United
States*, he simply announced that the institution was another of

11. J. Beattie to T. Blacklock, August 1, 1768, Acc. 4792, in Fettercairn Papers,
Dep. 2, uncataloged, SNL; D. Hume, "Of National Characters," (1756 version),
in T. H. Greene and T. H. Grose (eds.), *Essays Moral, Literary, and Political* (2
vols.; London, 1875), I, 252n; J. Beattie, *An Essay on the Nature and Immutability of Truth, in Opposition to Sophistry and Scepticism* (2nd ed.; Edinburgh,
1771), 507–12; *An Essay on the Causes of the Variety of Figure and Complexion
in the Human Species*, ed. W. D. Jordan (Cambridge, Mass., 1966).

"the brutal deeds of American republicanism and voluntaryism."[12] The voluntary churches, both the Congregationalists and the older secession groups, tried to prevent exposure to this kind of slur by putting as much public pressure as possible on their American brethren. By the mid-forties, their doing so was a pointed allusion to the shortcomings of their archenemy the Free Church of Scotland, which had lost considerable credit by falling into the trap of accepting funds from Presbyterian sympathizers in the slave South. By this time, too, the controversy had become more complex, for the publication of James Gillespie Birney's *The American Churches the Bulwarks of American Slavery* created a new interest in the drastic step of denying communion and other church privileges to Americans connected with slavery.[13]

It was not in Scotland alone that the slave became a pawn in clerical feuds. In America, it is often difficult to decide whether the controversies of the antebellum churches caused discussion of slavery, or discussion of slavery caused the controversies. Even Mrs. Stowe, when she depicted the Old School and New School Presbyterian ministers in *Dred* happily discussing reunification, was using slavery to discredit her Congregationalist family's rivals. In England, too, it was important as late as 1860 that denominations should keep their antislavery credentials clean.[14] In the forties, indeed, all British abolitionists became involved in two incidents where debate over the slavery issue was overlaid with real denominational tensions.

The first arose in 1843, over the British response to the division

12. G. Lewis, *Impressions of America and the American Churches* (Edinburgh, 1845), 66, 87, 97, 119, 263; A. Barnes, *Picture of Slavery in the United States of America: Being a Practical Illustration of Voluntaryism and Republicanism* (Glasgow, 1835), 5.

13. Aberdeen *Herald*, April 15, 1837; *American Slavery: Remonstrance of the Congregational Union of Scotland* (n.p., 1840); *Deliverance of the Reformed Presbytery of Edinburgh on American Slavery* ... (Edinburgh, 1845); *Memorial and Remonstrance Respecting Slavery, to the Synod of the United Secession Church* (Glasgow, 1846); *An Expostulation with Those Christians and Christian Churches in the United States of America That Are Implicated in the Sin of American Slaveholding, by a Committee of the Reformed Presbyterian Church in Scotland* (Glasgow, 1848); Minute for October 20, 1842, GESMB, II.

14. H. B. Stowe, *Dred: A Tale of the Great Dismal Swamp* (London, 1856), 375–97; W. H. Pullen, *The Blast of a Trumpet, Calling Upon Every Son and Daughter of Wesley, in Great Britain and Ireland, to Aid Their American Brethren in Purifying Their American Zion from Slavery* (London, 1860).

in the Indiana Yearly Meeting of Friends. The decision of the London Yearly Meeting was to support what appeared to be the proslavery side. This brought sharp criticism from radical provincial Friends like Webb, Smeal, and Elizabeth Pease. Though they were joined on this issue by Joseph Sturge, they may have shared the sense of alienation from the Society of the Friends in its modern established form, which had been the fuel for the Hicksite secession in the United States and which had probably contributed to the antislavery secession from the Indiana Yearly Meeting itself.[15] The focus for this internal opposition to the decision of the London Yearly Meeting was the *British Friend*, a paper founded and edited in Glasgow as a specific protest against the failure of the London *Friend* to cover the activities of the radical American abolitionists. Webb's protest against what he saw as a respect for "hollow unity &'. . . dead rules" was to resign from the Society.[16] The Friends who attacked the London abolitionist leadership had already denounced it in 1841, as Garrisonians at odds with the Quaker committee of the BFASS, but they were also a specific group within the Society of Friends.

They were much less successful over Indiana than in the second major controversy over the church response to slavery. This arose in 1846 with the foundation of the Evangelical Alliance, a body aimed at informal ecumenical cooperation between the "evangelical denominations" of Britain, America, and Europe.[17] It specifically excluded Unitarians and Quakers. Since the Unitarians and radical Friends controlled the provincial antislavery movement,

15. W. Edgerton, *A History of the Separation in the Indiana Yearly Meeting of Friends, Which Took Place in the Winter of 1842 and 1843, on the Anti-Slavery Question* (Cincinnati, 1856); T. E. Drake, *Quakers and Slavery in America* (New Haven, 1950), 162–68; R. W. Doherty, *The Hicksite Separation: A Sociological Analysis of Religious Schism in Early Nineteenth Century America* (New Brunswick, 1967), 33–36.

16. *British Friend*, April 29, 1843, May 31, 1843, June 30, 1843, October 31, 1843, November 30, 1843, February 29, 1844, July 31, 1844, December 31, 1844, April 30, 1845; A. M. Stoddart, *Elizabeth Pease Nichol* (London, 1899), 147–49; R. D. Webb to M. W. Chapman, February 29, 1844, in BPL-G.

17. R. W. Dale (ed.), *Life and Letters of John Angell James, Including an Unfinished Autobiography* (London, 1861), 396–423. There is a list of denominations, with members attending, in *Evangelical Alliance: Report of the Conference Held in Freemasons' Hall* (London, 1846), appendices, xcviii. Its aims are outlined in *Brief Statement of the Proceedings of the Conference Held in Liverpool for Promoting Christian Union* (London, 1846).

and the conservative Friends controlled the BFASS, its most powerful enemies had a quick eye for its antislavery shortcomings. With the help of George Thompson and the radical American visitors Frederick Douglass and William Lloyd Garrison, this unlikely coalition was able to dramatize the issue of slavery in a way that divided southern delegates from British and northern ones, and made the alliance as originally envisaged unworkable. It simply became a loose confederation of independent national alliances, which must have been most satisfying for those denominations, like the Friends, who had objected from the outset to its "disposition to lengthen the creeds and shorten the commandments." The triumph must also have been sweet for the Scottish Garrisonians.[18] Several of their local enemies, like Dr. King and Dr. Wardlaw of Glasgow, or Dr. Robert Candlish of Edinburgh, had been heavily committed to the alliance. The Scots, however, had meanwhile become involved in a controversy of their own over the shortcomings of the Free Church of Scotland. In bitterness and scope it makes these English skirmishes seem insignificant.

The story of the Free Church's birth still has to be written, though the Disruption was the most important event of the Scottish nineteenth century. What it involved was the secession of over a third of the twelve hundred or so ministers of the established Church of Scotland. Their leader was Thomas Chalmers, a social theoretician and economist of considerable stature, who had worked and written extensively in Glasgow on the problem of churching the urban working class. He had also held a chair at Saint Andrews. He became the first moderator of the Free Church.[19] Neither Chal-

18. H. Richard, *Memoirs of Joseph Sturge* (London, 1864), 374–76; London *Inquirer*, September 5, 1846; *Evangelical Alliance: Report of the Conference*, 290–309, 320–40, 371–459; *ASR*, September 1, 1846, November 2, 1846, December 1, 1846; Minutes for September 18, 1846, October 30, 1846, November 2, 1846, BFASS Minute Books, II, in ASP; London *Patriot*, September 3, 1846, September 17, 1846; *Nonconformist*, September 23, 1846; *WLG*, III, 150–86; W. L. Garrison to H. B. Garrison, August 18, 1846, September 17, 1846, W. L. Garrison to R. D. Webb, August 19, 1846, W. L. Garrison to S. May, December 19, 1846, all in BPL-G.

19. Ferguson, *Scotland, 1869 to the Present*, 311–17; W. O. Henderson, *Heritage: A Study of the Disruption* (Edinburgh, 1958); J. Brown, *Annals of the Disruption* (3 vols.; Edinburgh, 1876–77); J. W. Nisbet, "Thomas Chalmers and the Economic Order," *Scottish Journal of Political Economy*, XI (1964), 151–57; H. Watt, *Thomas Chalmers and the Disruption* (Aberdeen, 1943); W. Hanna, *Memoirs of Thomas Chalmers* (4 vol.; Edinburgh, 1852–53).

mers nor his followers were in the slightest bit radical, either socially or theoretically. Their interest in benevolence was a keen one, but it was a benevolence of the kind that, rightly or wrongly, has been decried in the American case because of its associations with social control.[20] Their concerns were those of middle-class evangelicals on both sides of the Atlantic, and their view of society was one based on individual moral autonomy, redemption by example, and the beneficence of the invisible hand.

The specific issue that caused the Disruption was the exercise of lay patronage in the choice of ministers, by heritors whose powers were independent of the will of the congregation. During the long controversy before 1843, this practice had been doggedly defended by the moderates, whose intellectual stature had declined lamentably since the brilliant days of Robert Wallace or Alexander Carlyle. Many of the evangelicals had originally intended to regulate rather than destroy the patronage system, but the increasing bitterness of the controversy led to their secession in 1843 as a "nonintrusionist" body. If the issue of patronage is set aside, the Old Kirk and the Free Kirk were doctrinally and organizationally as dissimilar as Tweedledum and Tweedledee. The nonintrusionists still accepted the establishment principle, and they still hated and feared the voluntaries—which may, indeed, have been one of the reasons for their increasing anxiety over patronage. Nevertheless, the conflict was one of central importance, for the patronage issue had become one upon which entirely different views of the place of the church in the nation had crystallized. This was not a question of the relationship between church and state, but one of defining the mutual responsibilities of the church and the communities it served. At the same time, the debate raised questions about property rights and about the moral autonomy of evangelical Christians. It also involved the trauma of destroying Scotland's only remaining national institution other than her courts. When Thomas Chalmers led his four hundred and seventy follow-

20. C. S. Griffin, "Religious Benevolence as Social Control, 1815–1860," *MVHR*, XLIX (1957), 423–44; *idem, Their Brothers' Keepers* (New Brunswick, N.J., 1960); M. J. Heale, "Humanitarianism in the Early Republic: The Moral Reformers of New York, 1776–1825," *Journal of American Studies*, II (1968), 161–75. Two significant alternative explanations of American benevolence are C. S. Rosenberg, *Religion and the Rise of the American City: The New York City Mission Movement* (Ithaca, N.Y., 1971); L. W. Banner, "Religious Benevolence as Social Control: A Critique of an Interpretation," *JAH*, LX (1973), 22–41.

ers out of the Old Kirk assembly and down the Mound to their own gathering, he was sacrificing not just a church but one of the last attributes of nationhood. Even in short-term retrospect, the schism took on a kind of desperate bitterness that would make it only too easy to be used as a touchstone for defining positions in other controversies.

This is exactly what happened when the Free Church was forced to make a response to American slavery. Its most immediate difficulties after the Disruption were financial. The virtue gained by leaving the fleshpots of Erastianism did not provide new fleshpots to put in their place, and it became a matter of real urgency to find stipends and church buildings for the Free Kirk ministers. The first General Assembly authorized the establishment of a sustentation fund and a building fund. Both were to be opened with contributions from even the poorest communicants, voluntary only in theory. Thereafter money was to come from canvassing overseas. America was clearly the place to begin. Many Americans admired the new church for giving up material wealth for the principles of primitive Presbyterianism. Others developed the mistaken impression that it had made a godly sacrifice in support of the voluntary system of church organization.[21] The Free Church quickly sent a delegation to capitalize on American sympathy, and it was moderately successful. It was not surprising, given the strength of Presbyterianism in the South, that much of the three thousand dollars collected came from the slave states.[22] If the men and women whose money they had accepted were not slaveholders, they were at least lax enough to take communion with those who were and to remain silent as to their sins.

Those abolitionists who had no interest in the survival of the Free Kirk responded quickly to a betrayal of such magnitude. Those who had every reason to wish its ministers might starve to death and its churches never be built responded quickly and with

21. A. A. Maclaren, "Presbyterianism and the Working Class in a Mid-Nineteenth Century City," *SHR*, XLVI (1967), 128–30; T. Smyth, *Works* (Columbia, S.C., 1908), III, 482–505; statement of the Synod of New York and New Jersey, in New York *Observer*, January 13, 1844, rpr. in *Witness*, February 14, 1844.

22. *Witness*, May 25, 1844, December 25, 1844; *Proceedings of the General Assembly of the Free Church of Scotland, Held in Edinburgh, in May, 1844* (Edinburgh, 1844), 64ff.; Lewis, *Impressions of America and the American Churches*, *passim*.

venom. Those few who were Free Church members either remained shamefacedly silent or tried to defend the connection with
the South. The result was a most extraordinary controversy, which
lasted for several years. It attracted more attention than any other
event in nineteenth-century Scottish church history except the
Ten Years' Conflict and the Disruption itself. Externally, if there
was ever an incident which supports the view that Victorian Scots
were "theocratic madmen," this was it.[23] In fact, however, the
"Send Back the Money" campaign arose logically from both the
dynamics of the antislavery movement and the real tensions within and between the Scottish churches. It became a vehicle for
expressing the rivalries between different factions of abolitionists
and between different denominations. In the process it provided
the Scottish Garrisonians with some most improbable new friends.

The Free Church delegation to America had not been as remiss
in criticizing slavery as their enemies later insisted. On the voyage
home for instance, they had petitioned the captain to admit a
Haitian Negro to the cabin deck, only to be foiled by a counter-
petition to admit the ship's cow to the saloon. "The jest . . . was
not relished by the passengers."[24] Until abolitionist critics became
outrageous, indeed, the General Assembly showed some anxiety
over the extent to which accepting southern money had been
proper. But it was inevitable that the abolitionists should respond
aggressively, for in 1843 and 1844 they were working in a situation
in which a specially delicate equilibrium in America had brought
with it a greater sensitivity than usual to foreign opinion. In evangelical circles the prestige of the Free Church was great indeed,
and its lapse, as Lewis Tappan put it, would be enough to "para-
lize" abolitionist efforts.[25] Both the BFASS and the American and

23. See G. A. Shepperson, "Thomas Chalmers, the Free Church of Scotland and
the South," *JSH*, XVII (1951), 517–37; *idem*, "The Free Church of Scotland and
American Slavery," *SHR*, XXX (1951), 126–43; *idem*, "Frederick Douglass and
Scotland," *JNH*, XXXVIII (1953), 307–321; Ferguson, *Scotland, 1689 to the
Present*, 310.

24. Lewis, *Impressions of America and the American Churches*, 391. Extracts
rpr. as G. Lewis, *Slavery and Slaveholders in the United States of America* (Edinburgh, 1846).

25. *Proceedings of the General Assembly . . . 1844*, pp. 163–64; *Cf. Proceedings
of the General Assembly of the Free Church of Scotland, Held at Edinburgh,
May, 1845* (Edinburgh, 1845), 256–58; Shepperson, "The Free Church of Scotland
and American Slavery," 131; L. Tappan to J. Scoble, April 10, 1844, in A. H. Abel

Foreign Anti-Slavery Society were quick to petition the commissioners of the General Assembly to take a new stand. At first, too, the conservative leaders in Britain thought it worth encouraging efforts their old Garrisonian enemies were making in the same direction.[26]

The Scots themselves at first took up the controversy in a way that did not go outside the normal tactics of the new organization. One of the problems of the Scottish societies, inevitably, was to reconcile the demands of antislavery with a courtesy towards their own Free Church membership. In Edinburgh this made it impossible for the emancipation society to hold meetings on the subject. In Glasgow, the GES at first encouraged the cooperation of Free Church members who were ambivalent about the acceptance of slaveholders' money. One of them, James Macbeth, ruined his career over the issue. A second was the Reverend Dr. Robert Burns of Paisley, one of the delegates to America. He appeared at the 1844 annual meeting of the society and stated frankly that he thought policy would be changed in the future.[27] Elizur Wright, who was present, was pleased with his views, and indeed a GES subcommittee which was appointed to interrogate him had already reported rather sheepishly that his abolitionist principles appeared "perfectly sound." Another Free Church minister, the Reverend John Willis, was able to remain on the committee without serious embarrassment until mid-1846, at the peak of the controversy, when he moved on to become president of the Free Church Anti-Slavery Society.[28]

---

and F. J. Klingberg, eds., *A Side-Light on Anglo-American Relations, 1835–1858: Furnished by the Correspondence of Lewis Tappan and Others with the British and Foreign Anti-Slavery Society* (New York, 1927), 182. See also L. Tappan to J. Scoble, June 29, 1844, *ibid.*, 184–85.

26. *Letter of the American and Foreign Anti-Slavery Society to the Commissioners of the Free Church of Scotland* (Edinburgh, 1844), first published in New York *Commercial Advertiser*, extract, n.d., rpr. in *ASR*, May 15, 1844; *Address* of the BFASS, in *ASR*, July 1, 1844; Minute for May 16, 1844, BFASS Minute Books, II.

27. M. Welsh to M. W. Chapman, April 25, 1844, in BPL-W; Minute for April 10, 1846, in GESMB, IV. This was MacBeth, on whom see *A Real Statement of the Secret and Concluding Debate in the Assembly on Mr. MacBeth's Case . . . by a Lover of Justice and a Member of the Free Church*, broadsheet (Glasgow, 1849); Minute for August 1, 1844, in GESMB, III; GESR, 1844, pp. 18–22.

28. Minutes for July 1, 1844, August 1, 1844, in GESMB, III; M. Willis, *Strictures on the Proceedings of the Last General Assembly of the Free Church of Scotland, Regarding Communion with the Slaveholding Churches of America* (Edinburgh, 1847), 1; *ASR*, November 2, 1846; Glasgow *Argus*, November 21, 1846.

Long before then, cooperation of this sort had become atypical. The new development was that the ministers of the voluntary churches rushed to use the issue in their ongoing vendetta against the Free Church. One of them, George Jeffrey of the United Secession, the author of *The Pro-Slavery Character of the American Churches*, had denounced it at a GES meeting as early as March, 1844. Another, the radical Dr. Ritchie of Edinburgh, had done the same in response to Burns's conciliatory speech at the annual meeting of the same year. Such attacks did little to change the attitude of the Free Church itself. An exchange of letters with its moderator and a trip to Edinburgh to distribute antislavery propaganda outside its General Assembly did not prevent the commissioners from announcing that slaveholding was not *"per se* an insuperable barrier to the enjoyment of Christian privileges." This was at odds with every radical abolitionist view on the proper church response to slavery. It was more than enough to obscure the whole premise of the rest of the deliverance that stated, "There is no question here as to the heinous sin involved in the institution of American slavery."[29]

The Glasgow reaction was to move the whole debate to a new level. Smeal and Murray called a public meeting for the specific purpose of denouncing the Free Church. It had six speakers. One of them was the visiting American nonresistant Henry C. Wright, and another the Free Church minister John Willis. The other four were the Reverend Drs. John Ritchie and George Jeffrey of the United Secession Church; the Reverend Dr. Bates of the Reformed Presbyterian Church; and the Reverend C. S. Ingram, a Congregationalist. Of these four, only Jeffrey had been associated with the GES prior to 1844. Doubtless all shared the antislavery concerns of their evangelical generation, but the new enthusiasm that inspired them to make major speeches at twenty-four hours' notice was not a coincidence. What Smeal and Murray had done for their own radical abolitionist purposes was send the fiery cross round the Glasgow voluntaries. After this meeting, which they held on November 18, 1844, the controversy maintained its momentum because it had become a battle royal between different factions

29. Minutes for March 14, 1844, March 25, 1844, August 1, 1844, in GESMB, III; *Proceedings of the General Assembly . . . 1845*, pp. 256–58; W. Smeal and J. Murray to H. Grey, March 30, 1844, H. Grey to W. Smeal and J. Murray, June 21, 1844, both in GESMB, III.

of the Scottish churches. This did not mean that its antislavery content had become any less emotive. For the next three years the GES expended so much money on the Send Back the Money campaign that it almost bankrupted itself.[30]

The work of the Scots abolitionists was much influenced by the visits of Americans who came to help attack the Free Kirk. Frederick Douglass and Garrison himself arrived in Scotland in 1846, together with James N. Buffum, but none played as important a role as Henry Clarke Wright. He developed considerable personal influence, especially with the Paton and Smeal families. But his nonresistant and anti-Sabbatarian views provided the Free Church with a crushing counter-accusation against their old enemies and his new friends among the voluntary clergy. Wright was an extraordinary figure, a man whose espousal of nonresistance was more comprehensive than that of Garrison himself. He had been trained at Andover Theological Seminary after a short but discontented spell as a hatter, but had left the ministry in 1833 to work in the antislavery and peace movements. By the time of the American schisms, he had become a Christian anarchist with unusual polemical gifts.[31] Wright came to Britain late in 1842, when he was forty-five, as the agent of the New England Non-resistant Society. Like many of the Garrisonians, he combined a capacity for inspiring complete and lasting loathing among those who disagreed with him and an ability to attract the instant and deep affection of those already well disposed towards his views. Again like many of the Garrisonians, he loved children and was loved by them, perhaps because he shared their willingness to act upon impulse. He was a combination of playfulness, harshness, love, and idiosyncrasy. He must have horrified his British hosts by eccentricities like his love of raw cabbage. Like Collins before him, though the two men could not have been more different, he was

30. Minute for November 17, 1844, November 18, 1844, in GESMB, III; *ASR*, December 11, 1844, December 25, 1844; Glasgow *Argus*, November 21, 1844, broadsheet copy in Smeal Donation; extract from *Scottish Guardian*, November 22, 1844, in *Witness*, November 27, 1844; W. Smeal to L. A. Chamerovzow, April 16, 1953, in C36/52, ASP. See also Appendix F.

31. L. Perry, *Radical Abolitionism: Anarchy and the Government of God in Anti-Slavery Thought* (Ithaca, N.Y., 1973), 18–22, 52–53, 57–58, 89–91; P. Walker, *Moral Choices: Memory, Desire, and Imagination in Nineteenth-Century American Abolition* (Baton Rouge, 1978), 278–304.

quick to win the friendship of Elizabeth Pease. She wrote to the Phillipses that "his company is a brook by the way, an oasis in a desert, a bright, delightful, heart-cheering one in the midst of this ceremony-ridden, formality-loving, etiquette-worshipping, caste-enslaving world."[32]

When Wright moved to Scotland in the following year, it was a very short step to become a favorite son of Smeal, Murray, and the Glasgow Emancipation Society. Smeal was by then a professed nonresistant. Murray's attitude is more obscure, since he avoided public writing as much as he avoided public speaking, but both secretaries had had full access to the reports of the Massachusetts Anti-Slavery Society and the stream of nonresistance material that the American Garrisonians had been sending to Britain since 1840. In either case, they received Wright warmly, and he quickly made friends with the Glasgow businessman Andrew Paton and his sister Catherine. He spent much of his Scottish visit staying with them, either at their house in Roseneath or at Richmond Street in Glasgow. At the 1844 annual meeting, Smeal's group allowed him to propose and pass a resolution congratulating the American and Foreign Anti-Slavery Society on adopting the principle of "NO UNION WITH SLAVEHOLDERS." Although many of those present probably interpreted this as a specific response to the Texas problem and the candidacy of James K. Polk, its nonresistant implications became clearer at the next annual meeting. Wright and the GES then resolved that "it is the duty of the friends of liberty and equal rights throughout the world to combine, & by Christian, peaceful, & bloodless means, to seek the Dissolution of the American Union as the gigantic enemy of Freedom and the Rights of Man."[33] Since his first interest was in nonresistance, to which the attack on slavery was incidental, there was no reason for Wright to shrink from statements that might frighten converts away from abolition. In

32. A. M. Stoddart, *Elizabeth Pease Nichol* (London, 1899), 145; E. Pease to W. L. Garrison, June 17, 1843, in BPL-G; E. Pease to A. W. Weston, January 27, 1844, in BPL-W. On these aspects of abolitionist behavior, see L. Perry, "'We Have Had Conversation in the World': The Abolitionists and Spontaneity," *Canadian Review of American Studies*, VI (1975), 3–26.

33. W. Smeal to W. L. Garrison, February 1, 1841, in *Liberator*, March 12, 1841; C. Paton to M. W. Chapman, November 2, 1845, November 17, 1846, both in BPL-G; GESR, 1844, p. 26; Minutes for August 2, 1844, August 1, 1845, in GESMB, III.

132 THE SCOTS ABOLITIONISTS

Scottish terms, he was playing into the hands of the Free Church, by linking his frighteningly radical disunion standpoint with the Send Back the Money campaign. Later on, at a most infelicitous time, he publicized his views on Sabbath observance in the same way.[34] The irony was that while the Scots were using the divisions among the abolitionists to help them in their church rivalries, Wright and the other Americans were able to use the disagreement of the Scottish churches to give a new dimension to tensions in the world of radical reform.

Frederick Douglass, the great black leader, showed less of a tendency than Wright to fight American fights on British soil, though his personal tensions with the Garrisonian leaders became much more marked during his 1845–1846 visit. He had come over on board the *Cambria* in August, along with James N. Buffum and the Hutchinsons, an important evangelical singing group. His first venture was an Irish tour, and he was lionized in every city where he spoke, with two exceptions. One was Waterford, where black visitors had been unpopular since Moses Roper turned up to give a lecture, very drunk indeed. The other was Belfast, the citadel of Irish Presbyterianism, where Douglass set about denouncing the conduct of the Free Church of Scotland.[35] By the following year its sympathizers were placarding the city with the legend SEND BACK THE NIGGER, and it was still impossible to raise local support for American antislavery ten years later.[36] With the Irish Garrisonians, Douglass' relationships were less than happy because of a

34. H. C. Wright, *The Dissolution of the American Union Demanded by Justice and Humanity, as the Incurable Enemy of Liberty, with a Letter to Rev. Drs. Chalmers, Cunningham, and Candlish, on Christian Fellowship with Slaveholders, and a Letter to the Members of the Free Church Recommending Them to Send Back the Money* (Glasgow, 1845), and *First Day Sabbath not of Divine Appointment, with the Opinions of Calvin, Luther, Melancthon, Barclay, Paley, and Others: A Letter to the Committee of the Edinburgh Emancipation Society* (Edinburgh, 1846).

35. B. Quarles, *Frederick Douglass* (New York, 1948), 38ff.; F. Douglass, *My Bondage and My Freedom* (New York, 1855), Chap. 24 *passim*; I. Jennings to M. W. Chapman, n.d., H. Webb to M. W. Chapman, October 18, 1845, both in BPL-W; J. A. Calder to J. Scoble, December 24, 1845, C14/124, in ASP; *British Friend*, December 31, 1845; *ASR*, November 12, 1845.

36. R. D. Webb to M. W. Chapman, October 12, 1845, F. Douglass to R. D. Webb, November 14, 1845, both in BPL-G; R. D. Webb to M. W. Chapman, June 17, 1846, in BPL-W; J. A. Calder to R. Bolton, April 9, 1849, C24/22, J. A. Calder to L. A. Chamerovzow, April 9, 1849, C29/20, 23, both in ASP.

surprising personal incompatibility with Webb. This was worsened by an impertinent letter from Maria Weston Chapman warning the Irishman that his guest could not be trusted. Webb did not like Douglass, and he never came to like him. Several years later, when the split between the Garrisonians and the Rochester group was complete, he remarked that Douglass "outherods all the New Organisation Herods in bitterness, extravagance, and malignity." Perhaps Douglass would have fled sooner to the relatively uncomplicated Scottish environment if it had not been for his distaste for Wright, which again looks forward to his division from the Garrisonians.[37]

Although Douglass was invited to Glasgow by Smeal in October, 1845, it was only in the following January that he arrived to help in the attack on the Free Church.[38] In all his Scottish work, however, his instinct was to treat slavery as a strict single issue and to denounce the Free Church only insofar as it had compromised its abolitionist integrity. Exactly the same was true of his traveling companion Buffum, a matter-of-fact, self-educated, self-made carpenter from Massachusetts. His role was never more than a supporting one for Douglass, but it was consistently different from that of Wright.

Douglass was also supported by a rather less unequal partnership with George Thompson, who had likewise been attracted to Scotland by the propaganda possibilities of the Free Church affair. He had now returned from his Indian visit and was living on a retainer as the agent for the Rajah of Sattarah and on freelance fees as a lecturer on Indian affairs. Though he was kind to Wright from the outset, he soon began to balk at the violence of his onslaught upon Free Church ministers. As a professional reform lecturer, though he might at times have bitten the hand that fed him, he could hardly have been expected to help chew it off. At the same time, in spite of his genuine admiration and love for Garri-

37. M. W. Chapman to R. D. Webb, June 29, 1845, January 23, 1846, February 24, 1846, all in BPL-M; F. Douglass to M. W. Chapman, March 29, 1846, R. D. Webb to M. W. Chapman, May 16, 1846, both in BPL-W; R. D. Webb to S. H. Gay, March 1, 1851, in Gay Papers, Columbia University Library; F. Douglass to R. D. Webb, November 10, 1845, in BPL-G.
38. Minutes for October 17, 1845, in GESMB, III; F. Douglass to R. D. Webb, January 30, 1846, F. Douglass to F. Jackson, January 29, 1846, both in BPL-G.

son, he was a deeply traditional man who had always promoted reform through existing agencies. He had not become a Garrisonian on the same ideological basis as Wright, Webb, or even Smeal, but because of personal loyalty and the realities of his own position on the fringe of the national benevolent establishment. This does not make his position any less attractive. In either case, his Scottish work in 1846 was aimed purely at changing the standpoint of the Free Church on slaveholders' money. At this time, too, he was mellow enough for civility to the BFASS, and it was he who arranged his own and Douglass' trip to its anniversary meeting in May.[39]

Perhaps it was because of Thompson's sensitivity to Scottish conditions that Garrison's part in the Free Church affair was, for him, a subdued one. Wright had been an important correspondent of the *Liberator* during 1844 and 1845, and the Glasgow Emancipation Society specifically invited its editor to Scotland, at Thompson's suggestion, in April, 1846. In practice, he spent relatively little of his time north of the border. After arriving in Liverpool on July 31, he traveled with Wright and Webb to join Thompson and Douglass in London. There they became very much involved in purifying the World's Temperance Convention from its connection with slavery and in trying to found the Anti-Slavery League. This drew support from moral force Chartists like John Lovett and Henry Vincent, and it was intended to unite all British Garrisonian abolitionists as an old organization counterweight to the BFASS. Like Collins and like the leaders of the GES but, curiously, unlike Wright, Garrison was quite prepared to ally with respectable elements of the working class, whose political aims he would have found irrelevant a few years before. This added a new series of complications to the Scottish situation. Many Free Church sympathizers must have shared the view of the Bristol Unitarian John Bishop Estlin that "Henry Vincent was by no means a choice person for Mr. G. to fraternize with." Estlin concluded that he was

39. GESR, 1843, Appendix, 44–68; *British Friend*, all issues for 1843; G. Thompson, *Five Lectures on British India . . . Delivered in the Friends' Meeting House, Manchester* (Manchester, 1845); G. Thompson to H. C. Wright, January 22, 1845, May 23, 1845, July 26, 1845, G. Thompson to R. D. Webb, August 12, 1845, all in BPL-G; P. S. Foner (ed.), *The Life and Writings of Frederick Douglass* (New York, 1950), 66.

"under some sort of quixotic notion—that the more unpopular he made himself with the middle classes of society in this country, the more he should promote the A.S. cause."[40] In terms of American reform, Garrison was merely being consistent. During his short visit to Scotland in October, however, when he joined Wright as the guest of Andrew Paton, he was uncharacteristically silent over the extraneous issues. But he did everything he could to couple his criticism of the Free Church and the Evangelical Alliance with his efforts to found auxiliaries for the league. Despite the discretion of Douglass, Thompson, and Buffum, the intervention of Wright and Garrison equalized the debating capital of the two church parties. The Free Church had exposed itself by allying with slaveholders. Its voluntary enemies, however, had opened their flank by leaguing with infidels, Sabbath-breakers, no-government men, and Chartists. In terms of paper strength, it would have been hard to slip a razor blade between the two teams.

The controversy had been raging for two years when it reached a peak at the Free Church General Assembly in 1846. All the efforts of the abolitionists led up to its meetings in May and June, and they were followed by the whole Atlantic community of reformers. To Douglass its importance made "this the *time*, and Scotland the *place* for all my efforts." The abolitionist plan was either to force the Free Kirk to send back the money, which it had already spent, or to split in two. By this time, in fact, most conservative abolitionists had given up the affair unless they had ulterior motives, for they had found the letters sent to America by the 1845 assembly quite satisfactory. Upon Wright, their effect was the opposite one. By the end of 1845, he had not only denounced the Free Church in the most tactless way but had also linked his criticism to an exposition of his own views on nonresistance and the corruption of the American Union. Wright's influence over the GES committee was now complete, and it published

40. W. L. Merrill, *Against Wind and Tide: A Biography of William Lloyd Garrison* (Cambridge, Mass., 1963), 108–109, 188, 358n; Minutes for April 20, 1846, April 21, 1846, in GESMB, III; *Liberator*, May 29, 1846; W. L. Garrison to H. B. Garrison, July 25, 1846, August 18, 1846, September 3, 1846, W. L. Garrison to R. D. Webb, August 19, 1846, all in BPL-G; London *Patriot*, September 17, 1846; F. Douglass, *My Bondage and My Freedom*, 381–82; WLG, III, 151–74; J. B. Estlin to S. May, October 1, 1846, November 2, 1846, both in BPL-M.

his works under its auspices.[41] It cannot have been reassuring to conservatives to be told, for instance, that "when our obligations as members of a particular nation conflict with our duties as members of the human family, the former cease," or to read that the commander of American troops in Mexico was by definition more disreputable than a well-known murderer.[42] Much of the odium Wright attracted had to be shared by Douglass and Buffum when they arrived in January, though they did most of their work independently, probably in an effort to avoid being tarred with the nonresistant brush. Douglass' personal stature rose greatly during the visit, and he clearly became more than capable of acting independent of his white patrons. There was no color prejudice against him, or at least none he noticed. He recorded that "it is quite an advantage to be a 'nigger' here. I find I am hardly black enough for British taste, but by keeping my hair as woolly as possible I make out to pass for at least half a negro at any rate."[43] Even this did not prevent his being denounced for an alliance with nonresistance, which he had rejected, and a cooperation with voluntaries, which he could not avoid.

For the first three months of the year, Douglass and Buffum visited provincial towns as far north as Aberdeen. They included some improbably small market, weaving, or fishing communities, where the Free Church was often strong. It was easy for its ministers to argue that criticism from men and women who were radicals or the friends of radicals should be ignored, easy to extrapolate the damning accusation of infidelity from the more complicated case of nonresistance and anticlericalism. In Scottish terms, too, it

41. F. Douglass to J. Scoble, May 9, 1846, C16/75, G. Thompson to J. Scoble, May 14, 1846, C22/61, both in ASP; G. Thompson to H. C. Wright, May 7, 1846, in BPL-G; ASR, 1845, June 11, 1845; Proceedings of the General Assembly ... 1845, pp. 256–58; H. C. Wright, American Slavery Proved To Be Theft and Robbery, Which No Circumstances Can Justify or Palliate, with Remarks on the Speeches of the Rev. Drs. Cunningham and Candlish Before the Free Presbytery of Edinburgh (Edinburgh, 1845); W. L. Garrison, Letter to the Committee of the Glasgow Female Anti-Slavery Society (Glasgow, 1845); Minute for November 5, 1845, in GESMB, IV.
42. Wright, Dissolution of the American Union Demanded by Justice and Humanity, 4, and Dick Crowninshield, the Assassin, and Zachary Taylor, the Soldier: The Difference Between Them (Edinburgh, n.d.).
43. Minute for January 12, 1846, in GESMB, IV; F. Douglass to F. Jackson, January 29, 1846, in BPL-G.

was simple to point to the sinister inconsistency between the old
voluntary enthusiasm for the American churches, and their new
demand that relations with them should be broken. It was quite
true that the voluntaries wished to help Douglass and Buffum. In
Dundee, for instance, their host was the great littérateur and establishment hater from the Congregationalist church, the Reverend
Dr. George Gilfillan.[44]

The response of the Scots had precious little to do with slavery. When Douglass found that it was easy to have urchins rush
through the streets of the towns he visited chanting "Send back
the money!" he had not, as he thought, mobilized Scotland against
American slavery. What he had done was unite the many elements
in her society that had grudges against the previously impregnable
Free Kirk. Some of its provincial defenders were statesmanlike
enough to turn from the delicious opportunity of mounting a counterattack against their old voluntary enemies, but they were few
indeed.[45] Since establishment ministers like Patrick Brewster of
Paisley were also working for the abolitionists, it was easy to
decry the unlikely alliance of the secession churches and "a church
which you designate as enslaved, and bondaged, and erastianised,"
or to conclude that the whole campaign was underwritten by
"an intense hatred of evangelical truth and vital godliness."[46] The
position of the Free Church was also strengthened by Henry
C. Wright's making incautious statements about "tipplers" and

44. *Northern Warder*, February 12, 1846; *The Free Church and Slavery . . . a
Series of Papers from the Dundee Courier* (Dundee, 1846); *Relation of the Free
Church to the American Churches: Speeches Delivered at the Free Synod of Angus
and Mearns, on Tuesday, 28th April, 1846* (Dundee, 1846), 3–12, 19; R. A. and
E. S. Watson (eds.), *George Gilfillan: Letters and Journals, with a Memoir* (Lon-
don, 1892), 79; *Report of Speeches Delivered at a Soiree Held in Honour of
Messrs. Douglass, Wright, and Buffum, on 10th March, 1846* (Dundee, 1846);
Fifeshire Journal [of May 7, 1846, May 14, 1846]: Send Back the Money, broad-
sheet (Dundee, 1846).
45. F. Douglass to F. Jackson, February 12, 1846, F. Douglass to R. D. Webb,
February 10, 1846, both in BPL-G; *An Appeal to the Members of the Free Church
on the Subject of Fellowship with Slaveholders, by Humanus* (Aberdeen, 1846);
*Should the Free Church Hold Fellowship with Slaveholders? And Should the
Money Lately Received from the Slaveholding Churches Be Sent Back?* (Linlith-
gow, 1846); J. Dick, *In Favour of the Free Church and Also of the Abolition
Cause* (Montreal, 1847).
46. J. Macnaughton, *The Free Church and American Slavery: Slanders Against
the Free Church Met and Answered* (Paisley, 1846), 8; *Relation of the Free
Church to the American Churches*, 3.

"drunkards" in its congregation at Hawick. He was forced to apologize for them after a controversy in the *Northern Warder* and the *Border Watch*, which was triumphantly presented as a "striking illustration of Messrs. Wright and Co.'s veracity."[47] The travels of the Americans brought the issue to the towns of Angus, Fife, and the northeast; to the farming and weaving communities of the southwest; and to the Borders. For all their energy and all their shortcomings, there was nothing they could have done to prevent slavery from becoming a weapon in a bewildering series of local church vendettas.

As the summer approached, exactly the same happened at national level. Thompson came north a month before the assembly at the end of April. The sides began to polarize more rapidly, partly because there was nothing he or Douglass could do to curb Wright. Free Church waverers were unlikely to be won over by the news that they had "betrayed the world's Redeemer . . . for money!! . . . betrayed Christ into the hands of His deadly enemies," though it was doubtless pleasing to the voluntaries and the establishment. By this time, though Dunlop and Greville had at first done what they could, the Edinburgh Emancipation Society had dropped out of the controversy under the combined strain of Wright's extremism and its own Free Church membership.[48] The Garrisonians were unsuccessful in founding a "Scottish Anti-Slavery Society" in its place, and what help they got in Edinburgh came from the Ladies' Emancipation Society. Its committee was a small one, and it was easy for its leaders to keep control of a group that was not well-informed and no longer had many Free Church members. It did everything it could to help the Glasgow

47. Extracts and correspondence in *Agitation Against the Free Church: Acknowledged Slander by H. C. Wright Against the Ministers, Elders, and Congregation at Hawick* (Glasgow, 1846). *Cf.* the attempted counterattack in *"Acknowledged Slander" Again! Free Church Assembly and Slavery Contrasted with the Irish Assembly and Slavery, and "Acknowledged Slander" Against Mr. Frederick Douglass, by the Rev. Dr. Smyth of Charleston* (Glasgow, 1846), 11, 12.
48. *The Free Church and Her Accusers in the Question at Issue: A Letter from George Thompson, Esq., to Henry C. Wright; and One from Henry C. Wright to Ministers and Members of the Free Church of Scotland* (Glasgow, 1846), 10, 12; *Witness*, December 18, 1844, December 25, 1844, January 1, 1845; J. Dunlop to J. H. Hinton, April 23, 1844, C156/256, in ASP; R. K. Greville, *Slavery and the Slave Trade in the United States of America* (Edinburgh, 1845), 15–20. *Cf.* M. Welsh to M. W. Chapman, April 25, 1844, in BPL-W.

society, which launched the summer campaign on April 22 with a mass meeting to celebrate Thompson's arrival and invite Garrison to Scotland.[49] A few days later Thompson and the Americans moved to Edinburgh and began whipping up opinion there with a rally they held, significantly, in Rose Street Secession Church. After this the ladies' society itself began spreading propaganda against the Free Kirk. In mid-May, however, Thompson and Douglass went off to London, whence the former wrote Wright pointedly, "We must be *high-toned, temperate,* and *resolute,* and by persuasion *we shall triumph.*"[50] This did not prevent Wright from choosing this crucial time to ram home the attack on the clergy by publishing his *First Day Sabbath not of Divine Appointment,* for the attack on slavery was in his eyes secondary to a much wider series of issues. When the four visitors met again in Edinburgh just before the opening of the assembly, they found, no doubt to Douglass' and Thompson's disgust, that every thinkable radical cat had been let out of the bag.

Although Wright had handed every ace to the Free Church leaders, it is only just to say that they played them with great skill. Thompson's speeches during the assembly were largely defensive, for he had to contend with the Reverend Andrew Cameron's brilliant *Letter to George Thompson.* It was typical of the more astute Free Church propaganda in that its accusations were unanswerable except in nonresistant terms, the use of which would only lose more friends for the abolitionists. Apart from elementary questions of truth and consistency, Cameron argued that the shared views of Thompson and Wright would "necessitate the excommunication . . . of almost every professing Christian in this country," because of their indirect involvement in the physical mechanism

49. L. Cruickshank to J. Scoble, November 10, 1846, C15/126, in ASP; *Free Church Alliance with Manstealers; Send Back the Money; Great Anti-Slavery Meeting in the City Hall, Glasgow* (Glasgow, 1846); *Liberator,* May 29, 1846; extract from Glasgow *Argus,* n.d., in Aberdeen *Journal,* April 29, 1846; Minutes for April 20, 1846, April 21, 1846, in GESMB, IV.

50. *Free Church Alliance with Manstealers,* 45ff; *Report of the Edinburgh Ladies' Emancipation Society . . . Passed at Their Annual Meeting, Held May 27, 1846, with an Appendix Containing Their Remonstrance to the Assembly of the Free Church of Scotland* (Edinburgh, 1846), 6–7; *Annual Report of the Edinburgh Ladies' Emancipation Society, with a Supplement Relating to the Proceedings in the Free Church General Assembly, on the 29th of May Last* (Edinburgh, 1847); G. Thompson to H. C. Wright, May 14, 1846, in BPL-G.

of the state. He pointed again to the past admiration of the voluntaries for the American churches. He closed with a series of embarrassing "queries," one of which asked whether, since Thompson's ally Dr. James Ritchie had received his D.D. from "a log-college in the Western States," he should therefore "send back the degree." It was not a very telling defense for Thompson to cry out that the views of his American friends were "a red herring."[51]

It was no surprise when the 1846 assembly moved to the right of the relatively conciliatory views some of its members had held two years before. It quickly excluded discussion of all external petitions, on procedural grounds. Among these there was a memorial from the inhabitants of Edinburgh, or at least the inhabitants who were in the voluntary churches or the Old Kirk.[52] Dr. Robert Candlish, the great tactician of the Disruption, then reported for the committee on correspondence with the American churches. His position was a respectable, moderate abolitionist one, but he was able to make much emotive capital by arguing that to reject fellowship with the southern churches would be to distort the relations between church and state and "run to an extreme form of voluntarism." His colleagues did not like voluntaries. After this there was little future in Lauriston Church's James Macbeth pointing to the sinister Erastian tendencies of the southern clergy. He was now completely isolated, and his fellows ostentatiously read their copies of the *Witness* while he spoke. It would be a pleasant duty for them, three years later, to drive him from the church after an affair with his housekeeper. In 1846 he was powerless to prevent the assembly from adopting an anodyne letter to American Presbyterians. It reminded them that no Christian

51. G. Thompson and H. C. Wright, *The Free Church of Scotland and American Slavery: Substance of Speeches Delivered in the Music Hall, Edinburgh, During May and June, 1846* (Edinburgh, 1846), 32; A. Cameron, *The Free Church and Her Accusers in the Matter of American Slavery; Being a Letter to Mr. George Thompson Regarding His Recent Appearances in this City* (Edinburgh, 1846), 11–24, 29–31; *Witness*, July 8, 1846; *A Letter to the Managers of Rose Street Secession and College Street Relief Churches, Denouncing their Conduct for Admitting Infidels and Sabbath-Breakers to Slander the Free Church* (Edinburgh, 1846).

52. *Address Adopted at a Public Meeting of the Inhabitants of Edinburgh, Convened in the Music Hall . . . to the . . . General Assembly of the Free Church* (Edinburgh, 1846). The assembly's deliberations were reprinted from an appendix to *Proceedings of the General Assembly of the Free Church of Scotland, Held at Edinburgh, May, June, 1846* (Edinburgh, 1846), as *Free Church: Report of the Proceedings of the General Assembly . . . Regarding the Relations of the Free Church and the Presbyterian Churches of America* (Edinburgh, 1846).

could possibly regard his slave as one, whatever their respective positions in the eyes of the law.[53]

The attitude of the assembly had hardened, and it continued to do so during the following eighteen months. Free Churchmen reacted violently to George Thompson's being given the freedom of Edinburgh, ostensibly for his services to free trade, by the enemy majority of the Town Council. "I do not know," said one of the minority, "that the circumstance of a man being hired to conduct a public discussion marks him out for any particular reward." There was probably some uneasiness among the church's younger intellectuals over the position taken by their senior colleagues. The New College Missionary Association wrote to their counterparts at Princton Theological Seminary along relatively radical antislavery lines.[54] Principal James Cunningham, who had himself been one of the Free Church commissioners to America, wisely ignored their scruples. For William Lloyd Garrison, the Scottish controversy had become a sideshow in his efforts to denounce the Evangelical Alliance and gain support for the Chartist/abolitionist front of the Anti-Slavery League. He did speak in several Scottish cities during September and October of 1846. Even in a small place like Kirkcaldy, he was still able to raise an audience of six or eight hundred, and the Glasgow Emancipation Society briefly forgot its now overwhelming financial problems in the enthusiasm caused by his visit. He was also provided with a silver service by the "ladies of Edinburgh," and he inspired the Edinburgh Ladies' Emancipation Society to continue its work against the Free Church.[55] Otherwise his visit did little to change the situation.

The tensions that whipped feelings up again before the 1847

53. *Free Church*, 13–28, 30ff., 50–52; Douglass, *My Bondage and My Freedom*, 383–84; J. MacBeth, *No Fellowship with Slaveholders: A Calm Review of the Debate on Slavery in the Free Assembly of 1846* (Edinburgh, 1846).

54. *Review of the Proceedings of a Minority of the Town Council of Edinburgh, in Presenting the Freedom of the City to Mr. George Thompson* (Edinburgh, 1846), 2; *Slavery in the Gentile Churches During the Apostolic Age, and the Present Duty of the Free Church of Scotland, Especially Addressed to the Students of the Free Church of Scotland, by a Fellow-Student* (Edinburgh, 1846); *Five Minutes Review of the Scriptural Argument in Favour of Fellowship with Slaveholders* (Edinburgh, 1846); Shepperson, "Thomas Chalmers, the Free Church of Scotland and the South," 530–35.

55. W. L. Garrison to H. C. Wright, September 23, 1846, October 25, 1846, W. L. Garrison to R. D. Webb, September 25, 1846, September 30, 1846, W. L. Garrison to E. Pease, September 25, 1846, all in BPL-G; GESR, 1846, pp. 9–10; Minutes for September 30, 1846, October 28, 1846, in GESMB, IV.

General Assembly were purely Scottish. In May of that year, a so-called Free Church Anti-Slavery Society was founded, quite deliberately without connections with the Garrisonian abolitionists. This could not disguise the fact that it was supported by a coalition of voluntaries and Old Kirk leaders who were known to detest the Free Kirk. Although its committee was a Free Church one, headed by Willis and Macbeth from Glasgow, it later complained that since only two of the church's ministers had been "faithful to the cause of justice and humanity," it had to seek support elsewhere. It did manage to publish a vigorous *Address* to the assembly, perhaps written by the talented Macbeth.[56] But the real clue to the society's support was that every one of its general pamphlets was written by a minister known to have grievances against the Free Church. One of their authors was George Gilfillan, the Dundee Congregationalist. A second was George Jeffrey, the pastor of Lothian Road Secession Church in Glasgow. Dr. David Young, an Old Kirk minister from Perth, contributed an evocative pamphlet entitled *Slavery Forbidden by the Word of God*. The final author was Isaac Nelson of the Presbyterian Church of Ireland.[57]

This team was hardly one likely to influence the Free Church. The 1847 assembly was even less cooperative than its predecessor. By this time Thompson was in London, Douglass and Garrison were back in America, and Wright was in Ireland busily denouncing the Society of Friends for accepting money from the South for famine relief. Yet the purely local opposition of other denominations was quite odious enough in itself for the assembly to dismiss the *Address* of the Free Church Anti-Slavery Society out of hand.

56. A. B. Murdock to J. Scoble, May 25, 1847, C20/26, June 1, 1847, C20/27, both in ASP; *ASR*, June 1, 1847; *Strictures on the Proceedings of the Last General Assembly of the Free Church of Scotland, Regarding Communion with the Slaveholding Churches of America* (Edinburgh, 1847), 9; *An Address to the Office-Bearers and Members of the Free Church of Scotland, on Her Present Connexion with the Slaveholding Churches of America, from the Committee of the Free Church Anti-Slavery Society* (Edinburgh, 1847).

57. G. Gilfillan, *The Debasing and Demoralising Influence of Slavery on All and Everything Connected with It: A Lecture* (Edinburgh, 1847); G. Jeffrey, *The Pro-Slavery Character of the American Churches . . .* (Edinburgh, 1847); D. Young, *Slavery Forbidden by the Word of God: A Lecture* (Edinburgh, 1847); I. Nelson, *Slavery Supported by the American Churches, and Countenanced by Recent Proceedings in the Free Church of Scotland . . . a Lecture* (Edinburgh, 1847).

None of the ministers present dissented from Dr. Candlish's view that the whole affair had been "an ingenious device of Satan to injure the Church." The abolitionists had lost. Macbeth, Willis, and the Reverend Dr. William King ultimately emigrated to carry on their antislavery work in Canada.[58] Perhaps, indeed, it had always been unthinkable that the Free Church, which was so generously provided with enemies at home, should send back the money and alienate the few friends it possessed abroad.

Nevertheless, the reasons for its increasing obstinacy are complex. The appeals of the voluntaries and the establishment were counterproductive, for the Free Churchmen had good reason to suspect they could not have cared less about American slavery. Their ears were also closed to abolitionist criticism by their fright at the specters of nonresistance and infidelity, for Wright had quite misread the Scottish situation. For the middle class at least, the Presbyterian churches were national institutions, and his anticlericalism was unlikely to make much impression on a body with the prestige of the Free Church.

What made an even worse impression was that the church's critics, unlike all previous abolitionists except John Collins, were prepared to court working-class support. The real reason for the vendetta against Macbeth may have been that he did not share his colleagues' belief in keeping the lower orders out of religious and benevolent decision making. "An appeal to the people," he had written, "in high and special emergencies, is part of the Presbytery." Wright, too, was anxious to spread antislavery among the "people," and he had appeared in Glasgow along with Henry Vincent. Garrison's Scottish visit was largely devoted to explaining the virtues of his alliance with the Chartists. Thompson had steered clear of this kind of complication, for he understood the horror with which the world of evangelical reform regarded Garrison's new friends. The Americans, who were being perfectly consistent within the context of their own views on reform, could not be expected to be sensitive to this problem. Ironically, it was the

58. H. C. Wright, *Slaveholders or Playactors, Which Are the Greater Sinners? To ... the Central Relief Committee of the Society of Friends in Ireland* (Dublin, 1847); D. Riach, "Ireland and the Campaign Against American Slavery, 1830–1860" (Ph.D. dissertation, University of Edinburgh, 1975), 356–75; *Proceedings of the General Assembly, 1847,* pp. 264–73; ASR, July 1, 1847.

gentler and more tactful Douglass who did most to create the impression of revolutionary designs. It was all very well to have the urchins of Edinburgh cut SEND BACK THE MONEY, in gigantic letters, out of the turf on Arthur's Seat, the great crag above the city. It was less effective to have them mob the most respected clergymen in the country. It was not for nothing that Mr. William Nixon of Montrose sneered nervously at this alliance with the "more ill-conditioned portion of our mechanics."[59] Douglass had raised the ghost of 1793.

On the other hand, Scotland's ostensibly democratic religious tradition made it important that each side should be able to claim popular support. A good deal of spurious balladry was produced to this end, and with some ease, for everyone involved in the controversy still spoke what would now be considered very broad Scots. The establishment was quick to produce ballads that concluded for instance:

> The Auld Ane's the best o' them, Kate,
>   Altho' muckle ill they've put till her;
> Ye have only to pay for your seat,
>   And they ask for nae mair o' your siller.[60]

The voluntaries, for their part, adapted the traditional "My Son David" as "The Kirk and Her Boy Tammy." Much used by Douglass, this version has Mother Kirk interrogating Tammy Chalmers, who eventually blurts out:

> Be mercifu'! An' say nae mair, my kind mammy;
> Ye'll drive me headlong tae despair, my kind mammy;
> "Send back the . . ." Oh! it canna be;
> Ye're gyte! that would destroy, ye see,
> *The Kirk's Infallibility.*
>   Ca' canny—Oh! Ca' canny!

59. *The Church and the Slaveholder: Or, Light and Darkness . . . Addressed to the Members of the Approaching Assembly* (Edinburgh, 1845), 36; C. Paton to M. W. Chapman, November 2, 1845, in BPL-W; J. Dunlop to A. Phelps, June 16, 1846, in BPL-P; Minute for August 1, 1845, in GESMB, IV; *Should the Free Church Hold Fellowship with Slaveholders?*, 8; *Relation of the Free Church to the American Churches*, 3.

60. *The Free Kirk and the Siller* (Edinburgh, May, 1846), copy in Bodleian Library, Oxford University. See also *My Faith, We'll Keep the Money* (Edinburgh, May, 1846), copy in *ibid.* The establishment had often used Scots propaganda in the past, as in *A Crack Aboot the Kirk for Cintra Folk*, in various editions, 1843.

Mother Kirk finally points out:

> There's aye some crotchet in your views;
> Ye'll stain my robes—ye'll toom my pews—
> They're flocking back to Granny.[61]

The trouble with the use of such popular critiques was that they gained their own momentum. There is at least one genuine working-class ballad demanding that the southern money be given to the poor.[62] The issue was also gleefully picked up by student satirists. One group, probably from New College, wrote a marvelous parody that had Thompson gloating over his plans: "They'll fill my pockets in a crack, / Th' Established chaps." He is interrupted by Douglass:

> Ah! Massa Thompson, what you tink?
> I heard de sound ob money's clink,
> So widoub noise I in did slink.

Thompson, "pale *with rage*," is forced to give him twenty pounds.[63] Another parody denounced all sides indiscriminately, and summarized the conflict between Douglass and Chalmers:

> Chalmy and Blackie ran a race,
> Chalmy fell and broke his face,
> Quo' Blackie I have won the race,
>   And the sow's tail till him yet,
>   And the sow's tail till him yet,
>   And the sow's tail to Chalmy.[64]

By analogy with the childrens' jingle on which it was based, the last line would have been sung "An' the soo's erse tae Chalmy!"

61. *The Kirk and Her Boy Tammy*, broadsheet (Edinburgh, 1846), copy in SNL.
62. *Oh, Don't Send the Money Back Again* (Edinburgh, n.d.), copy in Bodleian Library.
63. *Send Back the Money: A New Version* (Edinburgh, 1846), copy in Bodleian Library.
64. *The Yankee Looking Glass, or, "Measure for Measure", Containing a Report of the Speeches Delivered at the Disorderly Meeting Held on Friday Last, in the Music Hall, with a Letter from Tomkins to his Friends in Affliction in Edinburgh* (n.p., May, 1846), a copy in Bodleian Library. There is also a great deal of stilted Victorian verse on the subject, as in *The Sighs of the Slave in the Free Church of Scotland: A Poem* (Edinburgh, 1846), copy in AUL; "Send Back the Money," in *Anti-Slavery Songs* (Edinburgh, 1846).

It must have been specially appealing to "the more ill-conditioned portion of our mechanics," and to any voluntaries who could forget their piety sufficiently to chant obscenities in the streets. To that extent it can only have added to the intransigence of the Free Kirk.

The Send Back the Money campaign was an extraordinary episode. It was a classic example of the way in which Scotland used "events in the New World to bring into focus its own situation in the Old." It certainly weakened the Scottish antislavery societies. The Glasgow society had spent so much on publishing that it remained inactive until 1851, and the Edinburgh one collapsed under the strain of losing its Free Church goodwill. The Edinburgh Ladies' Emancipation Society never quite recovered from the disrepute attached to Wright's views.[65] Wright, indeed, had only diverted his energy into antislavery temporarily, and he had not understood how much his work would weaken his friends' capacity for helping the American cause. Perhaps his wider concerns made that consideration irrelevant, but for the Scots and their leader George Thompson it had presented a real dilemma. As Eliza Wigham put it, they had had to choose to reap "the fruits of Christianity from stigmatised infidels."[66] It was only for the core of committed abolitionists, however, that the problem was one of antislavery tactics. For most evangelical Scots, the controversy was a means of acting out the bitter tensions of their own church history.

The Free Church affair was not the last time slavery became a major issue for the Scottish churches. It is true that the urgency of their rivalries lessened, as the bitter years of the Ten Years' Conflict and the Voluntary Controversy receded into the past. The fifties, relatively speaking, were an age of equipoise in Scottish church history, partly because of the success of the Free Church in providing a buffer between the establishment and the true

---

65. Shepperson, "Writings on Scottish-American History: A Brief Survey," *WMQ*, Third Series, XI (1954), 173; GESR, 1851, *passim*; W. Smeal to L. A. Chamerovzow, April 16, 1853, C36/52, J. Calder to L. A. Chamerovzow, September 26, 1853, C29/20, October 19, 1853, C29/21, all in ASP; Jane Wigham to A. W. Weston, November 18, 1852, November 9, 1853, E. Wigham to M. Estlin, April 28, 1853, all in BPL-W.

66. E. Wigham to L. C. Chamerovzow, November 15, 1853, C160/218, in ASP.

dissenters in the voluntary churches. This did not prevent the churches from responding to slavery in ways that directly reflected their denominational concerns. This became clear once again in the confusion of the United Presbyterian Church over the policy of its mission at Old Calabar on the Niger Delta. The UP Church was formed in 1847, when the Original Secession Church and the Relief Secession Synod merged. Under its aegis the new denomination brought a majority of the ministers who were bitterly opposed to the Old Kirk, the Free Kirk, and the establishment principle in general.[67] They were the very men who had jumped to use the slavery issue for their own voluntary purposes during the Send Back the Money campaign.

In 1854, it became clear that the UP mission at Old Calabar, founded in 1846 by the United Secession Church, was accepting local slaveholders into communion. There was a long tradition of abolitionist concern over the proper missionary response to indigenous slavery, and indeed the Scots had paid close attention to the travail of the American Board of Commissioners for Foreign Missions at the time of the Free Church affair.[68] The problem of Old Calabar was first publicized by Dr. William Lillie, a UP minister who later became a close friend of Lewis Tappan. At the 1855 synod, it quickly became clear that he was powerless to make his church change the guidelines along which it was running its mission. This was not surprising, for a refusal to accept converts at the communion table until they had given up practices like polygamy and slaveholding, which were politely described as "organic sins," would have brought the work of almost every major Christian mission in Africa to a halt. Though the United Presbyterians had previously had good antislavery credentials—they had sent the black abolitionist Henry Highland Garnet to Jamaica as a missionary in 1851—a curb on missionary activity would have

67. Ferguson, *Scotland, 1689 to the Present*, 312; W. H. McKelvie, *Annals and Statistics of the United Presbyterian Church* (Edinburgh, 1873).
68. *The American Board of Commissioners for Foreign Missions, and the Rev. Dr. Chalmers, on Christian Fellowship with Slaveholders: An Address to Christians of All Denominations, But Especially to the Members of the Free Church of Scotland* (Glasgow, 1845); J. Dunlop, *American Slavery: Organic Sins, or, the Iniquity of Licenced Injustice* (Edinburgh, 1846); idem, *American Anti-Slavery Conventions* (Edinburgh, 1846), 11ff.

been specially disastrous for a church that controlled no less than five theological colleges, with an annual graduation of almost thirty students. Missions were an important outlet for young ministers who could not find immediate employment in a denomination of only some four hundred congregations.[69] Abolitionists had a different concern, for the parallels that could be drawn between slaveholding in Nigeria and in the South were obvious. The antislavery response, however, again became blurred by the divisions between factions in the movement, for the obvious group to put pressure on the UP Church was the Glasgow New Association for the Abolition of Slavery, which had recently been founded as a conservative counterweight to the old Garrisonian GES. Unfortunately almost all its leaders were themselves UP ministers who had a vested interest in maintaining existing arrangements at Old Calabar. Their position was compromised in exactly the same way, for instance, as that of the BFASS over Indiana, or even of the EES over the Free Church.

The controversy, like the Free Church one, was tailor-made for focusing tensions within the abolitionist movement and, to a lesser extent, within the rivalries between the Scottish churches. It is significant that the only general newspaper to denounce the synod decision was the Tory voice of the established Old Kirk, which hated secessionists even worse than it hated the Free Church. Perhaps Lillie himself was haunted by the inconsistency with the stated policy of the secession churches in 1846, when he wrote that his denomination had "hitherto borne a consistent testimony against admitting slaveholders to Christian fellowship." Most Scots abolitionists seem to have felt much the same, unless they happened to be UP members. Lillie had been corresponding with Lewis Tappan and had been assured that what the church was doing would "weaken our hands and obstruct our usefulness."[70]

69. W. Lillie to L. A. Chamerovzow, October 11, 1854, C33/100, in ASP; *Missionary Record*, October, 1854; *ASR*, November 1, 1854; L. Tappan to W. Lillie, May 26, 1857, August 29, 1857, in Letterbooks, VIII, Tappan Papers; *United Presbyterian Record*, June, 1855; W. H. McKelvie, *Annals and Statistics of the United Presbyterian Church* (Edinburgh, 1873), 678ff.

70. Edinburgh *News*, May 19, 1855, June 2, 1855; W. Lillie to L. A. Chamerovzow, June 4, 1855, C33/101, C. Kynoch to L. A. Chamerovzow, July 10, 1855, C33/63, both in ASP; L. Tappan to W. Lillie, March 16, 1855, in Letterbooks, IX, Tappan Papers, W. Lillie to G. Thompson, February 14, 1855, February 23, 1855, in Tappan Papers; *ASR*, November 1, 1856.

Although the BFASS did cover Lillie's efforts in the *Reporter*, the Scottish Garrisonians were quick to make capital out of the affair. They concluded that the problem lay in the new organization character of the Glasgow New Association, and complained bitterly of the failure of the London group to point this out.[71] The Garrisonian *Anti-Slavery Advocate*, edited by Richard Webb, noted the shortcomings of the upstart group in Glasgow, the annual report of which had specifically endorsed the offensive decision of the 1855 UP synod. In Edinburgh, the Ladies' Emancipation Society suddenly found itself faced with a new Douglassite rival, the Edinburgh Ladies' New Association. It too was silent on Old Calabar, because, as Eliza Wigham wrote bitterly, its leaders were UP members who had formed it "to prove *their* anti-slavery."[72]

Because the GES had weakened, because there were no American visitors, and because church rivalries had on the whole softened, the UP controversy was not nearly so lively as the Free Church one. Perhaps, too, the missionary problem was too touchy for the churches to become heavily involved in. Few had been able to get financial contributions from the South, but all relied on sending out some of their young ministers as missionaries. Nevertheless, the Old Calabar affair does show the strength of the voluntaries in the movement and the extent to which their activities could be curbed, just as they could be inspired, by their denominational concerns. It was not at all surprising that the UP Church, and indeed so many Scots abolitionists, remained silent. Most of them, like the Glasgow New Association, were "bound as an A.S. Association to endorse their own acts as a *Mission Board*."[73]

The relationship of the churches to slavery was the most vital of all questions for British abolitionists. It was specially so for the Scots, for their concern was deepened by the possibility of expressing their church rivalries as disagreements over antislavery tactics.

71. E. Wigham to L. A. Chamerovzow, April 18, 1856, C37/76, May 3, 1856, C37/75, in ASP. Miss Wigham's criticism was partly successful, in *ASR*, November 1, 1856.
72. *Anti-Slavery Advocate*, May 1856, commenting on Lillie to editor of Glasgow *Chronicle*, March 29, 1856; E. Wigham to S. May, April 4, 1856, in BPL-M.
73. E. Wigham to L. A. Chamerovzow, May 3, 1856, C37/75, in ASP.

This could produce startling shifts in their perception of antislavery duty, as it clearly did for the United Presbyterians between 1844 and 1856. This does not mean that their distrust for slavery was insincere, or their pity for the slave any less deep. However, the range of ways in which that pity could be expressed was wide enough to give much scope for disagreements, which added a reassuring moral dimension to feuds with other Scottish churches. The only consistent actors in the controversies over the role of the churches were the tiny handful of Scottish Garrisonians. They never swung from their view that all churches were obliged to come out of their connection with slavery, whatever the institutional cost. William Smeal was a good Friend, but his horror at the Hicksite controversy did not debar him from friendship with Mrs. Mott. Nor, for that matter, did his loyalty to the Society weaken his sympathy for the Indiana secessionists, any more than it did Eliza Wigham's. John Murray, from the Relief Secession Synod, was dead in 1855, but it is hard to imagine that Dr. Lillie would not have found him by his side over Old Calabar. What differentiated the Scottish Garrisonians from other middle-class reformers is that they did not see the preservation of existing institutions, even ones dear to them, as an end that in itself argued against implementing their values. Most of their countrymen were very fond of institutions, especially church ones. Perhaps this is why the fifties saw their enthusiasm for antislavery run into new channels.

CHAPTER 6

The Fifties: Mrs. Stowe
and a Romantic Unity

In 1841, one of Elizabeth Pease's American correspondents wrote
of the schisms in the antislavery movement that "a little forbearance, a little toleration, a little of that charity which 'never faileth'
would have saved us all this trouble and dishonour."[1] Twenty
years later, as the Civil War opened, it was clear that in the British case at least she had been wrong. For a time during the fifties,
both the BFASS and its radical rivals in the provinces showed considerable forbearance towards one another and made real efforts
to overcome their mutual hostility. Unfortunately the divisions had
become an integral part of the movement at its local level. It had
become a reflex to interpret all disagreements in terms of old vendettas. Even the horror of the Fugitive Slave Law, and the stream
of black leaders who came to Britain to denounce it, could not
re-create habits of cooperation that had been so thoroughly un-
learned. In Scotland and in Britain at large, the old and new organizations continued their infighting, at a time when the attention
of American abolitionists had moved on to the problems of pure
politics and violent resistance. On both sides of the Atlantic, it was
only the coming of the Civil War that drew the movement together again.

What did happen during the course of the fifties is that the
schisms between British abolitionists became irrelevant. This was
not just because there was no clear role for foreigners in the work
of violent confrontation and political organization that now absorbed the American movement. The old-style societies were
becoming less important in both countries, but in Britain their
activities were partly obscured by a new and wider romantic
commitment to antislavery, inspired by the fad for *Uncle Tom's*

1. M. Grew to E. Pease, March 18, 1841, in BPL-G.

Cabin and Harriet Beecher Stowe. This affected the abolitionists themselves, for the sentimental theme that Mrs. Stowe exaggerated had always had its place in their own more balanced concern for black people. None of them was immune to fantasies in which he became the Man of Feeling. The Scots in particular were enthusiastic about Mrs. Stowe, and indeed one group of them was responsible for inviting her to Britain in the first place. Yet the Uncle Tom cult was quite distinct from the dogged commitment of the past. Richard Davis Webb dismissed the "Uncle Tom Penny Offering" out of hand as "a very paltry moral bellows." "To honour her," Eliza Wigham wrote sadly, "is small anti-slavery."[2] What they could not deny was that this curiously dowdy academic wife had done the impossible. She had put the British old and new organization groups together in harness with important middle-class groups that neither of them had been able to reach in the past. Her success in drawing recruits to the antislavery cause was startling, beyond the wildest dreams of a Gurney or a Webb, a Dunlop or a Smeal—all the more so since the American campaign had entered a political phase wherein it was less susceptible than ever before to British influence.

Not even the glamour of the Stoweite movement can hide the extent to which the Scottish and indeed the British antislavery societies were beginning to fall on hard times. Their vigorous maintenance of the old quarrels is less a sign of vitality than of desperation. The foundation of new schismatic groups was part of an anxious quest for a platform that would re-create the united enthusiasm of a past that younger abolitionists had not even been alive to experience. In all factions, complaints of declining membership and funds recurred. The national society's *Reporter* was decreased in size in 1853, and the audiences attracted to its annual meetings were much smaller than in the forties, except when Mrs. Stowe was present.[3] When the London leadership tried to encourage local societies by publishing details of their history and present activities, it only succeeded in demonstrating that they were

2. *ASR*, May 2, 1853; *Anti-Slavery Advocate*, January, 1853; E. Wigham to M. Estlin, March 22, 1853, in BPL-W.
3. *ASR*, June 1, 1852, June 1, 1854, June 2, 1856. *Cf. Anti-Slavery Advocate*, June 1, 1854.

all finding it difficult to make ends meet and to maintain a following. In Dublin, Webb's helpers in his efforts to channel British support to the Garrisonians were now a handful, and the public meetings organized by the Hibernian society were few and far between. The days when its committee had met at ten every Thursday and held an open meeting in the Royal Exchange on the fourth Wednesday of every month might have gone by in another world. The old Glasgow Emancipation Society, too, was weakened by its overexpenditure in the Send Back the Money campaign and by John Murray's death in 1849. It did not meet from 1848 to 1851 and never recovered its old energy in the new decade. William Smeal and his brother Robert responded closely to the changing interests of the provincial Quakers for whom they produced the *British Friend*. It had made emancipation the issue of the day in the forties. In the fifties it all but ignored it. A little society like the Aberdeen one, which was probably representative of its size and organization, found it could not hold any meetings after 1850 except when Mrs. Stowe was in town.[4]

There was no longer a trace of the small-town enthusiasm Douglass had been able to tap in 1846. Although the Scots, after 1838, had never been as interested in imperial questions as the English, they too found it difficult to maintain public interest in slavery once such questions had been broadly settled.[5] Though they were in the first instance interested in American slavery precisely because it was a foreign problem, their ongoing commitment had gained strength from intermittent discussion of colonial problems that were now solved or shelved. Again, the twenty years that had passed since West India emancipation inevitably meant that there were many men and women in the reform world who remembered the excitement of 1833 only dimly if at all. More fundamentally, the British middle class as a whole was no longer undergoing a profound shift in its values. The age of equipoise is

4. *ASR*, May 2, 1853, July 1, 1853; Minute for January 31, 1850, in GESMB, IV; GESR, 1851, *passim*; W. Phillips to J. Murray, Jr., May 29, 1849, Ms. 3925, f.206, in Small Collections, SNL; W. Smeal to A. L. Chamerovzow, April 16, 1853, C36/52, D. Macallan to Chamerovzow, September 16, 1853, C33/127, both in ASP. See also Appendix F.
5. E. I. Pilgrim, "Anti-Slavery Sentiment in Great Britain: Its Nature and Decline, 1841–1854" (Ph.D. dissertation, Cambridge University, 1952), 273ff and *passim*.

a reality in that it marks the point where that value shift had become a *fait accompli*. External threats to the code of respectability had diminished because of its acceptance by the monarchy and much of the aristocracy, and by a substantial element in the skilled labor force. The overt threats of Chartism and violent revolution had receded. In the middle class itself, a new generation had internalized respectable values. Even evangelicals suffered less from the anxieties over personal purity, which they had soothed earlier in the century by a constant reaffirmation of moral commitment. Antislavery and other reforms were less attractive psychologically once the middle class had adapted to a changed and now relatively stable social structure. For the Scots, too, the relative softening of their denominational rivalries meant that it was less attractive to use slavery as a lever against other churches. In any case, the Compromise of 1850 had brought the American conflict to a point of physical and political confrontation where the practical role of foreign sympathizers was more circumscribed than ever.[6]

More immediately, the British movement had been seriously weakened by its own disagreements. Injudicious factional hostilities, much as they might stir up interest in the short run, dissipated the energies of abolitionists, smirched their public image, increased their operating difficulties, and weakened their long-term support. It must have been a real relief to turn from their exhausting polemics to the uncomplicated benevolence required by Mrs. Stowe. After the War, Eliza Wigham remembered little of the rancor of the old schisms, but could still write with warmth about "that marvellous book."[7] Whatever fault has since been found with *Uncle Tom's Cabin*, no one has suggested that it needs the same level of energy from its readers as *Right and Wrong in the Anti-Slavery Societies*.

As the Scottish societies continued their quarrels, the balance shifted further against the Garrisonians. Once they were fully

6. W. H. and J. H. Pease, "Confrontation and Abolition in the 1850's," *JAH*, LVIII (1972), 923–37; J. B. Stewart, *Holy Warriors: The Abolitionists and American Slavery* (New York, 1976), 124–77.

7. E. Wigham, *The Anti-Slavery Cause in America and Its Martyrs* (London, 1863), 99; E. Wilson, *Patriotic Gore: Studies in the Literature of the American Civil War* (New York, 1962), 3–58.

understood, views on universal reform which had a coherent tactical purpose in the American context were counter-productive in the churchly circles where the Scots leaders hoped to find supporters. Jane Wigham, William Smeal's sister, once wrote plaintively to her friend Ann Warren Weston that "I wish if thou hast any influence with W. L. G., thou would advise him to leave the Bible alone—if all acted to its instructions there would be neither war nor slavery." She would have sympathized with Mary Estlin, her ally in Bristol, who recorded that when she read the American papers to her father, "he goes to sleep over Mr. H. C. Wright's letters, wh. is a great comfort to me as I can skip the greater part without detection."[8] The opposition to Eliza and Jane Wigham's group in Edinburgh and to the Smeal and Paton group in Glasgow skillfully capitalized on suspicion of the extraneous issues.

The Scottish radicals had to steer a precarious course between the realities of the Scottish situation and the vindictiveness of Maria Weston Chapman, towards whose Garrisonian Boston Bazaar, an annual fund-raising sale that largely supported the *Anti-Slavery Standard*, their energies were principally turned. Of all the American abolitionist visitors to Britain, she was equaled in sheer malevolence and incomprehension of foreign conditions only by Parker Pillsbury.[9] Her dismissal of Eliza Wigham for allowing J. W. C. Pennington to speak in Edinburgh along with the popular fugitive slaves William and Ellen Crafts and William Wells Brown was a classic case of her setting the power of her own faction, as an end in itself, above the welfare of the movement as a whole. The discussion was based on the simple local consideration that more people in Edinburgh would come to hear four ex-slaves than three, and that Pennington invited could do a great deal less harm than Pennington snubbed. It must have been hard to have this become the basis for an accusation of treachery.[10] Even with such

8. Jane Wigham to A. W. Weston, November 18, 1852, M. Estlin to M. W. Chapman, February 13, 1851, both in BPL-W. See also E. Wigham to M. Estlin, April 28, 1853, Jane Wigham to A. W. Weston, November 9, 1853, both in BPL-W; E. Wigham to M. Estlin, September 13, 1850, in BPL-E.

9. *Cf.* J. H. Pease and W. H. Pease, *Bound with Them in Chains: A Biographical History of the Anti-Slavery Movement* (Westport, Conn., 1972), 28–59.

10. R. D. Webb to M. Estlin, May 13, 1851, in BPL-E; M. Estlin to A. W. Weston, May 8, 1851, in BPL-W; W. Estlin to A. W. Weston, May 16, 1851, in BPL-W, misfiled under 1857.

compromises, indeed, the Scots Garrisonians made little headway against their opponents. They had to contend not only with the faction directly in alignment with the BFASS and its American allies, but also with the Rochester group headed by Frederick Douglass, with the supporters of the New York and Philadelphia Vigilance Committees, and with a wide range of efforts to educate fugitive slaves in Canada. There was also a new threat in the strengthening free-produce movement, led in Britain by Eliza Wigham's aunt, Mrs. Anna Richardson of Newcastle. Her group hoped to starve out slave agriculture by finding alternative sources of tropical produce. All these factions could claim to be free of the heresies that had discredited the Garrisonians after 1841. The British Garrisonians, like Mrs. Chapman, were inclined to see the whole lot as offspring of their bitter enemies in the new organization.

By 1850, though the Glasgow Emancipation Society and its ladies' auxiliary were moribund, James Pennington still thought it worth trying to kill them once and for all. The New York Vigilance Committee, for which he sought support, was aimed primarily at helping black refugees endangered by the new Fugitive Slave Law. To this extent it offered an attractive and apparently non-partisan focus for British activities. Yet his Glasgow New Association for the Abolition of Slavery was clearly intended to harm the Garrisonians. The first act of its women's branch was to issue an *Appeal*, which played astutely on Scottish fears of becoming smirched with unorthodoxy, and suggested that work for Mrs. Chapman's Boston Bazaar should be stopped. Perhaps this was because some of the group's committee members were wives of voluntary clergymen, who were glad to take an opportunity of disassociating themselves from the embarrassingly radical views of their old allies in the attack on the Free Church. They pointed out that the American radicals "entail upon all in this country who cooperate with them, no small share both of the odium and the responsibility which attach to their irreligious views." These views were summarized as opposition to the Sabbath, the Christian ministry, and the authority of Scripture. Both Webb and his friend Dr. Estlin of Bristol rushed to point out that the American society was not responsible for the views of its individual members. Mrs.

Chapman, who was then in literary exile with her younger sisters in Paris, did not even stoop to argument. She simply assured the "Glasgow Female Seceders" that "you have been in the wrong. Do not hesitate to say so, and you will be in the right again."[11]

This was not enough, and the Glasgow New Association remained as the focus of women's antislavery activity in Glasgow for the rest of the decade. In 1853, it sent four hundred pounds to the New York Vigilance Committee, out of total receipts of £711.10.6. This sum was four times the income of the old GES and five times that of the Glasgow Female Anti-Slavery Society founded by John Collins in 1841. The new body showed considerable interest in all antislavery activities that were not Garrisonian, which was probably one of the reasons for its relative success. Before coming under the influence of Frederick Douglass' British agent Julia Griffiths, it was drawn into the free-produce movement by Henry Highland Garnet. His Scottish audiences failed to detect Garnet's increasing interest in violence, and he was eventually sent to Jamaica as a missionary by the United Presbyterian Church, from which the New Association drew its strength. Pennington as a new organizationist, Garnet as a free-produce man, Douglass on purely personal grounds, were equally distasteful to the Garrisonians. The male New Association, with its strong representation of voluntary ministers, also proved a respectable base for those abolitionists who had compromised themselves in their enthusiasm for the radical front against the Free Church. In spite of its understandable silence on the Old Calabar issue, it throve much more than the GES. In fact its first and most spiteful triumph over its rival was to gain national publicity by inviting Harriet Beecher Stowe to visit Scotland.[12] In the west of Scotland as a whole, the

11. Printed circular *Appeal* of the New Glasgow Ladies' Anti-Slavery Association provisional committee, May, 1850, copy in BPL-W; R. D. Webb to J. Barclay, June 3, 1850, copy in Hannah Webb's hand, in BPL-W; J. B. Estlin, *Reply to a Circular Issued by the Glasgow Association for the Abolition of Slavery, Recommending a Discontinuance of British Support for the Boston Anti-Slavery Bazaar* (Paris, 1850), 4 and *passim*; M. W. Chapman to the Glasgow Female Seceders, printed circular, June 8, 1850, in BPL-W.

12. *ASR*, May 2, 1853; *Slave*, February, July, 1852; A. Paton to A. W. Weston, November 19, 1850, in BPL-W; circular in behalf of Douglass, n.d., in BPL-M; *BCR*, 23–24; W. Smeal to A. L. Chamerovzow, C36/52, in ASP; W. Smeal to W. L. Garrison, March 4, 1853, in BPL-G; G. A. Shepperson, "Harriet Beecher Stowe and Scotland," *SHR*, XXXII (1953), 44.

only major radical abolitionists consistently active were William Smeal himself, Catherine Paton, and her brother Andrew, whose truculence and observance of the literal canon of Garrisonian reform were equal to Mrs. Chapman's own.

The fortunes of the Edinburgh Garrisonians were scarcely better. There had never been any prominent male Garrisonian there except Dr. Ritchie of the United Secession Church, later the UP Church, and he had always channeled most of his efforts through Glasgow. Here too, abolitionist activity in general declined as a reaction to the excitement of the Free Church affair. It was only in the summer of 1854 that the old emancipation society was replaced by a New Edinburgh Anti-Slavery Association. Its president was Duncan Maclaren, who had been chairman of the Central Board of Scottish Dissenters, was then Provost of Edinburgh, and was eventually to represent Edinburgh in Parliament. Two Free Church leaders, Dr. Candlish and Dr. Duncan, joined the committee, as did Dr. Lillie of the UP Church. Among their colleagues were several members of the old EES, including the Quakers Henry Wigham and Andrew Cruickshank, and the Episcopalian botanist Dr. Greville. The new association's only aims were immediate and universal emancipation, and its members were to be all who accepted these principles. It was nevertheless perceived as an anti-Garrisonian group, and the apparent catholicity of its views did not prevent Webb from observing that "a society hampered at its outset by dislikes, jealousies, and bigotry ... can never labour with much heartiness or efficiency."[13] In practice it never became very active, but even its formation was a reaffirmation of antislavery commitment purified of the alarming views put forward in the forties.

The threats faced by Garrison's female sympathizers in Edinburgh were more specific and more sustained. Jane and Eliza Wigham had never found it easy to overcome local distrust of the extraneous issues, especially of the alleged tendency to question the authority of Scripture. One of their advantages, however, was the connection of their Ladies' Emancipation Society with Mrs.

13. W. Ferguson, *Scotland, 1689 to the Present* (Edinburgh, 1968), 306, 308, 322–23; *Scottish Press*, June 23, 1854; *ASR*, October 1, 1854, November 1, 1854; *Anti-Slavery Advocate*, August, 1854.

Chapman's annual Boston Bazaar. Besides raising money primarily for the *Anti-Slavery Standard*, the bazaar also had great publicity value, especially in conjunction with the *Liberty Bell* gift annual that it sold each year. In British terms, all factions stressed the importance of gathering money, but the accumulation of donations had none of the fascination of work for the Boston Bazaar and the *Bell*. For women in particular, the creation and collection of goods to send across the Atlantic extended the role of antislavery as recreation, and it also gave a sense of personal contribution and active involvement that no other group in America could offer. The bazaar sold an extraordinary range of goods, from Parisian clothes sent over by Mrs. Chapman to locks of Dwarkanauth Tagore's hair. It also accepted all sorts of local produce, like New England maple sugar, which would avoid the consumption of slave-grown cane, or Scots shawls and Irish linen, which would exclude or at least supplement the wearing of slave-grown cotton. The bulk of its wares, however, ran through the whole gamut of Victorian craftwork, from elevating needlepoint mottoes to beautiful painted albums like the one prepared by the educational reformer Mary Carpenter of Bristol, which happens to have survived to the present day.[14]

A society which, like the Edinburgh one, was involved with the bazaar, was able to offer those committed to work against slavery a tangible and measurable form of activity. This was far more attractive, far more comforting, than the occasional lecture or rally presented by rival organizations. While such work was going on, the Scottish leaders, like their friend Mary Estlin in Bristol, must often have taken the opportunity of "dinning Anti-Slavery alphabets and grammars into the ears of raw beginners." It is not easy to see how they would have managed even to find beginners to indoctrinate if it had not been for the attractive sense that working for the bazaar meant *doing* something for the slave. Even with this advantage, Jane and Eliza Wigham could not prevent their more conservative friends from stopping their annual bazaar box in

14. W. H. and J. H. Pease, *Bound with Them in Chains*, 34–35, 44–47; R. Thompson, "The *Liberty Bell* and Other Gift Books," *NEQ*, VII (1934), 154–68; J. Estlin to S. May, October 2, 1848, in BPL-M; M. Carpenter, "Offerings of English Women," *Liberty Bell* (Boston, 1848), 238–42. Carpenter's album (1848) is preserved in the BPL.

1850, because of "a progressive feeling of dissatisfaction . . . respecting the religious arguments of the American abolitionists."
Nevertheless, it was agreed that individual contributions might
still continue through Catherine Paton's box from Glasgow, and
these rose steadily over the next few years. Unfortunately the
amount of energy available for this kind of work was finite. When
a Peace Bazaar was held in London, the two hundred pounds'
worth of goods it attracted from Scotland came directly out of the
box for Boston.[15] There was therefore a special danger in the work
of Julia Griffiths, Frederick Douglass' agent from Rochester. Since
her plan was to set up a rival bazaar at the expense of Mrs. Chapman's, the loyalty she offered had the same scope for involvement
as the Garrisonian bazaar, with none of its ideological complications.

Julia Griffiths arrived in Edinburgh at the beginning of 1856.
The Edinburgh New Ladies' Anti-Slavery Association she founded
was committed to supporting Douglass and to sending contributions of money and work to the annual Rochester Bazaar in aid of
Frederick Douglass' Paper. To this extent it was even more threatening to the Garrisonians than to the free-produce groups founded
by Henry Highland Garnet, or the new organization Vigilance
Committee elements drawn together by J. W. C. Pennington.
Douglass was always to be the black fallen angel, the only apos-
tate whom Garrison never forgave. The Edinburgh New Ladies'
Anti-Slavery Association also met specifically Scottish needs. It
was built principally upon suspicion of radical infidelity. Eliza
Wigham, who was a gentle soul in whom the bile of a true blue
Chapmanite was often wanting, wrote furiously that "they are
forming a *Christian* Anti-Slavery Society in Edinburgh and leaving on the *left hand* our poor Society which in truth has been
innocent enough."[16] More significantly, the new group was helped

15. M. Estlin to E. Weston, October 15, 1851, E. Wigham to M. Estlin, September 13, 1850, both in BPL-E; *Expressions of Sentiment Tendered by Members
of the Edinburgh Ladies' Emancipation Society and the Meeting of the Committee,*
circular (August, 1851), and Minute of Edinburgh Ladies' Emancipation Society,
for August 1, 1850, copies of both in BPL-W; John Wigham to G. Combe, October
22, 1850, Ms. 7311, f.107, in Combe Papers, SNL.
16. *Anti-Slavery Advocate,* May, 1858; E. Wigham to L. A. Chamerovzow, April
18, 1856, C37/76, in ASP; *Report of the Edinburgh Ladies' New Anti-Slavery
Association, for the Years 1856 and 1857* (Edinburgh 1858), 2–7.

by the anxiety of one denomination to maintain clear antislavery credentials without being tainted by the extraneous issues. In the wake of the Old Calabar affair, most of its leaders were United Presbyterians who "to prove *their* Anti-Slavery have formed their Socy to help Julia." The rest were apparently Free Church members trying to recover their antislavery face after the events of ten years before—ladies who were "glad to show anti-slavery in opposition to a troublesome association like ours." Unlike the sporadic events sponsored by the New York Vigilance Committee or the free-produce group, the Rochester Bazaar was organized with the same regularity and efficiency as Mrs. Chapman's.[17]

The Garrisonian group bravely continued the unequal competition until 1858. Mrs. Chapman then informed them, per Mary Estlin, that bazaars had outlived their usefulness. She directed that any future contributions should be sent to Mrs. Mott's less well known Philadelphia Fair, to prevent them from falling into Douglass' hands. After fifteen years of hard work, not even Jane and Eliza Wigham's adulation, poor women, stretched to accepting this meekly. Even if Mrs. Chapman had not habitually behaved like the Doge of Venice, Scotland would not have produced many Garrisonian sympathizers in the late fifties. Unless it was made attractive by some countervailing consideration like the rivalry of different churches, or immediate distrust of direction from a national organization, the old organization concept of reform, once it was fully understood, was distasteful to a middle-class community with so deep a respect for institutions, particularly religious ones. It must have been all the harder to win converts to the Garrisonian critique when so large a part of what remained of a national institutional and political life was enshrined in the churches it seemed to threaten, when the shreds of nationality left to a class that was systematically cutting itself off from other aspects of its culture were so predominantly religious. Even the influence of George Thompson had waned, for after his election for Tower

17. E. Wigham to S. May, April 4, 1856, in BPL-M; E. Wigham to A. L. Chamerovzow, May 3, 1856, C37/75, in ASP; *Cf. Report of the Edinburgh Ladies' Emancipation Society . . . Together with Some Account of the Twelfth Boston Anti-Slavery Bazaar* (Edinburgh, 1846), and F. Douglass, *The Nature, Character, and History of the Anti-Slavery Movement . . . A Lecture, Delivered Before the Rochester Ladies' Anti-Slavery Association* (Glasgow, 1855), 31–32.

Hamlets in 1847 he paid less attention to the Scots and more to his friends in London and in the English provinces. By the end of the fifties the only consistent devotees left were the Patons, the Smeals, and the Wighams. They would all have understood only too well what Richard Webb meant when he wrote that "I feel all my time in an ice house—the more sympathy one has with the true Garrisonians the fewer you find to agree with you."[18]

There was only one encouragement for the little band of Scots Garrisonians. In the fifties, radical and antislavery views that had previously been confined to Scotland and Ireland were picked up by small but active new groups in the West Country and the North Country, areas that likewise had their traditions of cultural autonomy. An Emersonian tendency to fragmentation afflicted the British movement every bit as much as the American one. Parker Pillsbury, who was not a tolerant man, wrote home in 1854 that there were "all sorts of creatures traveling in the name of American Anti-Slavery, and picking the people's pockets for *Vigilance Committees, Canada Missions, Chaplain Funds, Coloured Schools* in the West, & Coloured Churches in Canada . . . they are an outrage on all decency, & a scandal to the name of Anti-Slavery." Though his judgment was clouded by his own failure in Britain, his observations on the diversification of the British movement were basically correct. The free-produce campaign in particular went from strength to strength in the fifties, stimulated by the colorful oratory of Garnet, the devotion of Elihu Burritt, and the careful organization of Mrs. Richardson of Newcastle. Although few of the Scots abolitionists went off on this tack, the first issue of the *Slave* was able to record that no fewer than twenty-six free-produce associations had been set up in other parts of the country.[19] All of Pillsbury's other enemies were repre-

18. M. W. Chapman to M. Estlin, March 8, 1858, in BPL-E; Pease and Pease, *Bound with Them in Chains*, 45–46; E. Wigham to S. May, April 16, 1858, in BPL-M; R. D. Webb to S. H. Gay, June 7, 1850, in Gay Papers, Columbia University Library.
19. P. Pillsbury to S. May, October 5, 1854, in BPL-M; L. Billington, "Some Contacts Between British and American Reform Movements, 1830–1860" (M.A. thesis, Bristol University, 1966), appendix; E. Burritt, *Twenty Reasons for Abstinence from Slave Produce*, broadsheet, in various editions, 1853, rpr. in *ASR*, August 1, 1853; *British Friend*, October 30, 1847; *Anti-Slavery Advocate*, January, 1853, November, 1854; *Slave*, January, 1851.

sented too, but the principal division in the movement, often the focus for lesser schisms, was still the one between old and new organization. As the total force behind the movement slackened—perhaps partly because of frustration over its weakness—the old feuds gained momentum with the emergence of new Garrisonian groups in England. All their leaders were either friends of the Scots radicals, or became so as their sympathies became clear.

When the Bristol and Clifton Ladies' Anti-Slavery Society broke away from the BFASS, it replaced the Glasgow Emancipation Society as Dublin's main Garrisonian ally. It was inspired and financed by the pioneer ophthalmologist John Bishop Estlin, the son of a Unitarian minister whose circle had included Priestley, Southey, and Coleridge. He was himself a close friend of Samuel May of Leicester, whom he had met at the Western Unitarian Association in 1843. As a Unitarian, Estlin was doubtless distrusted by the orthodox Quakers at Broad Street. Though he did not accept the full Garrisonian position on universal reform, he had written glowingly about the American radicals.[20] Ever since meeting May, he had exposed his daughter Mary to the *Liberator*, the *Nonresistant*, and the *Standard*, and she had been one of the earliest British contributors to the Boston Bazaar. Garrison stayed with them when he visited Bristol in 1846. Though he noted uneasily that "so much formality and *selectness* takes all the warmth out of me," he seems to have impressed Mary well enough. As in other cities, the auxiliary he planned for the Anti-Slavery League in Bristol quickly collapsed, but Mary Estlin and a slightly older fellow Unitarian, Mary Carpenter, continued to gather goods for the bazaar.[21] Both were articulate, pleasant women, and it was not hard for them to make converts in the local ladies' society, which had been founded in 1840 as a BFASS auxiliary. They were helped in this by John Scoble's refusal to give a satisfactory explanation of the American schisms and by a number of visits from

20. W. James, *A Memoir of John Bishop Estlin, F.L.S., F.R.C.S.*, rpr. from *Christian Reformer* (London, 1855); Bristol *Mercury*, June 16, 1855; *Anti-Slavery Advocate*, July, 1855; *A Brief Notice of American Slavery and the Abolition Movement* (2nd ed.; Leeds, 1851), 28–30. *Cf.* M. Estlin to M. W. Chapman, February 13, 1851, in BPL-W.
21. M. Estlin to M. W. Chapman, October 28, 1844, in BPL-W; W. L. Garrison to H. C. Wright, August 26, 1846, in BPL-G; J. B. Estlin to S. May, January 12, 1847, in BPL-M.

the Crafts and William Wells Brown in 1850 and 1851. In February of the latter year, they expressed sympathy for the American society and agreed to send an annual box to the bazaar. Mrs. Chapman, a few months later, was sure that the bells of Bristol were ringing "Sturge is done."[22]

The newly radicalized society worked energetically for the rest of the decade. Apart from a number of Congregationalist supporters, the denominations from which it drew its support were quite different from those in Scotland. The most active members were Unitarians, and many of its rank and file Baptists. They put a great deal of effort into arranging testimonies against slavery for the benefit of American visitors to the Great Exhibition. Although the Unitarian abolitionists were not entirely successful within their own denomination, they did hold a meeting in London, at which they were joined by Mrs. Chapman, Caroline and Emma Weston, Susan Cabot, and her sister Eliza Lee Cabot Follen, the radical editor of the *Child's Friend*.[23] In Bristol, Mary Estlin felt there was no hope of defeating the new organization "by starting . . . with the violent measures you prescribe." It was only in the autumn of 1851 that carefully stage-managed visits by Mrs. Chapman, her sisters, Thompson, and Webb explained the old feuds to the Bristol ladies in bitter terms that were really irrelevant to the changed American situation of the new decade. The opponents of her group, Mrs. Chapman announced blithely, together amounted to "a harmless remnant" who were made into "instruments of mischief" solely by the patronage of the BFASS.[24]

22. M. W. Chapman to M. Estlin, September, 1851, J. B. Estlin to M. W. Chapman, July 2, 1852, both in BPL-E; M. Estlin to A. W. Weston, February 13, 1851, March 1, 1851, M. Estlin to E. Wigham, May 3, 1851, all in BPL-W; Minutes for February 13, 1851, March 27, 1851, BSMB; *BCR*, 5–15.

23. M. Estlin to A. W. Weston, May 8, 1851, in BPL-W; Minute for March 27, 1851, in BCMB; *BCR*, 16–20; *Clerical Teachings on American Slavery, Selected from American Publications*, broadsheet (Bristol, 1851), copy in BPL-M; J. C. Crandall, "Patriotism and Humanitarian Reform in Children's Literature, 1825–1860," *AQ*, XXI (1969), 16; *American Slavery: Report of a Meeting of the Members of the Unitarian Body, Held at Freemasons' Tavern, June 13th, 1851, to Deliberate on the Duty of English Unitarians in Reference to the United States* (London, 1851).

24. M. Estlin to C. Weston, June 3, 1851, in BPL-E; *BCR*, 31–38; Minutes for September 11, 1851, September 16, 1851, September 28, 1851, October 2, 1851, November 13, 1851, in BCMB; G. Thompson, *Speech . . . Delivered at the Anti-Slavery Meeting, Broadmead, Bristol, September 4th, 1851* (Bristol, 1851).

A few weeks later, the Bristol and Clifton Ladies' Anti-Slavery Society broke its ties with London and became independent. "It is pleasant," wrote Mary Estlin, "to have no anxiety about them." The secret was that she and Mary Carpenter kept the members loyal by absorbing them in working for the Boston Bazaar and preparing and distributing literature defending the Garrisonians.[25] Above all, they were set to work for the new *Anti-Slavery Advocate*, a brilliant monthly largely financed by Dr. Estlin and edited from Dublin by Richard Webb. By now he was a regular contributor to radical American periodicals, and an important pamphleteer in his own right.[26] The Bristol group became heavily involved in helping him with this new national magazine, which had a circulation of two hundred in Glasgow alone. It was also strengthened in the winter of 1852–1853 by being able to work with two American visitors, Sarah Pugh and Abby Kimber, both Hicksite Quakers and veteran abolitionists from Philadelphia. A visit from James Miller McKim had the same effect, and they were also briefly joined at one time or another by radical leaders like Jane Wigham, Richard Webb, and Elizabeth Pease Nichol. Apart from her personal charm, Mary Estlin's success was based on offering attractions the conservative national society simply could not match. The first was individual participation in the work of spreading propaganda and transmitting support to America. The second was a realistic chance for even the humblest supporter to meet leaders of what was, with all its shortcomings, a national American movement. No one in the Bristol society could complain, as Webb had done at the World's Anti-Slavery Convention, that she could only look upon visiting luminaries "from a distance, like the cat and the King." At the same time, like Eliza Wigham in Edinburgh, the Bristol group, and even the *Advocate*, showed

25. M. Estlin to M. W. Chapman, October 10, 1853, in BPL-W; *Statements Respecting the American Abolitionists by Their Opponents and Their Friends, Indicating the Present Struggle Between Slavery and Freedom in the United States* (Dublin, 1852); BCR; E. Quincy, *An Examination of the Charges of Mr. John Scoble and Mr. Lewis Tappan Against the American Anti-Slavery Society* (Dublin, 1852).

26. S. H. Gay to R. D. Webb, July 31, 1848, in BPL-G; R. D. Webb to S. H. Gay, July 31, 1848, in Gay Papers; S. H. May to R. D. Webb, February 19, 1850, in BPL-M.

a willingness to make haste slowly which was tailored to British conditions.[27]

For its size, Mary Estlin's society was able to make a substantial number of important Garrisonian converts in other English provincial cities. One was the slum missionary from Liverpool, the Reverend Francis Bishop, a Unitarian West Countryman from Exeter.[28] Another of their friends, also a Unitarian from the West Country, was the Reverend S. A. Steinthal, from the little market town of Bridgewater. After some indoctrination from Mary Estlin and a visit from the sensitive and tactful McKim, he was able to old organize the little local society, which was mainly supported by Unitarians and Baptists. In the North Country, too, the contact between the Estlins and another Unitarian family, the Luptons of Headingly, was central in the emergence of a new Garrisonian society in Leeds. It was while old Dr. Estlin and Sarah Pugh were staying with the Luptons over the Christmas of 1852, working on the *Advocate*, that the Leeds group began to show a new independence. Mary Estlin was at this time in Dublin helping Webb with the same work.[29]

The most important Leeds abolitionist, however, was Wilson Armistead. He is most unusual in that he did not accept Estlin's view that "it is not the kitchens & workshops that need Anti-Slavery agitation for America's sake, but the drawing rooms and the salons of the wealthy, & the libraries of the learned." He himself was a successful Quaker mustard miller, who devoted his considerable erudition to studies of black improvability. The propaganda schemes he developed were unique. He was willing to try anything to bring all elements of society into the movement—from selling lithographed autographs at inflated prices and flooding the country with cheap publications aimed at the poor and ignorant,

27. "Jottings for Maria Weston Chapman," February 22, 1842, in BPL-G; M. Estlin to M. W. Chapman, December 2, 1852, in BPL-W.

28. F. Bishop to M. Estlin, September 30, 1850, October 4, 1850, in BPL-E; Bishop to J. M. McKim, October 1, 1853, Bishop to W. L. Garrison, November 23, 1853, both in BPL-G; C. Wicksteed, *The Englishman's Duty to the Free and Enslaved American: A Lecture, Twice Delivered at Leeds in January, 1853* (Leeds, 1853), 12.

29. M. Estlin to J. M. McKim, September 4, 1853, in McKim Papers, NYPL; E. Matthews to [?], September 2, 1853, E. Mitchell to A. W. Weston, November 20, 1853 (misfiled under 1833), in BPL-W; S. Pugh to M. Estlin, December 14, December 15, and December 24, 1852, all in EP.

to indoctrinating the very young by means of juvenile tracts, or the cultured through essay competitions.[30]

Nevertheless, Armistead's work would have been impossible without the support of the Leeds Anti-Slavery Association, which Sarah Pugh and John Estlin helped found in 1853. The association was built on a tenuous tradition of support for the Boston Bazaar, and the enthusiasm whipped up by McKim and other American visitors. It was an extraordinary organization, the only British one ever floated on the full Garrisonian principle of being a joint society with a "promiscuous" committee of both sexes. Its composition is fascinating. It had few members with orthodox views similar to those of the Calvinist secession ministers who were so important in Glasgow. Apart from Armistead, who was president, there were none of the Quakers who dominated the national society. The Unitarians were dominant, with Joseph Lupton as vice-president and his daughter Harriet as secretary, but otherwise the members ranged from Baptists to High Churchmen.[31] Armistead later organized a Leeds Young Men's Society to do his tract work, but this heterodox new association was yet another independent group aimed at channeling local support to the American Garrisonians.

The apparent revival of Garrisonian sentiment in England brought hopes that a new national group might be organized to break the supposed BFASS monopoly of British antislavery opinion. One such attempt was the Manchester Anti-Slavery League. It was founded in 1854, and it was rather different from the Anti-Slavery League Garrison and Douglass had planned eight years

30. J. B. Estlin to S. May, October 1, 1846, in BPL-M; W. Armistead, *A Tribute for the Negro* (Manchester, 1848); *The Garland of Freedom: A Collection of Songs, Chiefly Anti-Slavery* (London, 1853); *A Cloud of Witnesses Against Slavery and Oppression* (London, 1854); *God's Image in Ebony* (London, 1854); W. Armistead to C. Sumner, November 8, 1854, in Sumner Papers, Houghton Library, Harvard; *Five Hundred Thousand Strokes for Freedom* (Leeds, 1853) [his collection of cheap tracts]; Armistead to L. A. Chamerovzow, April 7, 1853, C27/49, in ASP; *ASR*, June 1, 1854, April 1, 1857.

31. S. Pugh to M. Estlin, February 22, 1853, in BPL-E; W. L. Garrison to H. B. Garrison, September 10, 1846, in BPL-G; H. Lupton to M. W. Chapman, October 12, 1846, in BPL-W; J. Lupton to S. May, September 17, 1851, October 12, 1853, both in BPL-M; S. Pugh to M. Estlin, October 23, 1853, in EP; *Prospectus of the Leeds Anti-Slavery Association*, February 22, 1853, broadsheet, in May Collection, CUL, has denominations and occupations of members inked in.

before. At first it tried to attract all factions by avoiding an offensively specific commitment to those abolitionists who were known to be heretics. It epitomized the view of Wilson Armistead, one of its leaders, that the movement's real problem was "a lack of cordiality and sympathy with one another." Though there were "different *modes of operation yet all may tend* towards the promotion of the same great end." Nevertheless, the new league was perceived by the independent provincial radicals as an alternative loyalty to Broad Street. Its most influential leader was George Thompson. He had again gone to America in 1850–1851, in a vain attempt to make good the financial liabilities he had incurred as radical M.P. for Tower Hamlets, the large London constituency that appears as "Pottery Hamlets" in Anthony Trollope's *Phineas Finn.* He had returned reinforced in his friendship for Garrison. Not surprisingly, he lost his seat in the following year, soon after the death of his son Garrison and the engagement of his daughter to Frederick W. Chesson, with whom he soon became coeditor of their own general reform paper the *Empire.* Unlike most abolitionists, the consistency of his commitments was much affected by the necessity of making a living. He was still the same Thompson, "a fine, good hearted, magnanimous fellow, but always living from hand to mouth, always poor—always unbusinesslike." Chesson eventually became an important figure in the benevolent world as secretary of the Aborigines' Protection Society, but for Thompson the Manchester league was a final excursion into antislavery before his paper's bankruptcy in 1856 drove him into uncertain employment as a commercial traveler in India.[32]

The league arose from the ruins of a Manchester Union Anti-Slavery Society. Thompson had founded it in the previous autumn as an experiment in cooperation with Joseph Sturge and Louis Alexis Chamerovzow, the new secretary of the BFASS. Chesson had produced three issues of a little monthly, the *Anti-Slavery Watchman,* on its behalf. It followed Armistead's policy of trying to bring antislavery to the literate working class. Unfortunately

32. W. Armistead to L. A. Chamerovzow, November 27, 1854, C27/62, in ASP; G. Thompson to A. W. Weston, October 3, 1850, in BPL-G; G. Thompson to A. W. Weston, March 26, 1851, R. D. Webb to M. W. Chapman, February 23, 1851, both in BPL-W; R. D. Webb to S. H. Gay, July 1, 1851, in Gay Papers; S. May to W. L. Garrison, January 17, 1859, in BPL-G.

Chesson's insistence on filling it with denunciations of Garrison's enemies led to an unseemly fracas that ended in his and Thompson's resignations. The last issue contained a letter from John P. Nichol of the GES, Elizabeth Pease's husband, denouncing the sectarianism of the Union. Indeed the Union does not seem to have found much support among the few remaining Scottish Garrisonians.[33]

Its successor was officially entitled the North of England Anti-Slavery and India Reform League. Its radicalism was better calculated to please men like Professor Nichol, though there were serious doubts about young Chesson's abrasiveness and the quality of his leadership. Even Chamerovzow, who was doing everything in his power to bridge the gap between old and new organization, was unable to miss the sad significance of having "two Richmonds in the field."[34] The national conference held by the league in August, as a rival to the one he himself was planning for the BFASS, amply proved him right. Although it was attended by relatively conservative Garrisonians, like Dr. Estlin and the "ragged schools" pioneer, Dr. Thomas Guthrie of the Free Church of Scotland, it was dominated by the visiting Garrisonian Parker Pillsbury. Its discussion of "the charges preferred against the American abolitionists," as an agenda item, gave rise to violent controversy, especially over Sabbath observance. Chesson was the only British Garrisonian to whom Pillsbury's vindictiveness was not alien, but the issues that had been raised were enough to make it impossible for abolitionists who were not totally committed to the old organization view to continue cooperating in the league. Perhaps, indeed, this was why Pillsbury, as a tactically sound Garrisonian, had raised them. In any case, there were simple reasons for the league's life not being a long one. Chesson and Pillsbury had much spleen to provide propaganda, but no money to print it. Chesson, who was as poor as a church mouse, had received no dowry from

33. *ASR*, December 1, 1853, March 1, 1854; *Anti-Slavery Watchman*, November December, 1853, January, 1854; *Anti-Slavery Advocate*, October, 1853, January, February, 1854.
34. M. Estlin to E. Weston, January 16, 1854, in BPL-E; J. M. McKim to R. D. Webb, January 8, 1854, S. Pugh to R. D. Webb, February 24, 1854, L. A. Chamerovzow to M. Estlin, July 24, 1854, August 1, 1854, all in BPL-G; *Cf.* M. Estlin to L. A. Chamerovzow, July 31, 1854, copy, in BPL-G.

a man who was perhaps even poorer. Unable to work without pay, he returned, still just twenty, to work on the *Empire*.[35] With Estlin in failing health, Webb isolated in Dublin, and Armistead absorbed in his cheap publication schemes, the league, as Mary Estlin had prophesied, perished "for want of a soul in the three kingdoms qualified to take the helm." It was all but defunct by the time Chamerovzow's conference met in November.[36]

Louis Alexis Chamerovzow, unlike his malicious predecessor John Scoble, was a warm and decent man who saw no reason why the national society should not harness the energies of the provincial radicals with whom it was at loggerheads. Most of them received his first overtures well, in spite of Pillsbury's outraged and outrageous pun, "I see no hope of any but a *Cham* union."[37] All Chamerovzow's efforts were dogged by Pillsbury's ill will—an ill will that perhaps stemmed less from intrinsic malice, though that was not wanting, than from a realization that Garrison's British supporters were really more interested in antislavery per se than in the full spectrum of American radical reform. If they were won back to cooperation with the national society over slavery, there would be little basis for their continuing cooperation with the old organization on wider issues. Pillsbury is the least attractive of all the American radicals, and even Mary Estlin remarked upon "the diseased way in which his mind fastens upon erroneous views of a subject." To James Russell Lowell:

> Old Sinai burns unquenchably
> Upon his lips; he might well be a
> Hot blazing soul from fierce Judea,
> Habbakuk, Ezra, or Hosea.

35. *ASR*, September 1, 1854; *Scottish Press*, September 22, 1854, extracts and subsequent correspondence rpr. in *Anti-Slavery Advocate*, November, 1854; F. Chesson to S. May, August 28, 1854, in BPL-M; *Cf.* E. Wigham to L. A. Chamerovzow, November 15, 1853, C160/218, in ASP. On Chesson's subsequent career, see *Aborigines' Friend*, March, 1889.
36. M. Estlin to E. Weston, January 16, 1854, in BPL-E; F. Chesson to L. A. Chamerovzow, November 16, 1854, C29/26, in ASP.
37. P. Pillsbury to W. L. Garrison, October 5, 1854, in BPL-M. *Cf.* S. Pugh to S. May, October 8, 1854, in BPL-G; M. Estlin to A. W. Weston, March 4, 1853, R. D. Webb to M. W. Chapman, May 29, 1853, both in BPL-W; E. Wigham to L. A. Chamerovzow, April 1, 1853, C37/61, October 19, 1853, C37/62, W. Smeal to L. A. Chamerovzow, April 16, 1852, C36/526, all in ASP.

Unfortunately the demands of prophethood meant it was out of the question to engage in any form of dialogue with the Beast, and Pillsbury systematically snubbed all Chamerovzow's politeness during the summer of 1854. He wrote sadly to Mary Estlin that it was difficult to know how to please her friends.[38] What probably annoyed Pillsbury more than anything else what that although the much-adulated Mrs. Chapman had promised to "deal with" Chamerovzow, she gave him a perfectly civil interview in Paris. Chamerovzow did invite the British Garrisonians to his 1854 general conference, and although Steinthal and Armistead could not attend, Bishop, Thompson, and Professor Nichol did. Pillsbury came too, though he had publicly ridiculed and refused the invitation. Finding "the enemy" in control, with Thompson "fast in their fangs," he could not resist demanding and being refused a specific endorsement of the American Anti-Slavery Society. He then denounced the BFASS, stressing its lapse over Indiana in 1843, an especially infelicitous skeleton to drag across the decade, given the fact that most of the London Yearly Meeting was in the audience. He was silenced from the chair, and left the meeting.[39]

Chamerovzow's honeymoon was over. In fact his wish to cooperate with the radicals had not necessarily meant that they were to be treated as equals. In 1853, for instance, the Garrisonians invited to the BFASS anniversary had been pointedly seated at the back of the hall. Nevertheless, Pillsbury's intervention did exactly what he intended it to do, and expressed the old tensions in a way that destroyed the possibility of cooperation once and for all. There were still plenty of Britons who would take his part. Webb, for instance, concluded that the whole incident proved the movement was "a real struggle with the powers of evil, and not an

38. Ms. note on the relation between Pillsbury and Chamerovzow, March, 1855, in BPL-M; J. R. Lowell, "Notes from Boston," in *Complete Political Works* (Boston, 1896), 112, quoted in O. Sherwin, *Prophet of Liberty: The Life and Times of Wendell Phillips* (New York, 1958), 79–80; A. L. Chamerovzow to M. Estlin, July 24, 1854, in BPL-W; P. Pillsbury to S. May, June 2, 1854, in BPL-M.

39. S. Pugh to M. Estlin, August 28, 1854, in EP; C. Weston to M. Estlin, August 20, 1854, L. A. Chamerovzow to M. Estlin, August 24, 1854, both in BPL-G, misfiled in 1855 file; P. Pillsbury to W. L. Garrison, October 5, 1854, F. Bishop to W. L. Garrison, November 30, 1854, both in BPL-G; P. Pillsbury to M. W. Chapman, January 7, 1855, in BPL-W; P. Pillsbury to S. May, December 21, 1854, in BPL-M; *Anti-Slavery Advocate*, January, 1855.

intellectual Turkish bath for the promotion and indulgence of pleasing states of tranquility."[40] Even the Garrisonians who had been encouraging to Chamerovzow now deserted him. He had never made much impression on the Irish and Scots. Steinthal duly resigned from the BFASS, and Estlin followed suit as soon as he saw that the published proceedings of the conference made no mention of Pillsbury's speech.[41] Armistead had already been infuriated by finding that his plea for unity with the Garrisonians and cooperation in an attack on the churches had not been put on the agenda. Thompson, whose instinct as a trimmer remained strong, disgraced himself after the conference by publishing a pro-Garrison speech that no one who had been present could remember hearing him deliver.[42] All these leaders worked independent of the national society for the rest of the decade.

These efforts to reunite British abolitionists were doubtless produced by an awareness of their declining support, and their failure was widely seen as proof that the movement's disagreements were irreconcilable. Yet it is clear that the decline was itself caused in part by disunity. This was not because the participants or the public found controversy distasteful, though it must have become wearying in the long run. The structure of mid-Victorian reform societies made their work efficient in direct proportion to their size. Fragmentation meant smaller funds for each group to produce publications, and shrinking propaganda meant fewer adherents. More important, since only the national society could afford to pay a permanent staff, each group had to find amateur officials so dedicated to the cause that they would put in the endless hours of work in correspondence, memorializing, report writing, and fund raising upon which a society depended. The number of such individuals was strictly limited, all the more so in the fifties as this form of antislavery involvement lost its momentum. Every

40. S. Pugh to R. D. Webb, May 28, 1855, in BPL-G; *Anti-Slavery Advocate*, January, 1855; R. D. Webb to M. Estlin, March 5, 1855, in BPL-M.
41. S. A. Steinthal to L. A. Chamerovzow, April 4, 1855, C36/104; J. B. Estlin to L. A. Chamerovzow, May 21, 1855, C157/57, both in ASP; *Anti-Slavery Advocate*, May, 1855, June, 1855.
42. W. Armistead to L. A. Chamerovzow, December 4, 1854, C27/63, in ASP; *Anti-Slavery Advocate*, February, 1855; P. Pillsbury to S. May, February 2, 1855, in BPL-M; A. W. Weston to M. Estlin, January 21, 1855, G. Thompson to M. Estlin, July 31, 1855, both in BPL-E.

subdivision meant that more societies were sharing fewer leaders and less money.

The erosion of old-style antislavery sentiment had deeper causes than administrative fragmentation, and in spite of Chamerovzow's optimism it is hard to imagine any compromise that would have reunited the movement. It is still true, however, that the vitality of the schisms in the fifties, and the failure to paper them over, at a time when American abolitionists had turned their attention to issues not susceptible to foreign influence, weakened a weakening movement still further. This was all the more so for the Scots abolitionists, whose divided past had been specially bitter and who suffered from intricate local divisions as well as national ones. If it had not been transformed by Mrs. Stowe, their antislavery situation would have been a sad one indeed.

It was not Mrs. Stowe who introduced the Scots to a romantic admiration for the Negro. In the eighteenth century, they had produced a body of extraordinarily bad noble savage literature of their own. At times it could move from the pastoral to take on a tone of remarkable bitterness. There is even one piece that glorifies the success of the Maroons.[43] By the nineteenth century, however, there is little Scottish writing on the primitive virtues of the Negro, and virtually nothing in the abolitionist literature proper that concentrates on the cult of sensibility to African suffering, though it was always one theme away among many in the abolitionist attitude.[44]

On the other hand, sensibility in general, perhaps because it represented a comforting defense mechanism against the legacy of Calvinism, had always been appealing to Scots. It is well known that Robert Burns, who disliked Calvinists, considered Henry Mackenzie's *Man of Feeling* the most important of all books next to the Bible, and that he wore out his copy reading it behind the

43. "On the Execution of a Negro, Who Was Burned at a Slow Fire, Near Spanish Town, in August, 1785," in J. Marjoribanks, *Pieces of Rhyme* (Edinburgh, 1793), 11; "Zimeo, a Tale," in Edinburgh *Bee*, March 7, 1792, March 14, 1792, March 21, 1792. *Cf.* "Selico, a Tale," *Bee*, August 8, 1792, September 5, 1792.

44. D. B. Davis, *The Problem of Slavery in Western Culture* (Ithaca, N.Y., 1967), 391–445; E. B. Dykes, *The Negro in English Romantic Thought* (Washington, 1942); W. Sypher, *Guinea's Captive Kings: British Anti-Slavery Literature of the XVIIIth Century* (Chapel Hill, 1942).

plough.[45] Specific romantic stereotypes of the Negro were not in themselves disparaging, and there is no doubt that the English romantics at least refused to allow their distrust of abolitionists to lead them to approval of slavery. Even sensibility, the subromantic tradition that Mrs. Stowe herself epitomized and exploited, was not destructive so long as it was allied with the common evangelical assumptions on black improvability—which is exactly the place it occupied in the ideology of working abolitionists in the thirties and forties, and indeed in Mrs. Stowe's personal attitudes toward the Negro. In itself, however, sensibility was a different matter. It carried no coherent assumptions on the human capacity of the oppressed or the social duty of the privileged. The *Man of Feeling*, with all poor Harley's whimperings, would not have prevented Burns from going to the West Indies as an overseer if the success of the Kilmarnock edition had not removed the necessity for his doing so.

By 1850 sensibility was still a vital force in Scottish and English philanthropy. It did not exclude Mrs. Stowe's statement that the "African [is] naturally patient, timid, and unenterprising."[46] Indeed this implied that black people were the very kind of group upon whom sensibility might feed. It was all the more acceptable in that the British were entering a period of deep disillusionment with efforts to help the emancipated Negro himself. In Charles Dickens, who was himself much influenced by the cult of sensibility, this emerged less as criticism of Africans than of the white hypocrites and visionaries who had planned the settlement at Borioboola-Gha on the Niger. For Macaulay, the arguments of the abolitionists became "cant and silly mock reasons."[47]

Among Scots, there were doubtless some who shared this view of the futility of philanthropy, but there were others who turned their irritation against the Negro himself. One such was the Edinburgh surgeon Robert Knox, whose career had been ruined after the Burke and Hare body-snatching scandal. His pseudoscientific

45. H. W. Thompson, *A Scottish Man of Feeling* (London, 1931), 218.
46. H. B. Stowe, *Uncle Tom's Cabin* (Edinburgh: Gall & Inglis, *ca.* 1904), 60.
47. C. Dickens, *Bleak House* (London, 1966), 34–35; T. B. Macaulay, "Journals," July 8, 1858, quoted in J. Hamburger, "The Whig Conscience," in P. Marsh (ed.), *The Conscience of the Victorian State* (Syracuse, 1979), 26. *Cf.* Thomas, Lord Denman, *Uncle Tom's Cabin, Bleak House, Slavery and the Slave Trade* (London, 1853), 5–8, 18–24.

lectures were greatly admired by Darwin, and they were popularized to an extent that makes him "the real founder of British racism." Another was Thomas Carlyle, whose "Nigger Question" was reprinted as a pamphlet during Mrs. Stowe's 1853 visit. It heaped abuse on the devoted heads of the traditional antislavery workers, "one huge Gadarene-swinery, tail cocked, snout in the air, with joyful animating short squeaks."[48] Its views on Quashee and the ex-slaves "with their beautiful muzzles up to the ears in pumpkins," came straight from Carlyle's background in the manse at Ecclefechan. This was a characteristically Scottish response to the failure of black personality in the light of Calvinist concepts of duty and the calling.[49] These changing views did not have to be accepted in their entirety to contribute to a revulsion against the conception of black improvability, upon which both old and new organization societies had built their appeal. The simple message of *Uncle Tom's Cabin* was well suited to bridge the gap, for whatever Mrs. Stowe's more complex private views, her book relied for its attractiveness on a sensibility that accommodated compassion without admitting capacity.

Mrs. Stowe's final advantage was that she demanded much emotion but no work. Long before her visit to Scotland, another visitor to Edinburgh, Samuel Taylor Coleridge, had noted: "Sensibility is not benevolence. Nay, by making us tremblingly alive to trifling misfortunes, it frequently prevents it, and induces effeminate and cowardly selfishness. Our own sorrows, like the Princes of Hell in Milton's Pandemonium, sit enthroned 'bulky and vast:' while the miseries of our fellow-creatures dwindle into pigmy forms, and are crowded, an innumerable multitude, into some dark corner of the heart. There is one criticism by which we may always distinguish benevolence from mere sensibility—Benevolence impels to action, and is accompanied by self-denial."[50] It is not surprising that Mrs.

---

48. P. D. Curtin, *The Image of Africa: British Ideas and Action, 1780–1850* (Madison, Wis., 1964), 377–79; R. Knox, *The Races of Man* (Edinburgh, 1850); "Occasional Discourse on the Negro Question," *Fraser's Magazine* (December, 1849), rpr. as *Occasional Discourse on the Nigger Question* (London, 1863); Cf. *ASR*, January 1, 1850, February 1, 1850, March 1, 1850.

49. I. Campbell, "Carlyle and the Negro Question Again," *Criticism*, VIII (1971), 279–90; *idem, Thomas Carlyle* (London, 1974), 115–18.

50. S. T. Coleridge, "The Watchman," in *Collected Works*, ed. L. Patton (Princeton, 1970), 139–40.

Stowe's sensibility reached many men and women to whom the benevolence of the old-style abolitionists now seemed boring if not ridiculous.

The gulf between improvability and sensibility did not save the rank and file of the old movement from the Lorelei. After years of disappointment and dissension, it would have been a sore trial to remain aloof from this upsurge of feeling for the slave. Some, like Webb, had doubts about the fashionable shaking among bones previously thought dry, but they were very much the exception.[51] Sensibility had always been one among many antislavery weapons, and there was no reason why old-style abolitionists should at once detect the dangers of making it the only one. Like other Britons, too, they were already caught up by a swelling romantic excitement over slavery. This was independent from *Uncle Tom's Cabin*, but it obscured the extent to which Mrs. Stowe's supporters were at odds with the movement's traditional priorities. By the time her book came out, Richard Hildreth's *The White Slave* had already had a British success that was outstanding. The Compromise of 1850 and the reenactment of the Fugitive Slave Law made a deep impression on the British liberal mind. *Uncle Tom's Cabin* was only one of many attempts, fictional, semifictional, or historical, to make literary capital out of romantic, often Gothic, stories of escape from Yankee thralldom to Canadian freedom. Although some actually predated the compromise, their impact was increased tenfold as horror stories of recaptures in the North began to filter back to Britain, often carried by dignified black orators whose talents also spoke tellingly for Negro improvability.[52] It was easy for writers to fall into the habit of using fugitive stories to add romantic interest to their indictments of slavery. "The Law," announced Thompson, "has turned south-eastern Pennsylvania into another Guinea Coast." Printed slave narratives were all the more eagerly received because they were a genuinely exciting form of

51. *Anti-Slavery Advocate*, January, 1853; Minute for December 17, 1852, in BCMB. *Cf.* S. Pugh to M. Estlin, December 15, 1852, December 24, 1852, both in EP; G. Thompson, *A Lecture Delivered in the Music Hall, Store Street* . . . *Proving, by Unquestionable Evidence, the Correctness of Mrs. Stowe's Portrait of American Slavery in Her Popular Work, "Uncle Tom's Cabin"* (London, 1852).
52. G. Thompson to R. D. Webb, September 10, 1852, J. Barker to W. L. Garrison, October 24, 1850, both in BPL-G; M. Welsh to A. W. Weston, November 29, 1850, in BPL-W; B. Quarles, *Black Abolitionists* (New York, 1969), 116–42.

literature admissible in dissenting homes normally closed to the novel, which was still widely held to lack redeeming moral value. Again, they presented more covert or overt scenes of sexual license than any other form of antislavery literature, apart from deliberately designed atrocity manuals like Weld's *Slavery As It Is.* On the one hand these stories were just titillating food for bourgeois prurience, but they may also have given respectable evangelicals a means of projecting their deep anxieties over personal sexual control into disapproval of the South.[53] In either case, the circulation of the narratives was colossal.

Uncle Tom had all these advantages, but it made no troublesome assumptions on black equality, and it stressed a warm and simple sensibility at the expense of improvability. Though it is actually quite a good novel, and still an exciting one on its own merits, this combination of selling points goes far to explain why it sold a million copies in Britain alone before 1861, and how it managed to draw entirely new groups to an antislavery commitment. By the same token, it is easy to see why so few old-style abolitionists objected to or even perceived the new direction of sentiment among the Stoweites. *Uncle Tom* must simply have seemed an especially successful example of a genre of literature they were accustomed to accept without question. Moreover, the generally sentimental thrust of Mrs. Stowe's narrative did not prevent her from including characters among whom every group of antislavery tacticians, from colonizationists to revolutionaries, could find a favorite. Perhaps, too, the abolitionists' usually acute moral vision was blurred by the unaccustomed glory of working side by side with the aristocrats Mrs. Stowe had recruited. Garrison himself, though coy, had been pleased in 1840 when the duchess of Sutherland asked him to tea.[54]

During her 1853 visit, Mrs. Stowe was a glittering success wherever she went. Once the Civil War had begun, it still irritated Mary Boykin Chesnut that "the Mrs. Stowes have the plaudits of crowned heads; we take our chances, doing our duty as best we

53. *ASR*, February 1, 1851, March 1, 1851, April 1, 1851, May 1, 1851, *et seq.*; R. G. Walters, "The Erotic South: Civilization and Sexuality in American Abolitionism," *AQ*, XXV (1973), 177–210.
54. W. L. Garrison to H. B. Garrison, July 3, 1840, BPL-G.

may among the woolly heads." Simply because of her attendance, the BFASS was able to attract an unprecedented audience of six thousand to its annual meeting in May.[55] By this time, it had become clear that she was aiming for the sympathy of men and women who had not previously been connected with the movement. In the first instance, however, many veterans had been impressed with her, nowhere more so than in Scotland. In Glasgow, enthusiasm had risen before her trip was planned. Smeal welcomed *Uncle Tom* in the *British Friend*, and it was his old Glasgow Emancipation Society group that launched the "Uncle Tom Penny Offering" designed to make up for the royalties Mrs. Stowe could not receive on her British editions. The Glasgow New Association's inviting her to Scotland, through Smeal's old rival Ralph Wardlaw, was a brilliant scoop at the expense of their local Garrisonian enemies. Smeal explained darkly to Garrison that this would delude the public into the view that supporting the Boston Bazaar as opposed to the Vigilance Committee would be "to aid infidelity." His worst fears were justified. The Stowes stayed with Baillie William P. Paton, and went in Wardlaw's carriage to the huge soirees arranged for them.[56] None of the Glasgow Garrisonians met Mrs. Stowe. An address from Catherine Paton's Female Anti-Slavery Society only elicited a reply that, though civil, ended by stating that she did not agree "in some important respects" with the American Society.[57]

In Edinburgh and elsewhere in Scotland, the old wounds were not so raw as in Glasgow. While staying with the Wighams of South Gray Street, Mrs. Stowe was patronized by Duncan Maclaren, the husband of the Garrisonian abolitionist Priscilla Bright

---

55. B. A. Williams (ed.), *A Diary from Dixie* (Boston, 1949), 163; *ASR*, June 1, 1853. See also F. J. Klingberg, "Harriet Beecher Stowe and Social Reform in England," *AHR*, XLIII (1938), 542–52; G. A. Shepperson, "Harriet Beecher Stowe and Scotland," *SHR*, XXXII (1953), 40–46; H. R. Temperley, *British Anti-Slavery, 1833–1870* (London, 1972), 224–26; B. Fladeland, *Men and Brothers: Anglo-American Antislavery Cooperation* (Urbana, Ill., 1972), 350–58; F. Wilson, *Crusader in Crinoline: The Life of Harriet Beecher Stowe* (London, 1942), 368ff.

56. *British Friend*, November 1, 1852; Minute for November 16, 1852, in GESMB, IV; W. Smeal to L. A. Chamerovzow, April 16, 1853, C36/52, in ASP; Shepperson, "Harriet Beecher Stowe and Scotland," 44; W. Smeal to W. L. Garrison, March 4, 1853, in BPL-G; H. B. Stowe, *Sunny Memories of Foreign Lands* (London, 1854), 38, 42–43.

57. *ASR*, July 1, 1853.

Maclaren. Julia Griffiths' New Ladies' Anti-Slavery Association had not then been founded. On April 20, the old Edinburgh Ladies' Emancipation Society held a "temperance banquet" at which Smeal was present as a platform guest. It presented Mrs. Stowe with a silver salver and the first thousand pounds of the Uncle Tom Penny Offering. In Aberdeen, the pro-BFASS society entertained her at a "fruit festival."[58] Her hosts in Dundee were also conservative abolitionists, but the support for her was so united and so tumultuous that George Gilfillan, the friend of Emerson and Carlyle, noted that "whatever the Exeter Hall idiots might say," the meeting "seemed a minute of the Millenium sent before its time." When she went south to London, after a second short visit to Edinburgh, her reception was another triumph for the national society and the new organization. The Garrisonians invited to gaze upon Mrs. Stowe at the anniversary of the BFASS were badly enough seated for the piqued George Thompson to tell Chamerovzow, when they met later at the Estlins' lodgings, that "he believed the gulph [sic] that separated them to be impassable."[59] Mrs. Stowe, perhaps remembering the acrobatics of her father's abolitionism in the thirties,[60] was careful not to alienate either side. This did not prevent the British abolitionists who entertained her from using the kudos this earned them against their rivals.

In fact, Harriet Beecher Stowe's visit brought out much deeper tensions than the relatively simple ones over antislavery tactics. It soon became clear that many of those who lionized her came from social backgrounds much more elevated than the usual members of the abolition societies. The interest of the British aristocracy in the black slave had been dormant since 1838, but Mrs. Stowe's sentimental appeal had the effect of reawakening it. She showed every sign of enjoying the luster of contact with her new converts. Even in Glasgow, Pillsbury recorded, she was "as inac-

58. Stowe, *Sunny Memories*, 60–63, 73–74; *ASR*, May 2, 1853; W. Smeal to M. Estlin, May 17, 1853, in BPL-W; W. Smeal to L. A. Chamerovzow, April 16, 1853, C36/52, D. Macallan to L. A. Chamerovzow, September 16, 1853, C33/127, both in ASP; Aberdeen *Herald*, April 23, 1853.

59. G. Gilfillan to S. Dobell, May 1, 1853, cited in Shepperson, "Harriet Beecher Stowe and Scotland," 40; S. Pugh to R. D. Webb, May 28, 1853, in BPL-G.

60. L. Beecher to A. Tappan, April 23, 1833, quoted in B. M. Cross (ed.), *The Autobiography of Lyman Beecher* (2 vols.; Cambridge, Mass., 1961), II, 242.

cessible to *mortals* . . . as though they had seated her on top of Olympus." It was in Edinburgh, however, that Mrs. Stowe had her first delicious taste of life with the upper ten thousand. While living with the Wighams, she had her first letter from Lord Morpeth, by then the earl of Carlisle, and from Harriet Elizabeth Georgiana Leveson-Gower, the duchess of Sutherland. Even during this first visit, Eliza Wigham complained that she had little chance to talk to her, for she was always resting or attending meetings. On her second visit to Edinburgh, she had passed completely outside the sphere of the middle-class abolitionists. She made all her calls at the houses of landed magnates or of intellectuals whose celebrity equaled her own—Sir William Drummond of Hawthornden, the earl of Gainsborough, George Combe the phrenologist, and Sir William Hamilton of the chair of moral philosophy.[61] Once in London, though she still fraternized with the Gurneys and other great magnates of the London Committee, even the synopsis of her *Sunny Memories of Foreign Lands* mentions enough meetings with members of the titled aristocracy to satisfy the most snobbish American for a lifetime. It was the cachet attached to this group that gave Lord Shaftesbury's "Stafford House Address," named after the duchess' London residence and inspired by Mrs. Stowe, its momentum.

The new situation created by these alliances also gave fine opportunities for denouncing the British aristocracy through the use of the slavery issue. It was nothing new for slavery to become a vehicle for the canvassing of other problems. Wilberforce found that his views became a means of drawing attention to the depredations of the press gangs. W. E. Aytoun, the author of the nostalgic *Lays of the Cavaliers*, even expressed his distress at the failure of America to pay royalties to men like Dickens and himself by denouncing the republican thugs of the plantations. For Tories in general, it was tempting to point to the abuses of slavery as evidence of the flaws in democracy.[62] This was precisely why

61. P. Pillsbury to S. May, April 27, 1855, in BPL-M; Stowe, *Sunny Memories*, 60, 126–28; E. Wigham to M. Estlin, April 28, 1853, in BPL-W.

62. *A Letter to Wm. Wilberforce, M.P., on the Subject of Impressment: Calling on Him and the Philanthropists of This Country to Prove Those Feelings of Sensibility They Expressed in the Cause of Humanity on Negro Slavery, by Acting with the Same Ardour and Zeal in the Cause of British Seamen* (London, 1816);

the fashionable support for Mrs. Stowe was so enthusiastic, and in turn it gave splendid opportunities for denouncing aristocratic hypocrisy. It was all too easy to denounce the furor in Stafford House as "one of their periodic fits of benevolence," to look forward to a Scottish theme by making a special mention of the silence of the duchess and her friends over the misery of the Clearances, which saw cottar populations forcibly evicted to open parts of the Highlands to become sheep farms. The sympathies of the landlords, noted one critic, "demand something blacker and more distant."[63]

Mrs. Stowe's misfortune was that she arrived in Scotland at a time when the tensions between the landed rich and the poor had been accentuated by the Clearances, even in lowland areas that were not directly affected.[64] She did not avoid working people; if anything, rather the contrary. She was even pleased that the "workingmen's soiree" held for her in Glasgow had "more nationality" than the middle-class one. But she never seems to have understood the bitter divisions of the society in which she was campaigning. Even in lowland Aberdeen, an anonymous correspondent, in "a proud, testifying spirit," had presented her with a manifesto on poverty and prison statistics. It described the Scots whom she perceived so romantically as "a gey ignorant, proud, drunken pack; they manage to pay ilka year for whiskey one million three hundred and forty eight thousand pounds."[65] This was nothing to the storm she created by eulogizing the Clearances as "a sublime example of progress." She could hardly have written more ineptly: "As to those ridiculous stories about the Duchess of Sutherland . . . one has only to be here, moving in society, to see

W. E. Aytoun, "The American's Apostrophe to Boz," in *Stories and Verse*, ed. W. L. Renwick (Edinburgh, 1964), 314; N. W. Senior, *American Slavery: A Reprint of an Article on "Uncle Tom's Cabin" . . . and of Mr. Sumner's Speech, with a Notice of the Events Which Followed That Speech* (London, 1856), 38–39.

63. *The Fashionable Philanthropy of the Day: Some Plain Speaking About American Slavery—A Letter Addressed to the Stoweites of England and Scotland, by a Briton* (London, 1853), 7–8, 29. Cf. *Slavery Past and Present; or, Notes on Uncle Tom's Cabin, Edited by a Lady* (London, 1852).

64. A. Mackenzie, *The History of the Highland Clearances* (Inverness, 1883), 162–406; J. Prebble, *The Highland Clearances* (London, 1963); Stowe, *Sunny Memories*, 48–50, 93, 107.

65. "An Old Bachelor" to H. B. Stowe, April 21, 1853, dated Stonehaven, in Stowe, *Sunny Memories*, 78–80.

how excessively absurd they are.... Imagine, then, what people must think when they find in respectable prints the absurd story of her turning her tenants out into the snow, and ordering their cottages to be set on fire because they would not go out." Unfortunately the absurd stories were true, as the trial of Patrick Sellar, the duke of Sutherland's factor, later established. It was perhaps because Harriet Martineau knew of these other works of the house of Sutherland that she had written to Eliza Cabot Follen "denouncing in no uncertain terms 'the Duchess' and all her anti-slavery works."[66]

In Scotland the denunciation was fuller and more bitter. It was principally set out by one Donald McLeod, a Sutherlandshire stonemason who was eventually forced to emigrate to Canada. He was able to make great capital out of the duchess' unwillingness to extend her compassion from Negroes to crofters. He had no interest in supporting slavery, which, he wrote "is *damnable*, and the most disgusting word in the English or any other language." He had been spurred on by finding that the landlords had "procured an American literary luminary, who promises well to whitewash their foul deeds, particularly the Sutherlandshire depopulators (*of the long purse*)." He reprinted much of his correspondence to Scottish newspapers during 1853, and went on to denounce *Sunny Memories* specifically. The Clearances, he remarked, were "the shortest process of civilization in the history of nations ... the whole interior of the county of Sutherland ... in eight years converted to a solitary wilderness." He pointedly asked how the Uncle Tom Penny Offering money had been spent, and asked whether supporters like Thomas Guthrie of the Free Church might not have been influenced by the "cart loads and hurly loads of deer carcasses and of fowl" gifted by his parishioner the duchess. He concluded, with absolute justice, that "for the sake of aristocratic adulation and admiration ... you have exposed yourself to be publicly chastised by an old Highland Scotch broken down stone mason."[67]

66. *Ibid.*, 219–20, 227–28. *Cf.* I. Grimble, *The Trial of Patrick Sellar* (London, 1963); S. Pugh to M. Estlin, March 10, 1853, in EP.
67. D. McLeod, *Donald McLeod's Gloomy Memories in the Highlands of Scotland: Versus Mrs. Stowe's Sunny Memories in (England) a Foreign Land: Or a Faithful Picture of the Extirpation of the Celtic Race from the Highlands of Scotland* (Toronto, 1857), 76, 91, 82–88, 71.

The chastisement made not a whit of difference to the craze for Mrs. Stowe; if anything it was accelerated. For new middle-class adherents, the allure of the new movement was in its very connection with the aristocracy McLeod denounced. The "Stafford House Address" was offensive to most old-style abolitionists because of its outmoded gradualist position and its admission of the dangers of emancipation. Mary Howitt, who did join the committee promoting the address, was promptly visited by a delegation sent by the BFASS to ask her to change her mind. The *Reporter* tried to get up a parallel address on immediatist lines. The *Slave* gave only qualified approval. Webb's *Advocate* ignored it. Thompson expressed dissatisfaction with Shaftesbury's guarded language. The Bristol and Clifton Ladies' Anti-Slavery Society flatly refused to cooperate.[68]

One of the few British radical abolitionists who fully accepted the "Stafford House Address" was Wilson Armistead. He was willing to use *any* weapon against slavery, and he was quick to perceive the change in the nature of the movement's recruits. It was probably for them, at the start of his *Cloud of Witnesses*, that he produced the trump of the three duchesses, one marchioness, fifteen countesses, seven viscountesses, seven ladies of baronets, and an "etc." who had signed the address. The old abolitionists had been quite aware of the advantage of being able to use the right names in the right places. Two years before, while trying to prepare another address, Susan Cabot had observed that "there were two lists of names made out, [one of] those of whom work was expected, and the other whose names and station entitle them to consideration." But leaders like Smeal and Webb, Eliza Wigham and Catherine Paton, did not take to antislavery as a means of becoming associated with the great. They too may sometimes have hungered for status, but they did not expect to acquire it by slogging on with their work for the slave. Mrs. Stowe's new followers did expect this kind of advantage, for even dissenters could now safely look up to the aristocracy as moral and social models. When even the monarchy had adopted an ethic of respectability in which

68. M. Howitt (ed.), *Mary Howitt: An Autobiography* (2 vols.; London, 1889), I, 92; *ASR*, January 1, 1853, February 1, 1853; *Slave*, February, 1853; Thompson, *A Lecture Delivered in the Music Hall, Store Street*, 45; Minute for December 17, 1852, in BCMB; E. Wigham to M. Estlin, March 22, 1853, in BPL-W.

the middle class was itself now secure, there was little reason why the peerage should be perceived as anything but an elite extension of the bourgeoisie, even in itself a role model. In lauding Mrs. Stowe and signing the address, new converts who had previously given little thought to the slave were gaining cheap social cachet. Like Trollope's John Vavasour, in *Can You Forgive Her?* they were simply "growing up, towards the light, as the trees do."[69]

For the duchess of Sutherland and friends in her own class, the furor over Mrs. Stowe had a different function. Their commitment did not involve making a considered judgment on American slavery. What *Uncle Tom* had taught them was the pleasing lesson "that democrats may be tyrants, that an aristocracy of caste is more oppressive than an aristocracy of station." At the same time, they gained the cachet of good literary taste through their association with Mrs. Stowe. *Uncle Tom* was the most popular book of the generation, and strange as it may now seem it was then thought one of the best. Even the London *Times*, which disapproved of abolition and was surprised to find a woman who could write, admitted that it was "at every railway book stall in England, and in every third traveller's hand."[70] A more important reason for the extraordinary surge of fashionable interest in slavery was that Mrs. Stowe's appeal was grounded in a form of sensibility that was intellectually and morally less exacting than that of the less genteel abolitionist writers of the thirties and forties. The duchess of Sutherland had welcomed the American visitors to the World's Anti-Slavery Convention, and she had been known to contribute to the *Liberty Bell*. But it is not an accident that as she walked into the BFASS annual meeting with Mrs. Stowe at her side, she was heard to whisper that they were in for "one of our genuine Exeter Hall 'brays.'"[71]

It is unlikely that Mrs. Stowe herself saw the Negro either as a Sambo or as a creature not fully improvable. At least one edition

69. W. Armistead, *A Cloud of Witnesses Against Slavery*, 1; S. Cabot to M. Estlin, October 30, 1851, in EP; A Trollope, *Can You Forgive Her?*, ed. S. Wall (London, 1972, 1864), 240.

70. Senior, *American Slavery*, 38–39; London *Times*, September 3, 1852.

71. Wilson, *Crusader in Crinoline*, 229; "Extract of a Letter," *Liberty Bell* (Boston, 1844), 179–81.

of her *Dred* contains an edition of the *Confessions of Nat Turner*; and she was interested, though in a confused way, in various plans of black education, which culminated in her Mandarin settlement after the Civil War.[72] Still, the message of black inferiority is present in Uncle Tom for those who wish to find it. It was certainly found by those Britons and Americans who were going through the same revulsion as Knox and Carlyle against the old views of black improvability. Within the tradition of sensibility, this did not prevent a gush of pity for the slave, which could be projected into desultory good works on his behalf. *Uncle Tom* brought substantial sums of money into the underworld by giving new opportunities to blacks and their sponsors who played "the scaldrum dodge" as injured black slaves forced to beg for survival. Mrs. Stowe's message of compassion was a simple and appealing one, and it had a startling effect both on aristocratic and middle-class Stoweites. After an aristocratic hostess had shown her works by Claude, Murillo, and Velasquez, one American visitor was shocked to find that the next entertainment was "Negro Melodies!!!—'The Blue-Tail Fly' . . . received with acclamations of delight."[73] What it did not carry with it was the obligation accepted both by Garrisonians and Tappanites, sometimes even by Mrs. Stowe, that pity for the Negro carried with it a great deal of hard work, in helping him demonstrate his potential for equality, or in laboring patiently to convert the white world to abolition principles. They too were excited by fugitive-slave literature, by sensibility when in its proper place, sometimes even by *Uncle Tom* itself, but their excitement was modulated by a series of riders on black improvability and white duty. These gave their commitment an entirely different quality from that of the Stafford House enthusiasts.

Most of the remaining members of the antislavery societies would have agreed with Wendell Phillips that the fuss over *Uncle*

72. Cf. J. C. Furnas, *Goodbye to Uncle Tom* (New York, 1956), 47–51, and H. B. Stowe, *Dred: A Tale of the Great Dismal Swamp* (London, 1856), appendix; *Anti-Slavery Advocate*, July, 1853; E. Wigham to M. Estlin, April 28, 1853, in BPL-W. The Mandarin settlement is described in a series of letters from Mrs. Stowe to Mary Estlin, especially December 21, 1868 in EP.

73. K. Chesney, *The Victorian Underworld* (New York, 1970), 201; A. M. Fay, *Victorian Days in England: Letters of an American Girl, 1851–52* (Boston, 1923), 84.

Tom was "mere sentimental excitement."[74] It was once said of George Thompson, in many ways the typical voice of the Scots and other provincial abolitionists, that "his appeals are to the understanding & the conscience, & not to the sympathies, & hence the impression he creates will be permanent, & will not, like that of too many popular speakers, quickly pass away."[75] Mrs. Stowe's appeals left little scope for conscience or understanding, for their principal effect was to generate romantic pity for the Negro. In America, the movement had reached a stage at which it could profit from even the briefest flush of unthinking enthusiasm for the slave, whether it was expressed in voting behavior or in mass popular protest. In Britain, however, it was difficult for pity to be sustained or applied if it was not accompanied by a more complex commitment. The aim of the movement Thompson represented so well was to apply the institutional energies of the antislavery societies to the conversion of the individual. He might be converted by moral or theological argument, or by proof that slavery was inexpedient or unprofitable. In either case the central assumptions were that black people were potentially if not actually equal to whites and that conversion carried with it a lifetime obligation to convert others until slavery collapsed under the sheer weight of moral numbers. Mrs. Stowe may not have excluded these concepts, but most of her British followers did. It was for this reason that she disturbed the leaders of the old societies, but also proved able to raise short-term mass support of an order their unglamorous preoccupations could no longer hope to attract.

For the duchess and her followers, pity, legitimized by the long tradition of romantic sensibility, was a ladylike emotion. An intensely felt responsibility for individual conversion was not. The loyalty of the Stoweites also carried with it the satisfaction of buttressing existing prejudices against republicanism in general, but particularly in the United States. The old movement was based on a preference or even an admiration for American institutions.

---

74. W. Phillips to E. Pease, November 21, 1852, in BPL-G. See also E. Wigham to M. Estlin, March 22, 1853, in BPL-W; M. W. Chapman to M. Estlin, July 4, 1853, in BPL-E; S. Pugh to M. Estlin, June 26, 1853, in EP; *Anti-Slavery Advocate*, January, 1853.

75. S. S. Foster to W. L. Garrison, April 31, 1851, in BPL-G.

The new saw slavery as the final proof of their inadequacy.[76] In Scotland and indeed in Britain, Mrs. Stowe's success among the rich and powerful was dazzling. But it was bought at the cost of abandoning the old assumption that the black was as rational a being as the white, prevented only by his environment from realizing his true potential. John Murray would not have liked Mrs. Stowe. Indeed, the handful of Scottish Garrisonians he had left behind him had even less to gain from Mrs. Stowe's visits than their new organization rivals. Her second and third visits, in 1856 and 1859, changed the situation but little. The 1853 one fully bore out George Thompson's gloomy prophecy that she would "be almost fully in the hands . . . of those who have sought to deprecate and even destroy the true Anti-Slavery party in the U.S."[77]

After absorbing *Uncle Tom's Cabin* and Mrs. Stowe, Scotland certainly had more men and women who could loosely be classified as abolitionists than before. On the other hand, it had fewer who were regularly involved in the movement to the extent of frequent attendance at antislavery meetings or even voluntary reading of nonfictional forms of antislavery propaganda. This does not mean that Stafford House had killed the antislavery societies. They were already declining when the decade opened, and after Mrs. Stowe had gone home there would still be enough energy for the New Ladies' Anti-Slavery Association to be formed in Edinburgh. It is even likely that they profited slightly from the excitement she had caused. The Old Calabar affair, the attempts to unite the British Garrisonians, even Chamerovzow's ill-fated 1854 convention, all come after the Uncle Tom Penny Offering and the Stafford House Address. With the Civil War, in fact, the Scots themselves reunited in a vigorous campaign, first to promote emancipation and then to send help to the freedmen.[78] Though this is another story, there was still much antislavery energy to be tapped in Scotland.

Neither these continuities, nor the *Uncle Tom* excitement, can

76. *Cf.* H. Martineau, *The Martyr Age of the United States of America* (Newcastle, 1840), and Senior, *American Slavery*, 38–39.
77. G. Thompson to A. W. Weston, March 4, 1853, in BPL-W.
78. H. M. Finnie, "Scottish Attitudes Towards American Reconstruction, 1865–1877" (Ph.D. dissertation, University of Edinburgh, 1975).

obscure the sense that by 1853 the tempo had slackened, that the old themes had become blurred. The eschatological urgency of abolition had all but disappeared. By 1858, James Douglas of Cavers, now a very old man, was almost alone in pointing to American slavery as Satan and his lieutenants Mammon and Moloch embodied. Even the old feuds had lost the zest of the forties. Thompson founded a new and radical London Emancipation Committee in 1859, and when he and Douglass clashed flamboyantly in Glasgow in the following year it was like a breath from another world. The old passions had run down, and the energy going into the societies was minimal except when there were important visitors from overseas. In 1857 the Glasgow New Association for the Abolition of Slavery could announce that "a report of our last year's proceedings would scarcely be of sufficient importance to warrant our calling you together to hear it read."[79] That the fervor of the Stoweites could evaporate so swiftly is the best proof of its difference from the dogged work of the past. That it was not replaced by other activity shows how far the old movement had run into the sand. For all its pacifism, it was only the call of the Civil War that raised it from its slumber.

79. J. Douglas, *The American Revival* (Edinburgh, 1858); J. Botsford, "Scotland and the American Civil War" (Ph.D. dissertation, University of Edinburgh, 1956), 64–85; London Emancipation Committee, *Tract No. 5* (London, 1860); *Sixth Annual Report of the Glasgow New Association for the Abolition of Slavery* (Glasgow, 1857), 5.

CHAPTER 7

In Conclusion

In 1859, George Thompson, the English doyen of Scottish anti-slavery, was financially on his beam ends. The failure of the *Empire* had forced him to go to India as the agent for a dubious firm interested in pioneering new forms of textile fibers. The firm failed, and he returned to London after narrowly escaping death from a bout of "bilious fever," followed by some kind of paralytic attack. His confessed debts were only a little over a hundred pounds, but he had no money. His American friends still thought enough of his importance for the movement to get up a testimonial of $2,200. Mrs. Chapman herself sent fifty dollars. Nothing had happened, in almost thirty years, to shake the faith of American abolitionists in the British alliance. It was not necessary to be as radical as Parker Pillsbury to believe that its "moral influence against the awful iniquity is a voice of seven thunders in the ear of the oppressed."[1]

Thompson found that there was still much to be gained by continuing his work in antislavery. At the end of 1860 British abolitionists, like their American counterparts, reaffirmed their appreciation of his services with a small testimonial of five hundred pounds. As the war approached, the intensity of concern over America began to pick up again. When Sarah Remond was invited to Edinburgh by Eliza Wigham, it was once again possible to raise an audience of two thousand to hear her. Martin Delany, the black

1. F. Chesson to W. L. Garrison, January 16, 1856, in *Empire*, February 8, 1856, cutting in Thompson Scrapbooks, VII, in LC; S. May to W. L. Garrison, January 17, 1859, in BPL-M; G. Thompson to S. H. Gay, January 24, 1859, in Gay Papers, Columbia University Library; M. W. Chapman to W. L. Garrison, February 16, 1859, in BPL-G; W. Phillips to A. K. Foster, n.d., in Foster Papers, American Antiquarian Society; P. Pillsbury to F. N. Tribe, May 1, 1854, *Anti-Slavery Advocate*, June, 1854.

nationalist and Pan-Africanist, was also feted in Edinburgh when he came north after his appearance at the 1860 International Statistical Congress in London. George Barrell Cheever, of the Church of the Pilgrims in New York, found that the Scottish clergy, including old Free Churchmen like Dr. Candlish, rushed to testify against his congregation's attempt to silence him on slavery.[2] The Scots abolitionists, and indeed the British public as a whole, were rediscovering their interest in an American situation that was becoming more dramatic by the week. They too shared the awareness of their friends overseas that "the conflict between free institutions and slave institutions is seen and acknowledged to be irrepressible . . . all this is a sign that the end is rapidly approaching. Peaceably or by a bloody process, the oppressed will eventually obtain their freedom, and nothing can prevent it."[3]

Quick to sense the improving situation, Thompson founded his London Emancipation Committee in the summer of 1859. There was enough interest for him to continue working through it until after the beginning of the war and indeed to turn it towards channeling British support to the Union. He could even afford, once again, to follow up disagreements over tactics at the expense of unity within the movement. Although Douglass and he toured briefly together in the northern states early in 1860, their later Scottish quarrel was the last verse of an old song silenced only by the war.[4] As for the relationship with the BFASS, Thompson soon returned to denouncing Chamerovzow's "prostitution" of his official position.[5] Some of the old passion was already beginning to

2. "To the Friends of George Thompson," circular, August 9, 1860, E. Richardson to W. L. Garrison, December 12, 1860, both in BPL-G; *ASR*, November 1, 1860; J. Botsford, "Scotland and the American Civil War" (Ph.D. dissertation, University of Edinburgh, 1956), 105; R. Blackett, "In Search of International Support for African Colonization: Martin R. Delaney's Visit to England, 1860," *Journal of Canadian History*, X (1975), 29–34; G. C. Taylor, "Some American Reformers and Their Influence on Reform Movements in Great Britain from 1830 to 1860" (Ph.D. dissertation, University of Edinburgh, 1960), 139ff.; *ASR*, January 2, 1860; W. Wilson, *Memorials of Robert Smith Candlish, D.D.* (Edinburgh, 1880), 490.

3. W. L. Garrison to J. M. McKim, October 21, 1860, in BPL-G.

4. H. R. Temperley, *British Anti-Slavery, 1833–1870* (London, 1972), 254–55; *ASR*, January 2, 1860; London Emancipation Committee, *Tract No. 5* (London, 1860); Botsford, "Scotland and the American Civil War," 64–85.

5. G. Thompson to L. A. Chamerovzow, July 25, 1859, C37/7, July 28, 1859,

reemerge when the situation was transformed by the news of the war. It brought the Scottish reformers hurrying back to their anti-slavery posts.

The relationship of the Scots abolitionists to America during the war and Reconstruction was quite different from what it had been in the antebellum period. When George Thompson made his third visit to America in 1864–1865, he was reunited joyfully with Garrison. The two men, rich in years, went together as official guests to watch the Union flag rise again over Fort Sumter. Thompson, the man who had been unable to pay his way as radical M.P. for Tower Hamlets, was invited to the White House as the honored guest of President Lincoln.[6] To many, this seemed the apogee of a long tradition of cooperation. What it signified, in fact, was that the continuities had been broken. To a Union fighting physically to hold itself together, foreign support was not only a diplomatic guarantee but a psychological reassurance that the blood of brethren was not being spilled in vain. British approval was not merely welcomed, but sought after.[7] For the previous thirty years the antislavery connection had had very different functions. For the American abolitionists, internationalism had been in part a defense mechanism against their minority position in a Union that spurned them as a divisive and irresponsible faction. To their opponents, British support had been clear proof of a foreign conspiracy against the liberties of the republic, which was epitomized by the onslaught against slavery itself. The efforts of the Scots fitted neatly into this schema because of the remembered strength of Scottish loyalism in the revolutionary period, the prominence of Scots in the imperial army, and the supposed deviousness of the Scottish character. The net effect of interference was simply to confirm each party in its own views.

C37/7a, both in ASP. *Cf. ASR*, September 1, 1859, which reports Thompson's attendance at one BFASS rally in 1859. An Emancipation Committee address, July, 1860, C37/7c, in ASP, which criticized Broad Street, was discussed cordially in committee in Minute for August 3, 1860, BFASS Minute Books, III.

6. *WLG*, IV, 137–52; R. D. Webb to E. Quincy, March 27, 1851, copy from collection of Walter Merrill; M. W. Chapman to M. Estlin, October 29, 1855, in EP.

7. C. Bolt, *The Anti-Slavery Movement and Reconstruction, 1833–1877: A Study in Anglo-American Cooperation* (London, 1969), 26–170; H. M. Finnie, "Scottish Attitudes Towards American Reconstruction, 1865–1877" (Ph.D. dissertation, University of Edinburgh, 1975).

Nothing illustrates this better than Thompson's earlier visits to America. When he first crossed the Atlantic, thirty years before his invitation to the White House, Andrew Jackson in his annual message denounced him as a foreign incendiary. After his 1851 visit, he complained innocently that his activities had been misrepresented and denounced merely because he was a British member of Parliament talking on an American domestic question. The abolitionists themselves, to do them justice, were less surprised. One observed that "the appearance of a Foreigner in the field in an occasion of peculiar excitement gives the advocates of slavery an opportunity to change the issue." This could not have been more true. When Thompson lectured in Springfield, Massachusetts, a hostile mob hung his and John Bull's effigies side by side on the town green.[8] He was also mobbed in the 1850–1851 winter, though not so frequently as in 1834–1835. Few British efforts to help American abolitionists were as flamboyant, or as easy to react to, as Thompson's appearances on the other side of the Atlantic—but his reception epitomized the tendency of the British connection to polarize rather than convert. By the fifties, indeed, the Scottish movement was weakened, and it was not clear what reasonable people could actually do to influence the outcome of a conflict that was increasingly political.

The sixties were another story. The Civil War and Reconstruction gave new opportunities for foreign benevolence, and the last phase of the Scottish movement, after 1861, saw an extraordinary revival of interest in the Negro. Scottish opinion was by no means uniformly sympathetic to the North. In Glasgow, for instance, the city exported iron and shipping supplies to the South, and its pro-Confederate feeling was still strong when Jefferson Davis was triumphantly received there in 1869.[9] There was also a good deal of sympathy for the South as a young nation fighting in the romantic traditions of Mazzini and Kossuth. Scots of all opinions found the

8. G. Thompson, *Speech . . . Delivered at the Anti-Slavery Meeting, Broadmead, Bristol, September 4th, 1851* (Bristol, 1851), 20–21; J. Sargent to J. B. Estlin, December 6, 1850, in EP; G. Thompson to A. K. Foster, February 17, 1851, in Foster Papers. *Cf.* G. F. Simmons, *Public Spirit and Mobs: Two Sermons Delivered . . . After the Thompson Riot* (Springfield, 1851).

9. Botsford, "Scotland and the American Civil War," 337–38, 773–79; Finnie, "Scottish Attitudes Towards American Reconstruction," I, 50, 83. The following account is drawn almost wholly from Finnie's massive study.

war and its aftermath fascinating, and they followed American events closely as part of their "continuous appraisal of the complex experiment in democratic Republicanism." With occasional exceptions like Mrs. Stowe's admirer George Gilfillan, reform-minded Scots followed the lead of the *Caledonian Mercury* and John Bright's brother-in-law Duncan Maclaren, to whom the Confederacy was a conspiracy against democratic values. The Scottish churches were conscious that this was a period for closing the gulf slavery had opened between them and their American brethren. With the Old Calabar incident behind it, the United Presbyterian Church became pro-Union and to a limited extent even pro-Garrison. The Free Church itself plunged into freedmen's aid work, where two of the most prominent Scottish leaders were Robert Candlish and William Nixon, who had so belabored the radical abolitionists in 1846. Funds were sent to America by the churches as well as by strong freedmen's aid societies in Edinburgh, Glasgow, Dundee, and Aberdeen, and there was also activity in smaller towns like Perth, Banff, and Peterhead. The GES and the Edinburgh Ladies' Emancipation Society also helped, more modestly, in raising money. The total amount sent to America for the freedmen between 1865 and 1868 was about £10,500. The antislavery movement survived into the postwar period, but it did so without the rancor and backbiting that had characterized its earlier history. Even in 1863, Eliza Wigham was able to write her *Anti-Slavery Cause and Its Martyrs* without mentioning the divisions between the different American factions.[10]

When Jefferson Davis visited the battlefield of Culloden, he was pointed out to a local shepherd as the sometime president of the Confederacy: "And what was the Southern Confederacy, as ye ca' it? Was it in England? Or was it a Limited Liability Company?"[11] Probably he spoke for many Scots to whom the affairs of America were remote and the problem of slavery an abstraction. His ignorance, assuming it was unfeigned, comes as less of a surprise than

10. Finnie, "Scottish Attitudes Towards American Reconstruction," I, 19, II, 375, 419–20, 491–583, III, 165–207; E. Wigham, *The Anti-Slavery Cause in America and Its Martyrs* (London, 1863).

11. C. Mackay, *Through the Long Day* (2 vols.; London, 1887), II, 367–68, cited in Finnie, "Scottish Attitudes Towards American Reconstruction," I, 61.

the preoccupation of the Scottish abolitionists with the social institutions of a foreign country. For a period of forty-five years, the
country's whole churchgoing middle class was kept closely in
touch with events in America. An active minority of its members
was always involved in abolitionist societies that were principally
but not exclusively aimed at overthrowing slavery in the southern
United States.

The fortunes of these societies were not unmixedly prosperous.
In the thirties, they were broadly united, and the support they
attracted for American emancipation was occasionally not far short
of the levels it had reached in the campaign against West India
slavery. What was different was that the abolitionist leadership
was drawn from voluntary or dissenting denominations rather than
the established Church of Scotland that had dominated it before
1833. After 1841, Scottish abolitionists split up in a precise reflection of the schisms in the American movement. Slavery itself, and
the tactical disagreements of its opponents, thereafter became a
means of expressing the bitter controversies of Scottish church
life. Perhaps the excitement of the forties was artificially sustained
by the fascination of clerical squabbles, but in either case the fifties saw the Scottish antislavery societies enter a time of relative
weakness. This was partly due to the changed American situation,
which left little real scope for foreign abolitionists to work in concrete ways, and partly to the enervating effect of continuous internal feuding. British abolitionists continued to squabble furiously,
however small their numbers, and they continued to rank themselves along the line between old and new organization when the
gathering political momentum of antislavery had carried the attention of American abolitionists into new quarters. The outburst of
enthusiasm for Mrs. Stowe, after 1851, did help disguise the plight
of the abolitionist societies but did little to promote or sustain ongoing agitation of the old sort. Only the Civil War and Reconstruction presented new hopes and new opportunities to help the slave
directly. The sixties, like the thirties, were united, energetic, and
relatively uncomplicated. The Scottish reform public, stimulated
by the discoveries of David Livingstone, had meanwhile returned
to its original interest in the African slave trade. Nevertheless,
their intense interest in North American slavery had survived for
almost half a century.

The motives behind the Scottish antislavery commitment were complex, and it is easier to define what they were not than what they were. Above all, they were not selfish and they were not sinister. Coleridge, while staying in Scotland, had written long before that it was hard "not to become disgusted with active Benevolence, or despondent because there is a *Philanthropy-Trade*—It is a sort of Benefit Club of Virtue, supported by the contribution of *Paupers* in Virtue."[12] This would not have been a fair comment for the mid-Victorian abolitionists. It is probably true that the Scottish antislavery societies were part of the elaborate network of institutions by which the possession of status was defined in each city.[13] It is also likely that Mrs. Stowe's followers, with their anxiety to grow upwards towards the light, were interested in antislavery in part because of the status they might acquire through their involvement. But the concerns of the general run of old-style abolitionists were much deeper, more complex than a wish to regain status that was slipping away from them or to secure status to which they now felt entitled. This does not exclude a wish to be seen as recognizably good men and women, for the moral approval of others was an important supplement to the moral approval of self upon which the soothing of religious anxieties depended. Insofar as this was a factor, however, it was far removed from a hunger for social status understood in the Weberian sense. They did not share all the drives that seem to have carried middle-class Americans into benevolent work. Their sense of mission, their conception of a specific national preparation for the millennium, was no deeper than for normal evangelical protestants. In the Napoleonic Wars they had fought against the Beast, that is, exegetically on the correct side, so that if they had received a divine warning, it did not stem from anything so obvious as the War of 1812. They were also stable and well-adjusted men and women, for whom psychobiography would yield only a series of different individual conclusions.[14]

12. K. Coburn (ed.), *The Notebooks of Samuel Taylor Coleridge* (London, 1973), III, 4067.

13. C. D. Rice, "Abolitionists and Abolitionism in Aberdeen," *Northern Scotland*, I (1972), 86–87.

14. *Cf.* D. Donald, "Toward a Reconsideration of Abolitionists," in *Lincoln Reconsidered* (New York, 1961), 19–36; J. Gusfield, *Symbolic Crusade: Status Politics and the Temperance Movement* (Urbana, Ill., 1963); E. L. Tuveson, *Redeemer Nation: The Idea of America's Millennial Role* (Chicago, 1968); W. Gribbin, *The*

It is tempting, however, to speculate that the commitment of the Scots abolitionists can be explained by some of the same hypotheses that explain their American colleagues. The eschatological concerns that fueled the anxiety of converted evangelicals over slavery were shared throughout the Atlantic reform world. Slavery could become a symbol for the atonement, the accountability, for sin itself, for guilt. The most common ongoing phenomenon, however, was concern over slavery as a paradigmatic antithesis of moral free agency. Thompson spoke even more evocatively than he knew when he announced that the American slave was "an animated hoeing Machine in the Fields."[15] The slave's condition represented a total loss of moral autonomy. To a generation whose principal guide to behavior was the individual capacity to make internal ethical choices, denouncing slavery may have been a compelling way of expressing a personal self-confidence that was very often not there. Their intense interest in sexuality may tell the same story. The Scots and other provincial abolitionists were exposed to lurid documents like Weld's *Slavery As It Is* and to the titillating episodes of the slave narratives. They listened raptly to endless denunciations of the South as bordello, to cries like Thompson's "one vast brothel . . . a great lazar house . . . where the chastest female is liable to be compelled to yield herself up for the brutal lusts of the demi-devil that beckons for her from the field, or commands her to his house (intense sensation)." This was not just a prurient interest. Over sex, as over authority and free agency, the abolitionist middle class made slavery a symbol of what it agonizingly felt it might itself become without the restraints of personal control.[16]

Such hypotheses may or may not be accurate. Even if they are

Churches Militant: The War of 1812 and American Religion (New Haven, Conn., 1973); L. Perry, "Psychology and the Abolitionists: Reflections on Martin Duberman and the Neoabolitionists of the 1960's," *Reviews in American History*, II (1974), 309–22.

15. Masthead of the *Anti-Slavery Watchman*, November, 1853. The full quotation, which encapsulates much of the complexity of antislavery motives, is "The American slave is an animated hoeing-Machine in the Fields; a pampered or a scourged hound in the house; a dumb Chattel in the Court of Justice; a leper in the house of prayer; an Outcast even from the Christian churchyard."

16. G. Thompson, *Speech . . . Delivered . . . Broadmead, Bristol*, 17–18; R. G. Walters, "The Erotic South: Civilization and Sexuality in American Abolitionism," *AQ*, XXV (1973), 177–210.

accurate for Scottish reformers, they were certainly not unique to them. However, if they did suffer from anxieties about personal moral control at a time of a rapid change in values, this would help explain why the movement declined so in the fifties. Perhaps the age of equipoise was a reality, in that the new values of autonomy and self-control were now universally accepted by the churchgoing middle class. They had also been adopted by a large section of the respectable working class and by much of the aristocracy. It must have been deeply reassuring to find swelling numbers of skilled laborers intoning the Protestant ethic at temperance soirees. The Prince Regent, who had gone with his entourage to boxing matches and other scenes of vice, was a distant memory, the Prince Consort a new pledge for the virtue of the ruling class.[17] Victorian England, superficially at least, had become ethically homogeneous. At the same time, concern over the "hoeing machine" aspects of industrial organization lessened as the paternalistic image of a preindustrial society receded into the past. The anxieties left to express had become less pressing. Until new concerns were raised by the war itself, antislavery of the old sort only retained an appeal for the handful whose commitment had become so intense as to be an end in itself.

In either case, the Scots were kept interested in antislavery by peculiar stresses and tensions of their own. Their position within the total British society was a peculiar one. Their distance from the national political structure doubtless made it attractive to them to become involved in an international campaign in which the main action was foreign though in a sense not appreciably more remote to them than what happened at Westminster. It can be no accident that they showed so little interest, after 1838, in slavery in the colonies, and so much in slavery in America. Again, the problems of authority and subjection for which the the slave relationship could become a paradigm were especially pressing for a group uncertain about the position of their class within their nation, and their nation within their country. This problem was more acute for the voluntary denominations, for whom the surrogate

17. K. Chesney, *The Victorian Underworld* (New York, 1970), 266–67; I. Bradley, *The Call to Seriousness: The Evangelical Impact on the Victorians* (London, 1976), 55–56.

political life of the churches also revolved around anxiety over the distribution of authority. It is no coincidence that the voluntaries were the most important element in the Scottish movement after 1833.

Within the national context, too, the Scots made special use of the movement's disunity to express and further their own local concerns. They were always ambivalent about metropolitan control, and those who chose a Garrisonian position clearly resented the BFASS's attempts at centralization as much as its faulty ideology. They would all have understood what one of Mary Estlin's West Country friends meant when she wrote that "the *London* Society have treated the provincials as they almost invariably do . . . Vide Brit[ish] & For[eign] Schools—Home and Colonial Infant Schools—etc. etc. etc."[18] For those who felt that too many areas of their lives were already controlled from the center it must have been easy to slip into using antislavery as another device for expressing their resentment. Locally, too, the discussion of abolition could be used to project many forms of hostility. An antislavery consensus was now assumed, but it was still tempting for one church to use disagreements over tactics against others, especially given the emotive meanings attached to the very concept of slavery. This does not mean that the commitment of Scottish abolitionists should be seen as a mechanistic and cold one. The compassion they felt towards the slave was real, and it involved them in much hard work. But this was only one level of motivation. What brought them to the point of feeling and constantly reinforcing that compassion, to the point of translating it into action through antislavery societies, is a more complex problem. Not least among the deeper forces behind their commitment were the infinite ways in which slavery could be used to express other concerns.

William Lloyd Garrison took it for granted that the help of the Scots abolitionists was important to the cause. In 1865, as he welcomed Elizabeth Pease's stepson to Boston, he could still write fondly of his "dear and beloved friend, Eliza Wigham," of the

18. S. H. Dawson to M. Estlin, October 6, 1852, in BPL-W.

Patons, and of William Smeal's "Quaker simplicity and upright-ness."[19] The fact that Americans like Garrison valued the support and friendship of the Scots in itself meant that their work for the slave was valuable. Yet they never reached the goal of universal emancipation they had set themselves in 1833. They had neither the staying power nor the expertise to continue the fight against bondage in Cuba and Brazil. Genuine chattel slavery is still with us in the modern world. Even in the United States, freedom was not achieved by the weapons of moral suasion they had originally chosen. Much of their effort had been sidetracked into frustrated and undignified bickering. In fact, the American situation had passed beyond a point where foreigners could influence it fifteen years before the war, not least because of a national polarization that foreign interference only served to accelerate.

It was in contributing to this polarization, however modestly, that the Scots did something towards the end they had set out with. Mary Boykin Chesnut once noted plaintively that "we are human beings of the nineteenth century and slavery has to go, of course."[20] The Scots abolitionists were also children of their time, and they accepted getting rid of slavery as one of the obligations this entailed. In their dogged efforts against slavery, they became insignificant members of a massive team, a small detachment in the civilized forces ranged against the slave system. They helped stiffen the spines of their allies in America and push the slave-holding South into an increasingly defensive position. The ultimate result was the destruction of the American Union, and its resur-rection freed of slavery. The contribution of the Scottish aboli-tionists to this outcome was minor, perhaps even unconscious, but it was not discreditable given their disadvantages.

Though the Scots were much influenced by local considerations, they behaved in general very much like abolitionists in other parts of the world. In this sense, their history does not lend itself to a local conclusion, except in one limited sense. The intense strains within Scottish society, and the peculiarities of its position vis-à-

19. W. L. Garrison to J. Nichol, October 9, 1865, Ms. 3925, in Small Collec-tions, SNL.
20. B. A. Williams (ed.), A Diary from Dixie (Boston, 1949), 164.

vis England and America, put it in a uniquely tempting situation to use slavery as a vehicle for arguing out problems that had nothing to do with it. In this the Scots abolitionists were doing much the same as their colleagues elsewhere in the evangelical world, only more so. In Scotland more than anywhere else, slavery was all things to all men.

Abbreviations
Used in the Appendices

C.M.	Committee member
D.	Director
Dp.	Depository
G.	Governor
M.	Manager
P.	President
S.	Secretary
T.	Treasurer
Ts.	Trustee
V.P.	Vice-President

RELIGIOUS

B.	Baptist
C.S.	Church of Scotland
C.S.Ev.	Church of Scotland evangelical (*i.e.*, known to belong to party that eventually became the Free Church of Scotland).
E.	Episcopalian
I.	Independent (*i.e.*, Congregationalist).
M.	Methodist
O.S.	Original Secession Church
Q.	Quaker
R.P.	Reformed Presbyterian (*i.e.*, Cameronian).
R.S.	Relief Secession Synod
U.S.	United Secession Church

       Ecclesiastical Characteristics

In the following, the numbers after each denomination's name are the numbers of congregations it controlled in Edinburgh.*

      Church of Scotland, 18

1690   Cameronians, or Reformed Presbyterian Church, 0

1733   First Secession, which eventually gives rise to: *a*) Original Secession Church, 2, and *b*) United Secession Church, 9.

1761   Relief Secession, 5, unites with United Secession Church in 1847 to form United Presbyterian Church.

1843   Free Church of Scotland, 23, attracts many Original Secession and Reformed Presbyterian adherents. Most of it reunites with the Church of Scotland in 1929.

There were also:

      Episcopalians, 8; Methodists, 2; Independents or Congregationalists, 3; Baptists, 6; Unitarians, 1.

In 1835–1836, the Parliamentary Church Commission estimated Edinburgh Church accommodations as follows:

Established churches	20,419
Episcopal churches	3,327
All secession churches	15,793
Baptists, Independents	5,220
Methodists	1,470
Catholics	2,750
Unitarians	150
Friends	100
Jews, 20 families	

New Statistical Account of Scotland (15 vols.; Edinburgh, 1845), I, 668.

Philanthropic Activities of
Edinburgh Abolitionists, 1835

The committee listed below is that of the Edinburgh Society for the
Abolition of Negro Slavery (Throughout the World) in Oliver and
Boyd's *Edinburgh Almanac or Universal Scots and Imperial Register
for 1835*, p. 453. Information comes from the sections entitled "Charit-
able Institutions," "Religious and Missionary Societies," and "Miscellaneous" in the same issue of the *Edinburgh Almanac*. Denominations
have only been systematically researched for ministers and are not listed
for lay members unless information has cropped up incidentally.

Name and Position		*Philanthropic interests*	*Denomination*
Lord Moncrieff	P.		C.S.Ev.
Rev. Dr. R. Gordon	V.P.	M., Orphan Hospital; D., Scottish Bible Soc.; V.P., Edinburgh Assoc. in Aid of Moravian Missions; C.M., Gen. Assembly Comm. for Propagating Gospel in Foreign Parts; Edinburgh Soc. for Promoting Religious Interests of Scottish Settlers in British North America; C.M., Edinburgh Soc. for the Diffusion of Information on Capital Punishments.	C.S.Ev.
Rev. E. Craig, A.M.	V.P.	S., Church of England Missionary Assoc.; S., Edinburgh Aux. Bible Soc.; V.P., Edinburgh Assoc. in Aid of Moravian Missions; "Examinator," Edinburgh City Mission; C.M., Edinburgh Soc. for the Diffusion of Information on Capital Punishments; V.P., Edinburgh Soc. for the Suppression of Intemperance.	E.
Lord Cockburn	V.P.		C.S.Ev.
A. Cruickshank	T.	D., Edinburgh Education Soc.; C.M., Edinburgh Soc. for the Diffusion of Information on Capital Punishments; C.M., Edinburgh Soc. for the Suppression of Intemperance.	Q.

Name and Position		Philanthropic interests	Denomination
R. K. Greville, Ll.D.	S.	T., Church of England Missionary Assoc.; D., Scottish Missionary Soc.; C.M., Edinburgh Education Soc.; S., Edinburgh Soc. for the Diffusion of Information on Capital Punishments; V.P., Edinburgh Soc. for the Suppression of Intemperance.	E.
A. Macaulay, M.D.	S.	G., George Watson's Hospital; G., Merchant Maiden Hospital; D., Parochial Institutions for Religious Education of Children of the Poor; C.M., Edinburgh Bible Soc.; D., Scottish Missionary Soc.	E.
J. Ogilvy	S.		
H. Tod, W.S.	S.	C.M., Soc. for the Support of Gaelic Schools; C.M., Edinburgh Soc. for the Diffusion of Information on Capital Punishments.	C.S.Ev.
Rev. C. Anderson	C.M.	D., Irish Soc., Edinburgh Aux.; D., Soc. for Promoting Christianity Among the Jews; C.M., Voluntary Church Assoc.	[?]
R. Bald	C.M.		
P. Crooks, W.S.	C.M.		
H. D. Dickie	C.M.	C.M., Edinburgh Bible Soc.; D., Edinburgh Aux. Bible Soc.; T., Baptist Home Missionary Soc.	B.
Dr. J. Easton	C.M.	C.M., Edinburgh Bible Soc.; D., Edinburgh Soc. for Promoting Religious Interests of Scottish Settlers in British North America.	
Hon. H. D. Erskine	C.M.	D., Edinburgh Aux. Bible Soc.; C.M., Edinburgh Soc. for the Diffusion of Information on Capital Punishments; C.M., Edinburgh Soc. for the Suppression of Intemperance.	
J. A. Haldane	C.M.	C.M., Edinburgh Bible Soc.; S., Baptist Home Missionary Soc.; D., Edinburgh Gratis Sabbath School Soc.	B.
R. Haldane, W.S.	C.M.	S., Baptist Home Missionary Soc.	B.
R. Huie, M.D.	C.M.	M., Charity Workhouse; Physician, Magdalen Asylum; C.M., Edinburgh Assoc. in Aid of Moravian Missions; C.M., Edinburgh Education Soc.; D., Edinburgh Soc. for Promoting Religious Interests of Scottish Settlers in British North America.	
A. Hutchison, S.S.C.	C.M.	M., Charity Workhouse; D., Parochial Institutions for Religious Education of Children of the Poor.	

Name and Position		Philanthropic interests	Denomination
J. S. More, Adv.	C.M.	C.M., Edinburgh Bible Soc.; C.P., Edinburgh Gratis Sabbath School Soc.; D., Edinburgh Soc. for Promoting Religious Interests of Scottish Settlers in British North America; C.M., Edinburgh Soc. for the Diffusion of Information on Capital Punishments.	C.S.
J. McAndrew, S.S.C.	C.M.		
G. McCallum, M.D.	C.M.		
Rev. Prof. G. Paxton	C.M.	S., Friendly Soc. of Dissenting Ministers.	O.S.
D. Purdie	C.M.		
Rev. Dr. J. Ritchie	C.M.	D., Edinburgh Education Soc.; D., Friendly Soc. of Dissenting Ministers; C.M., Voluntary Church Assoc.; V.P., Edinburgh Soc. for the Suppression of Intemperance.	U.S.
T. R. Robertson	C.M.		
Capt. H. Rose, Gov. of Prison	C.M.	C.M., Edinburgh Bible Soc.; D., Scottish Missionary Soc.; C.M., Soc. for the Support of Gaelic Schools; C.M., Edinburgh Soc. for the Suppression of Intemperance.	C.S.[Ev.(?)].
A. Scott	C.M.		
P. Tennent, W.S.	C.M.	D., Scottish Missionary Soc.; D., Sabbath School Union for Scotland; S., Edinburgh Soc. for Promoting Religious Interests of Scottish Settlers in British North America; D., Anti-Patronage Soc.	C.S.Ev.
J. Wigham, Jr.	C.M.	D., Edinburgh Aux. Bible Soc.; C.M., Soc. for the Support of Gaelic Schools; T., Edinburgh Education Soc.; C.M., Edinburgh Soc. for the Diffusion of Information on Capital Punishments; C.M., Edinburgh Soc. for the Suppression of Intemperance.	Q.

Occupations and Denominations of
Edinburgh Abolitionists, 1834–1836

The leaders listed below are a combination of those on the Committee
of the Edinburgh Society for the Abolition of Negro Slavery, in the
Edinburgh Almanac or Universal Scots and Imperial Register for 1853,
p. 453, and the 1836 committee of the Edinburgh Emancipation Society,
in G. Thompson, *A Voice to the United States of America from the
Metropolis of Scotland* (Edinburgh, 1836), 3. Members listed on the
former are marked with an asterisk, those on the latter with a cross.
The Edinburgh Emancipation Society was an adaptation of the older
body, and the combination of these two lists gives a cross section of
abolitionists active in Edinburgh in the thirties. Occupations have been
traced, where possible, through titles on the lists, and through C. B.
Boog Watson (ed.), *Roll of Edinburgh Burgesses and Guild Brothers,
1761–1841* (Scottish Record Society, 1833). Denominations have been
traced for ministers where possible, through the Edinburgh *Almanac*,
Fasti Ecclesiae Scottincanae, and W. Ewing (ed.), *Annals of the Free
Church of Scotland, 1843–1900* (2 vols.; Edinburgh, 1914). Denominations of lay members are only listed where information has appeared
incidentally. Members who appear on both lists are noted by the highest
office in which they served.

Name	Office	Occupation	Denomination
Lord Moncrieff	P.*	Law Lord	C.S.Ev.
Rev. R. Gordon	V.P.*	Minister	C.S.Ev.
Rev. E. Craig	V.P.*	Minister	E.
Lord Cockburn	V.P.*	Law Lord	C.S.Ev.
A. Cruickshank	T.*	Hosier	Q.
R. K. Greville, Ll.D.	S.*	Botanist	E.
A. Macaulay	S.*	Doctor	C.S.
H. Tod	S.* +	Lawyer	C.S.Ev.
W. Somerville, Jr.	S.+	Stationer	
W. Oliphant	T.+	Bookseller	C.S.Ev.

Name	Office	Occupation	Denomination
Rev. C. Anderson	C.M.* +	Minister	
Rev. W. Anderson	C.M. +	Minister	R.P.
Rev. W. Goold	C.M. +	Minister	R.P.
Rev. E. Halley	C.M. +	Minister	U.S.
Rev. Prof. G. Paxton	C.M.* +	Minister	O.S.
Rev. Dr. W. Peddie	C.M. +	Minister	U.S.
Rev. W. Peddie	C.M. +	Minister	U.S.
Rev. Dr. J. Ritchie	C.M.* +	Minister	U.S.
W. Alexander, Esq.	C.M. +	Merchant [?] from Leith	
R. Bald	C.M.*	Engineer	
J. Brenner	C.M. +		
P. Brown	C.M. +		
P. Crooks, W.S.	C.M.*	Lawyer	
J. Campbell of Carbrook	C.M. +	Gentry	
E. Cruickshank	C.M. +		
H. D. Dickie	C.M.* +	Accountant	B.
J. Dickie, W.S.	C.M. +	Lawyer	
Dr. J. Easton	C.M.*	Doctor	
Hon. H. D. Erskine	C.M.* +	Gentry	
J. A. Haldane, W.S.	C.M.*	Lawyer	B.
R. Haldane, W.S.	C.M.*	Lawyer	B.
R. Huie, M.D.	C.M.*	Doctor	
A. Hutchison, S.S.C.	C.M.*	Lawyer	
G. Inglis, Jr.	C.M. +	Draper	
J. McAndrew, S.S.C.	C.M.* +	Lawyer	
G. McCallum, M.D.	C.M.*	Doctor	
J. Martin	C.M. +	Woolen draper	
J. S. More, Adv.	C.M.*	Lawyer	
D. Purdie	C.M.*	Merchant	
W. Oliphant, Sr.	C.M. +	Bookseller	
T. R. Robertson, W.S.	C.M.* +	Lawyer	
Capt. H. Rose	C.M.* +	Governor of prison	C.S.[Ev.(?)]
A. Scott	C.M.*	Merchant	
W. Somerville, Sr.	C.M. +	Stationer	
C. Spence, S.S.C.	C.M. +	Lawyer	
P. Tennent, W.S.	C.M.* +	Lawyer	C.S.Ev.
J. B. Tod	C.M. +	Broker	
J. Wigham	C.M.* +	Shawl maker	Q.
G. Wilson	C.M. +		

Philanthropic Activities of
GES Committee Members, 1835

The committee list used below is in entry for February 25, 1835, in Glasgow Emancipation Society Minute Books, I. Unless noted otherwise, all information is taken from D. Robertson, *The Western Supplement to [Oliver and Boyd's] Edinburgh and County Almanac of Scotland for 1835*. Unfortunately this does not list all benevolent institutions in Glasgow, which may explain why the interlocking of committee memberships does not appear to be as marked as in the Edinburgh case. With reference to the strength of voluntaries in the GES, mentioned in Chapter 2, note the number of members involved in the multidenominational Glasgow Voluntary Church Society. Denominations have only been checked formally for ministers.

Name and position in GES		*Philanthropic interests*	*Denomination*
R. Grahame, Esq.	P.		
Rev. Dr. R. Wardlaw	V.P.	Ts., Andersonian University; P., Glasgow Religious Tract Soc.; P., Glasgow Voluntary Church Soc.	I.
A. Wigham	V.P.	C.M., Aberdeen Aux. Bible Soc. (1840).*	Q.
Rev. Dr. J. Heugh	V.P.	S., Glasgow Voluntary Church Soc.	I.
J. Johnston	T.	C.M., Glasgow Voluntary Church Soc.	
J. Murray	S.	C.M., Glasgow Voluntary Church Soc.	R.S.
W. Smeal	S.		Q.
J. Smeal	S.		Q.
Rev. W. Anderson	C.M.	V.P., Glasgow Religious Friendly Soc.; C.M., Glasgow Voluntary Soc.	R.S.
Rev. W. Auld	C.M.	C.M., Glasgow Voluntary Church Soc.	R.S.
Rev. C. J. Brown	C.M.		C.S.

Aberdeen Almanac, 1840.

Name and position in GES		Philanthropic interests	Denomination
Rev. E. Campbell	C.M.		[?]
Rev. J. Duncan	C.M.		C.S.
Rev. J. Edwards	C.M.	C.M., Glasgow Voluntary Church Soc.	R.S.
Rev. G. Ewing	C.M.	C.M., Glasgow Voluntary Church Soc.	I.
Rev. G. Harvey	C.M.	C.M., Glasgow Voluntary Church Soc.	R.S.
Rev. A. Kidston	C.M.	T., Andersonian University; S., Glasgow Missionary Soc.	U.S.
Rev. D. King	C.M.	C.M., Glasgow Voluntary Church Soc.	U.S.
Rev. W. Lindsay	C.M.	C.M., Glasgow Voluntary Church Soc.	R.S.
Rev. P. McOwan	C.M.	C.M., Glasgow Voluntary Church Soc.	M.
Rev. J. McTear	C.M.		[?]
Rev. M. Willis	C.M.		C.S. Ev. [Until 1839, was Auld Licht Burgher (O.S.)]
D. Anderson	C.M.	C.M., Glasgow Voluntary Church Soc.	
J. Beith	C.M.	C.M., Glasgow Voluntary Church Soc.	
H. Brown, Jr.	C.M.		
W. Brown	C.M.	C.M., Glasgow Public Library; C.M., Glasgow Assoc. for Promoting Interest of Church of Scotland.	
R. Connell	C.M.	S., Glasgow Public Library.	
W. Craig	C.M.		
G. S. Dick	C.M.	C.M., Glasgow Voluntary Church Soc.	
W. Ferguson	C.M.	G., Wilson's School.	
J. Fleming	C.M.		
G. Gallie	C.M.	Dp., Glasgow Religious Tract Soc.; Temperance Worker.*	
R. Kettle	C.M.	T., Glasgow Religious Tract Soc.; Temperance Worker.†	
H. Langlands	C.M.		
P. Lethem	C.M.	T., Scottish Temperance Soc.; C.M., Glasgow Voluntary Church Soc.	

*The Autobiography of John Dunlop (London, 1832), 101.
†L. J. Saunders, Scottish Democracy, 1815–1840 (Edinburgh, 1950), 234.

Name and position in GES		*Philanthropic interests*	*Denomination*
J. Maxwell, M.D.	C.M.	Professional attendant, Glasgow Lying-In Hospital.	
T. Muir	C.M.		
C. McDougal	C.M.		
A. McGeorge	C.M.		
D. MacIntyre	C.M.		
A. McKeand	C.M.		
D. Maclaren	C.M.	S., Glasgow Religious Tract Soc.; C.M., Glasgow Voluntary Church Soc.	
J. McLeod	C.M.	C.M., Glasgow Voluntary Church Soc.	
J. McLeod (Argyll)	C.M.		
J. Reid	C.M.		
R. Sanderson	C.M.		
T. Slater	C.M.		
D. Smith	C.M.		
J. Stewart	C.M.		
P. Thomson	C.M.		
G. Thorburn	C.M.		
G. Watson	C.M.	C.M., Glasgow Voluntary Church Soc.	
A. Watson	C.M.		
A. Young	C.M.	C.M., Glasgow Voluntary Church Soc.	

Changes in GES Committee
Membership, 1841

Since resignations were not noted in the Glasgow Emancipation Society Minute Books except for the leaders of the society, it is not possible to give dates at which individual members resigned. Data has
been gathered by comparing the lists of the *Annual Reports of the
Glasgow Emancipation Society*, for 1840 and 1841. Other new members
appear in the list in *G.E.S. Reports, 1841*, having been added at the
anniversary meeting on August 2, 1841. Information on occupations
has been gathered from Glasgow post office directories and J. R. Anderson (ed.), *The Burgesses and Guild Brethren of Glasgow* (Edinburgh:
Scottish Record Society, 1935). Ministers are identified by denomination. The cases where duplication of names leaves occupation in doubt
are indicated by a question mark.

I. Members who resigned from committee.

Name and position in GES		*Occupation or denomination*
Rev. Dr. R. Wardlaw	V.P.	I.
Rev. Dr. J. Heugh	V.P.	I.
A. Wigham	V.P.	Ironmonger (Aberdeen)
W. P. Paton	V.P.	Commission merchant
Rev. Wm. Brash	C.M.	U.S.
Rev. J. Duncan	C.M.	C.S. Ev.
Rev. G. Ewing	C.M.	I.
Rev. A. Harvey	C.M.	R.S.
Rev. J. Johnston	C.M.	U.S.
Rev. D. King	C.M.	U.S.
Rev. W. Lindsay	C.M.	R.S.
D. Anderson	C.M.	Merchant
J. C. Blyth	C.M.	Boot and shoe maker
H. Brown	C.M.	Manufacturer
J. C. Dick	C.M.	Manufacturer
A. Fullarton	C.M.	Publisher and bookseller
G. Gallie	C.M.	Bookseller

R. Kettle	C.M.	Cotton yarn merchant
P. Lethem	C.M.	Manufacturer
N. McGilp	C.M.	[?]
D. Maclaren	C.M.	Accountant or commission merchant

II. Members who did not resign from committee

Name and position in GES		*Occupation or denomination*
R. Grahame, Esq.	P.	Tobacco merchant and landowner
T. Grahame, Esq.	V.P.	Tobacco merchant and landowner
Rev. Dr. A. Kidston	V.P.	U.S.
J. Murray	S.	Landowner
W. Smeal	S. & T.	Grocer
Rev. W. Anderson	V.P.	R.S.
Rev. W. Auld	C.M.	R.S.
Rev. J. Eadie	C.M.	U.S.
Rev. J. Edwards	C.M.	R.S.
Rev. J. Graham	C.M.	O.S.
Rev. J. McTear	C.M.	[?]
Rev. T. Pullar	C.M.	I.
Rev. M. Willis	C.M.	O.S.
W. Brodie	C.M.	Company name only in post office directory
W. Brown	C.M.	Boot maker
W. Buchanan	C.M.	Newspaper editor
R. Connell	C.M.	Teacher
W. Ferguson	C.M.	Accountant or wine merchant
J. Fleming	C.M.	[?]
W. Gunn	C.M.	Bagpipe maker
H. Langlands	C.M.	Partner in Reid, Robertson, and Co.
A. McKeand	C.M.	Warehouseman
J. McLeod	C.M.	Bookseller
C. McDougal	C.M.	Manufacturer [?]
R. Mathie	C.M.	Agent and house factor
Dr. Maxwell	C.M.	Medical doctor
J. Reid	C.M.	Bookseller [?]
R. Sanderson	C.M.	Ship and insurance broker
J. Stewart	C.M.	[?]
G. Thomson	C.M.	Sewed muslin manufacturer
A. Watson	C.M.	Partner of Fleming, Watson and Nairn
G. Watson	C.M.	Librarian and bookseller
J. Watson	C.M.	[?]
T. Watson	C.M.	[?]
W. White	C.M.	Tobacco pipe maker or glass merchant
A. Young	C.M.	[?]

III. Members added to the committee.

Name and position in GES		Occupation or denomination
J. Dennistoun, Esq., M.P.	V.P.	Lawyer and politician
J. Oswald, Esq., M.P.	V.P.	Landowner and politician; S., Glasgow East India Assoc.
Rev. G. Rose	C.M.	M.
E. Anderson	C.M.	Listed in directory without profession.
J. Barr	C.M.	Weaver
T. Brown	C.M.	[?]
J. Bruce	C.M.	Farmer [?]
P. Bruce	C.M.	[?]
J. Dunn	C.M.	Baker or sewed muslin manufacturer
W. Lang	C.M.	Merchant [?]
W. Lochead	C.M.	Wright
W. McLeod	C.M.	Weaver
J. McNair	C.M.	Merchant
H. Muir	C.M.	Teacher
A. Paton	C.M.	Maltman [?]
D. Russell	C.M.	Printer
J. Turner, Esq., of Thrushgrove	C.M.	Landowner and tobacco merchant
J. Ure, Esq., of Croy	C.M.	Landowner
R. Wright	C.M.	Provision merchant

Abstract of GES Finances

These figures are drawn from the Glasgow Emancipation Society Cash Books, in the Smeal Donation, Mitchell Library, Glasgow. Annual figures are difficult to calculate, since the books were balanced at irregular times, but this column of receipts at each audit gives a good idea of the rise and fall in the society's fortunes.

Receipts between audits			*Date of audit*
£	s	d	
200 ·	19 ·	8	Aug. 11, 1834
249 ·	19 ·	2	Feb. 6, 1836
425 ·	14 ·	0½	Mar. 13, 1837
693 ·	2 ·	0½	Aug. 2, 1838
397 ·	7 ·	6½	Aug. 1, 1839
213 ·	9 ·	11	Aug. 7, 1840
176 ·	16 ·	3½	Aug. 2, 1841
134 ·	10 ·	4	Oct. 24, 1842
126 ·	1 ·	2	Aug. 1, 1843
190 ·	12 ·	9	Aug. 1, 1844
96 ·	14 ·	3	Aug. 1, 1845
463 ·	6 ·	10½	Feb. 1, 1847
49 ·	19 ·	6	Jan. 13, 1848
77 ·	2 ·	9	Jan. 15, 1849
46 ·	13 ·	9	Jan. 15, 1850
61 ·	6 ·	10	Jan. 6, 1851
27 ·	18 ·	7	Jan. 14, 1852
39 ·	16 ·	11	Feb. 13, 1854
40 ·	15 ·	9	Mar. 13, 1855
46 ·	10 ·	10	Mar. 17, 1856
32 ·	16 ·	7	Mar. 16, 1857

Receipts between audits	Date of audit
£ s d	
20 · 12 · 8	Mar. 15, 1858
72 · 14 · 9	Mar. 15, 1860
94 · 9 · 3	Aug. 28, 1862
143 · 2 · 4	Jan. 4, 1864
29 · 7 · 8	Feb. 22, 1876
55 · 17 · 5	Feb. 4, 1884

Index

Abdy, Edward S., 7, 55, 68
Aberdeen, 32, 76, 179
Aberdeen Anti-Slavery Society, 22, 35, 49, 51, 62, 91, 153
Abolitionism. *See* American abolitionists; Antislavery movement; British abolitionists; Garrisonian abolitionists; Irish abolitionists; Scots abolitionists; Women abolitionists; and names of specific organizations
Aborigines' Protection Society, 57, 63, 65–66, 78, 168
Adam, William, 94, 99
Africa, 16–17, 39, 61, 65, 67, 104, 115, 116, 147–49, 174
Allen, Richard, 62, 92
American abolitionists: in Britain, 6, 53, 94–99, 101–13; schisms in movement, 29, 42, 80–87, 194; and churches, 84–85; description of, 93–94; and Scots, 199
American and Foreign Anti-Slavery Society, 87, 104, 114, 127–28, 131
American Anti-Slavery Society, 73, 86–87, 99–100, 103, 104, 171
Anti-Corn Law League, 12, 37, 57, 59, 103
Anti-Slavery Advocate, 17n28, 78, 92, 149, 165, 183
Anti-Slavery League, 141, 163, 167
Antislavery movement: international-ism, 3–5, 14–15, 27, 34, 36, 60, 61; religious rationale, 13–15, 22, 24–27, 30, 34–35, 51, 79, 121, 196; secular rationale, 26–27, 30–31, 34–35; slave as pawn, 28–29; violence against, 69–71, 75–76, 192. *See also* American abolitionists; British abolitionists; Garrisonian abolitionists; Irish abolitionists; Scots abolitionists; Women abolitionists; and names of specific organizations

Anti-Slavery Reporter, 17n28, 99, 149, 152, 183
Anti-Slavery Standard, 92, 101, 113, 155, 159, 163
Anti-Slavery Watchman, 17n28, 78
Armistead, Wilson, 166–72, 183
Aytoun, William, 118, 180

Bailey, Gamaliel, 88
Baptist church, 25, 26, 46, 48, 120, 164, 167
Barnes, Albert, 121
Beattie, James, 19–21, 120–21
Beith, James, 45
Bell, John Hyslop, 44
Bethune, George, 72
Birney, James Gillespie, 83, 86, 89, 94, 95, 98, 99, 122
Bishop, Francis, 166, 171
Blacks, *See* Slaves
Brewster, Patrick, 46, 49, 95, 110, 137
Bright, John, 44, 193
British abolitionists: interest in America, 5–10, 15–17, 27–28, 35–36, 61, 67; denounced in United States, 70–76, 103, 191–92; schisms in movement, 99, 102, 151. *See also* Irish abolitionists; Scots abolitionists; and names of organizations
British and Foreign Anti-Slavery Society, 17, 35, 50, 60–61, 64–66, 77, 78, 80, 87, 91, 92, 94, 98, 104, 105, 108, 114, 117, 123, 127, 134, 148, 149, 151, 156, 163, 164, 167, 168, 171, 172, 178, 184, 190, 198
British Friend, 42, 78, 123, 153, 178
British India Society, 57, 65, 102, 115
Buffum, James N., 130, 132, 133, 135–37
Burns, Robert, 128, 129, 173, 174
Burritt, Elihu, 6, 162
Buxton, Thomas Fowell, 16, 115